THE ECOLOGICAL OTHER

The Ecological Other

Environmental Exclusion in American Culture

Sarah Jaquette Ray

THE UNIVERSITY OF
ARIZONA PRESS

TUCSON

THE UNIVERSITY OF
ARIZONA PRESS

www.uapress.arizona.edu

Library of Congress Cataloging-in-Publication Data
Ray, Sarah Jaquette.
    The ecological other : environmental exclusion in American culture /
Sarah Jaquette Ray.
        p. cm.
    Includes bibliographical references and index.
    ISBN 978-0-8165-1188-4 (cloth : alk. paper) 1. Ecocriticism. 2. Ecology in
literature. I. Title.
    PN98.E36R39 2013
    809'.93355–dc23

                                    2012038182

Publication of this book is made possible in part by the proceeds of a permanent
endowment created with the assistance of a Challenge Grant from the National
Endowment for the Humanities, a federal agency.

Manufactured in the United States of America on acid-free, archival-quality paper
containing a minimum of 30% post-consumer waste and processed chlorine free.

18   17   16   15   14   13   6   5   4   3   2   1

Permission to reprint "Endangering the Desert" (part of chapter 3) is granted by
ISLE: Interdisciplinary Studies of Literature and Environment, and "Risking Babies
in the Wild" (part of chapter 1) is granted by *The Journal of Sport and Social Issues.*

Contents

Illustration

Acknowledgments

I OFTEN HEAR THE CRITICISM that humanistic scholars are so solitary in their work. We don't socialize in the lab or work in teams to collect data. We don't often publish multi-author work, and we spend a lot of time alone in the virtual stacks of research databases, reading and thinking. But as I sit to write this acknowledgment and imagine all the people, funds, and other forms of support that went into the production of this manuscript, I realize that this project has been decidedly collective, not solitary at all. Each page bears the influence of teachers, mentors, editors, conference discussants and fellow panelists, colleagues, students, and loved ones.

I am rich in mentors and humbled by their indefatigable cheerleading. I am grateful to professors who inspired me to pursue my doctoral degree, for which I wrote the dissertation that has evolved into this book: Steve Hopkins, Mark Wallace, Diana K. Davis, and Janet Davis. A handful of scholars have been particularly inspiring in their work and generous of their time and advice since I began graduate school: Joni Adamson, Catriona Mortimer-Sandilands, and Diana K. Davis. I seek to emulate their generosity and activism in my own approach to scholarship and students. I am especially grateful to my dissertation committee for polishing my thoughts and having faith in the import of this project, despite its sometimes-unwieldy interdisciplinarity: Shari Huhndorf, Louise Westling, Susan H. Hardwick, David Vazquez, and Juanita Sundberg. The communities of students, staff, and faculty in both the Environmental Studies Program (Gayla WardWell, Alan Dickman, and Lise Nelson especially) and the English Department at the University of Oregon (Elizabeth Wheeler, Karen Ford, and William Rossi especially) were essential to fostering the intellectual conditions necessary to produce a meaningful dissertation. In particular, I thank the students and faculty of the University of Oregon's Literature and Environment Discussion Group, Mesa Verde. Close friendships with Janet Fiskio, Chaone Mallory, Teresa Coronado, and Kelly Sultzbach, among others, helped blur the line between intellectual stimulation and psychological health, a requisite for getting through graduate school.

Funding support from the American Association of University Women allowed me to work on writing my dissertation in my final year. This dissertation fellowship helped shift my goal from getting a degree to publishing my dissertation as a book. Research grants from the Center for the Study of Women and Society, the Coeta Barker Foundation, the Center on Diversity and Community, the University of Oregon, and the Evelyn Rhoads Wilson Endowment Fund all helped immensely to conduct research for and share various chapters at conferences.

I am grateful for the fruitful feedback I received from the University of California–Davis' Environment and Societies Workshop, and the follow-up feedback from Diana K. Davis, Louis Warren, Traci Voyles, and Mary Mendoza that the workshop precipitated.

Thanks are due to University of Arizona Press, especially Kristen Buckles, who championed the book from the start, and to the publishing, editing, and marketing staff at the Press. I always tell my students not to be afraid of work returned covered in ink; it means I am taking their ideas seriously and want them to be expressed as well as possible. This is precisely how I received the extensive revision suggestions from two anonymous, incisive reviewers, whom I thank for the time they took to show me how to make my arguments better.

At the University of Alaska Southeast, colleagues from the Faculty Research Colloquium, especially Kevin Maier, have been seminal in developing my thinking, and the enthusiasm and help of administrative staff Virginia Berg and Margaret Rea buoyed me as I frantically worked on the book over the past year from within my windowless office. Thanks are due to the School of Arts and Sciences for funding an undergraduate Research Assistant, Kristie Livingston, who deserves commendation for her attention to detail in helping revise the final manuscript, and to Dominic Lodovici for indexing help.

Finally, my family's support in my degree, career, and book project has been humbling. I thank my dad, Dave Jaquette, and my brother,

Chris Jaquette, who shaped the environmentalist in me through years of rafting, kayaking, hiking, camping, and living simply. It is perhaps trite but still an understatement to say that I would not have done any of this—graduate school, the dissertation, the book, much less writing my first essay for college—had my mother, Jane S. Jaquette, not been the most amazing combination of therapist, editor, and, more recently, colleague. There are no words to thank her for her role in all aspects of my life.

My husband, James Ray, deserves more than a brief mention here. As a salmon biologist and cultural studies skeptic, he holds me accountable to the "so what" of my work and, most importantly, makes warm dinners on the long days. In the same year I completed this book, he and I had our first daughter, Hazel Ray, who reminds me of the playground lesson to leave the planet a better place than I found it and gives me reason to keep working on that goal. Mostly, though, I thank James and Hazel for dragging me away from the computer to look for birds and splash in puddles outside during those precious moments when the Juneau rain abates. What else, if not the ability to freely and safely work and play together, is environmental justice?

THE ECOLOGICAL OTHER

Introduction

The Ecological Other

If nature is to matter, we need more potent, more complex understandings of materiality.
— *Stacy Alaimo (2)*

CRITICAL RACE THEORISTS ARE ATTENTIVE to the power of disgust
in fortifying whiteness, and feminists are attentive to the ways that
disgust materializes and thereby diminishes femininity. Yet, despite
the environmental movement's focus on waste, trash, recycling, pollution, and toxicity, few have considered the role of disgust as an
environmental discourse. Thus, this book explores how the environmental movement deploys cultural disgust against various communities it sees as threats to nature. I argue that it does so through
discourses of the body.[1] Disgust shapes mainstream environmental
discourses and vice versa, and it does so by describing which kinds
of bodies and bodily relations to the environment are ecologically
"good," as well as which kinds of bodies are ecologically "other." *The
Ecological Other* seeks to understand how environmental discourse
as a discourse of disgust enforces social hierarchies even as it seeks
to dismantle other forms of hegemony. Mainstream environmentalism is promoted along lines of "purity and pollution," to use Jake
Kosek's term. That is, as a critique of the political economy of efflu-
via—by-products of production and consumption, and also what
we might call the "ecological shitprint" of human activity on the
planet[2]—environmentalism is rightly suspicious of the status quo. At
the same time, it uses discourses of dirt to delineate between pure
and impure bodies.

1

In this book, I do not see this simultaneous distaste for dirt and obsession with environmental purity (or absence of dirt) as paradoxical. On the contrary, I agree with many critical environmental scholars that environmentalism's focus on maintaining a pure nature is as much about social order as it is about ecological health. Making a case here for a *corporeal* ecology, I examine what I call an "environmentalist disgust," which determines which bodies are "good" for nature and which are not and justifies removing the "unnatural" from sight. I draw on and extend a growing corpus of critical scholarship on the intersections of disability, the body, and the environment, including work by Elizabeth Wheeler, Deborah Slicer, Stacy Alaimo, Hsuan Hsu and Martha Lincoln, Julie Sze, Rachel Stein, Priscilla Wald, Sandra Steingraber, and Linda Nash, as well as the collections *Changing Life: Genomes, Ecologies, Bodies, Commodities,* edited by Peter Taylor, Saul Halfon, and Paul Edwards; *Bodies of Nature,* edited by Phil Macnaghten and John Urry, and *Places through the Body,* edited by Heidi Nast and Steve Pile. Drawing on this scholarship, I provide a discursive genealogy of environmentalist disgust in US culture, which I contend originates in the mid-nineteenth century alongside the science of eugenics, in order to demonstrate how that disgust distinguishes between good ecological subjects and impure, dirty, unnatural "ecological others," as I call them.

Take, for example, the widespread acceptance of the local food movement, which teaches us that consuming locally is both environmentally ethical and healthy for our bodies. The locavore movement illustrates how environmental discourses focus on the body as a means of getting close to nature, or a means of recovering a lost connection to nature. Updating Frances Moore Lappé's 1971 *Diet for a Small Planet,* a rash of popular texts urge us to recognize the environmental, social justice, and health consequences of what we put in our mouths. From Barbara Kingsolver's *Animal, Vegetable, Miracle* and Michael Pollan's *The Omnivore's Dilemma* to the documentary *Food, Inc.* and even to Jamie Oliver's television show *Food Revolution,* which attempts to alter one American town's entire food production and consumption patterns to combat obesity, we learn that the body is a site of negotiation of and resistance to industrial food production, as well as all of the social and environmental injustices such production entails. These "environmentalist bodies," so to speak, seek a pure connection to the land that has been corrupted by industrialized food production and, in Marxist terms, the body's alienation from its means of production. Slow, pure, organic food becomes a symbol for enlightened consumerism in a world where food—its production and its consumption—is a primary means of destroying the environment and creating human insecurity.

These discourses of food tie the body to place in ways that are liberatory—they raise awareness of how the personal is political, how the local is global, and how our bodies bear the costs of the industrialization of food. But, just as we should be careful to avoid "utilizing class disgust as a vehicle for the truly feminine," as Laura Kipnis puts it (388), referring to anti-pornography feminism, in this case, environmentalists must be more nuanced in our theories of the environment so that we do not run the risk of using disgust as a "vehicle" for the so-called natural. The body has long been a site of environmental practices and a marker of environmental virtue. Thus, a historical perspective reveals the dangers in making the body a primary site of environmentalist practice, particularly because of the ways delineating virtuous "environmentalist bodies" from environmentally impure bodies serves to reinforce other social hierarchies based, for example, on race, gender, sexuality, nationality, and ability.

For example, Vasile Stanescu reads many aspects of the locavore movement as xenophobic, elitist, and misogynist, highlighting how this contemporary movement manifests and even exacerbates long-standing social divisions. "To stigmatize a food," Stanescu writes, "runs the extreme risk of serving as a proxy to stigmatize" the people who eat it (25). Here, the impulse to cultivate an environmentally pure body and get "back to the land" can mask a more conservative set of impulses to erect stronger borders, get women "back in the kitchen," and be disgusted by the fast-food habits of America's (increasingly obese) poor, whose bodies become, in this example, environmentally suspect, rendering them "ecologically other." In this logic, then, fat people are ecologically other, for example, because they have not been enlightened to the ecological consequences of their eating habits; neither do they choose active, outdoor lifestyles that might make them care about the environment. In the contemporary locavore movement, then, the body becomes an indicator of one's environmental distinctions.

While the locavore movement can be credited for having drawn attention to the ways in which our bodies are embedded in global political, economic, and environmental contexts (how they are "trans-corporeal," to use Stacy Alaimo's term), it individualizes the problems with these contexts and suggests that meaningful recourse is simply a matter of changing your diet. I do not mean to suggest that what we eat does not have geopolitical and ecosystemic implications (although whether a local or a vegetarian diet is the best way to reduce greenhouse gases is unclear (Weber and Matthews, qtd. in Stanescu 12)). But I am concerned that a consumption-based model of diet that is not paired with efforts to change the way corporations, industries, and governments produce, consume, and regulate lulls us into equating bodily purity with environmental health, as mainstream advertising would have us believe (following the logic, "a healthy body is a natural body is a healthy nature"). Indeed, the trend in local food does not necessarily insist on "consideration for the full panoply of social justice issues that a truly just and therefore truly 'green' diet must entail" (Stanescu 29). This political "food coma," if you will, deflects attention from issues of food security, distribution, and regulation; saves only those in the know and who have the means to avoid the dangers of industrialized food; and thereby reinforces the very social hierarchies that the locavore movement claims to challenge.

This example of the relationship between the body and social justice in the locavore movement suggests that environmentalism is fundamentally paradoxical: it functions as a critique of some dominant relations, especially capitalism, and yet it reinforces many social hierarchies along lines of race, class, and gender. Following Foucault, this book examines how this paradox is expressed at the level of the body, as I believe that a corporeal analysis reveals connections between environmentalism and social control that other forms of analysis do not. For example, it is only with a focus on the body that we can read *Food Revolution* in terms of what Timothy Luke and others call "eco-governmentality"—Jamie Oliver's impulse to combat obesity in America by telling people to stop eating fast food is a kind of dietary "regime of the self" that internalizes discipline in support of dominant interests (such as reducing state health costs and cultivating a healthy labor force, in this case). While combating obesity may be an admirable goal, *Food Revolution* focuses on individuals as the problem, rather than on the institutions that constrain individual choice, or on the cultural and socioeconomic contexts in which we all eat (call this "culinary situatedness," if you will). The narrative demands of a television show notwithstanding, this oversight merely perpetuates popular cultural forms of eco-governmentality, which regulate human interactions with the natural world in ways that ultimately serve dominant interests, rather than oppose them, as the slow-food and locavore movements would like to have it.

By constructing normative notions of the kind of body favored as good for nature—the environmentalist body, if you will—and its antithesis, the ecologically other body, the green cultural discourses and texts I analyze in this book, like *Food Revolution,* ultimately craft an environmental ethic that is neither ecologically nor socially healthy, much less sustainable.

Defining the Ecological Other

The locavore movement is just one example of how popular contemporary environmentalism can exclude a community because its environmental ethics and practices do not fit mainstream environmentalism's notion of what it means to be ecologically correct.[3] If, as Timothy Luke argues, contemporary environmentalism has created the "ecological subject(s)"—a green consumer whose everyday economic activities play a role in deciding earth's fate (Kollin 18), or, as Lorraine Code offers, "subjects that are well placed, collectively and singly, to own and take responsibility for their epistemic-moral-political activity" (qtd. in Alaimo 17)—then the ecological other is the antithesis of these empowered ecological subjects.

As much as we need ecological subjects in the world, they are often defined against an "other," much like "the West" is imaginable only over and against "the East," as in Edward Said's formulation of "the other." Unlike ecological subjects, whose aim it is to save the world from ecological crisis, ecological others are often those from whose poor decisions and reckless activities the world ostensibly needs to be saved. Susan Kollin hints at how an ecological other comes to be: "the loss of nature experienced by Euro-Americans often becomes directed toward the racial Other, who in turn is made responsible for that loss, becoming a target of environmentalism's denigration and blame" (140). It is this Other that I am terming the ecological other, and on which I elaborate in this book.

What critical scholarship has thus far failed to address, though, is the identity category that I believe underlies these exclusions, distinctions, and hierarchies—disability. The disabled body,[4] I show, is the consummate ecological other, forming the corporeal basis for other expressions of environmental exclusion. In this book I build on existing critical environmental scholarship but add an analysis of the *corporeal* underpinning of environmentalism's others. I argue that the figure of the disabled body is the quintessential symbol of humanity's alienation from nature, and that it underpins other kinds of ecological-othering, including racial, sexual, class, and gendered othering within the mainstream environmental movement. I argue that, historically, environmentalism played a significant role in constructing the disabled body, a historical legacy that continues to shape the corporeal bases for its various forms of exclusion. I do not argue that all othered bodies are disabled, or that all disabled bodies are equally othered in environmental discourse. Rather, I seek to outline a form of analysis that can sometimes (but not necessarily always) illuminate the basis for environmental exclusion and disgust.

Environmental purity is often portrayed as bodily wholeness and health, while environmental toxicity is measured at the level of the body, as environmental justice activists and scholars know. A material analysis of environmental thought reveals that the body has become a metonym for contemporary environmental values such as ecological health, planetary unity, and connection with nature. Indeed, in many ways, it *is* that connection with nature. Ecocritics and environmental justice scholars are "putting the body back in nature" in important ways. Eco-phenomenologists and some feminists reveal the ways in which the body is the first environment, following Adrienne Rich, for whom the "body is the geography closest in," and that knowledge about the environment can be understood only through the body. The body is a source of epistemological identification with nature, as ecofeminist Deborah Slicer suggests in her call for women to "attend to their bodies as materialized starting points for theorizing similarly materialized nature" (qtd. in Alaimo 33). These movements reveal a revision of Cartesian dualisms; inverting the privilege of the mind as the site of knowledge about the world, as in science and Cartesian thought, contemporary environmental thinkers posit that the mind is immaterial and therefore distanced from material nature. Thus, much environmental thought proposes that the body provides a more environmental way of knowing the world. If the body is to nature as the mind is to the abstraction of nature, the crisis of the environment is a crisis of the body. As Timothy Morton mockingly interprets this turn to the body in environmental thought, "Some philosophy wants the body to ride in like the cavalry and save it from Western dualism" (106).

But this move to consider the body as the means to becoming more attuned to ecosystems is unbalanced, in that it often ignores the ways in which the body is the means by which environmental injustices occur. To put it more simply, some bodies benefit from this dualism-inverting turn to the body, while others bear the costs of environmental exploitation. Other work, such as Stacy Alaimo's *Bodily Natures: Science, Environment, and the Material Self,* provides a much more balanced analysis of the body in contemporary environmental thought. Alaimo outlines the possibilities of analysis and justice that are opened by seeing the "traffic" between the body, the environment, the economy, and technology, connections that she calls "trans-corporealities." She outlines how a "material turn" in environmental studies helps us understand the ways in which environmental issues are at once global and local, political and philosophical, scientific and poetic. These distinctions are blurred in the material self, which provides a perspective of environmental issues that no other form of analysis can. For example, Ulrich Beck reminds us that even science—the consummate disembodied view of nature—has "sensory organs" (qtd. in Alaimo 19). So, despite the epistemological conceit of science as "above" the body (an interesting preposition, if we are taking matter seriously),[5] all knowledge of nature in fact originates in the body, even knowledge that is valued as objective, immune to the sensory, subjective limitations of the body. Moreover, environmental justice scholars insist that the health of the body is a measure of ecological quality, a point that Richard Lewontin and Richard Levins reveal when they write, "Your body knows your class position no matter how well you have been taught to deny it" (qtd. in Alaimo 27).

These examples of the material turn in environmental studies are a launching point for the concerns of this book. But, while
Alaimo refers to the contributions disability studies makes to thinking about trans-corporealities—the traffic between the body and
nature(s)—she does not go as far as I want to go here, which is to
demonstrate that the disabled body is the *defining* antithesis of the
whole bodies that her study scrutinizes. Indeed, Alaimo's theory
of trans-corporeality—in its insistence on recognizing the interconnections between bodies and environments and in its rejection of
the medical model of the contained, bounded body—is not new to
disability studies scholars. To the extent that scholars are arguing
that the body is the site of environmental injustice and the means of
recovering from those injustices, they fail to trouble the correlation
between the whole, healthy body and a whole, healthy environment,
an assumption that I argue is ableist and ignores the investments in
abled bodies that environmentalism has long held.

Toni Morrison's argument that an "Africanist presence" underpins American literature helps illuminate how I am theorizing the
disabled body in environmental thought. Morrison's theory provides a model for the "absent presence" of the disabled figure in
environmental thought. That is, just as the "major and championed
characteristics of our national literature" are in fact "responses to
a dark, abiding, signing Africanist presence" (5), I want to argue
that the uncritical focus on the body in environmental thought
"exposes the illusion" (as Rosemarie Garland-Thomson puts it) of
able-bodiedness. Theorizing a "disablist presence," as I call it, in
environmental thought allows us to see the ways in which Alaimo's
trans-corporealities are responses to a deep, abiding, "signing" (to
echo Morrison) anxiety about disfigurement as nature gone wrong.
Only within this logic, I argue, does it make sense to fix nature by
fixing our bodies.

Alaimo insists that we must recognize the ways that bodies and
environments are connected, and the ways in which environments
connect bodies and vice versa. In this book, I try to put the body
back in nature, but I do so by scrutinizing the very premise of this
connection in the first place. I argue that the historical origin of disability as a social construct is also the historical moment at which the
body became a means of reuniting with nature. In order to make this

argument, I map the origins of the concept of disability alongside the origins of the US environmental movement and examine three examples of how these connections manifest today—in discourses of risk in American outdoor adventure culture, in representations of the Native American body in environmental justice literature, and in attitudes toward the immigrant body in contemporary environmental discourse. These examples reveal how the body became the site of traffic between culture and nature in the first place, such that the category of disabled emerged at the same time as the notion of ecology. These examples of ecological others reveal environmentalism's investment in status quo social hierarchies, even as it is positioned as a critique of dominant structures.

Of particular importance to this theorizing is a closer examination of the environmentalist roots of social Darwinism, which treated evolutionary survival as *environmental* necessity, justifying programs of social control, such as eugenics, as part of the same nation-building project as wilderness preservation. Preserving the land was not about nature so much as it was about an imagined body politic. As Bruce Braun has argued, wilderness became a "purification machine" that produced ideal Anglo-American men. The protection of nature and the protection of the ideal American were part of the same biopolitical imperative in the Progressive Era. Both the early wilderness movement and the nascent field of ecology glorified the fit body. They deployed ideals of American national identity and American nature to justify social exclusion on the bases of physical and mental ability, race, and national origin. Privileged bodies could escape the dirty environments of the city, while less privileged bodies became associated with—even blamed for—the toxicity, poor hygiene, and dirt that become associated with urbanization.[6] In these senses, environmental values and discourses of "nature" gained meaning within the context of social engineering projects to purify the nation.

In each of the chapters that follow, I focus on three distinct case studies of ecologically other corporealities. First, I examine what I consider the prototypical corporeal other—the disabled body— which has operated (and continues to operate) as the implicit other against which environmentally healthy subjects are defined. Second, I draw on these assumptions about the disabled body to scrutinize the body of the Native American, which was "sacrificed" (in conjunction with "sacrificed" landscapes) through processes of colonialism in ways that make all the more insulting the dominant discourse of the ecological Indian, whose body is, paradoxically, "at one with" nature. Ecological subjects seek to emulate the Indian body's connection to nature, obscuring the ways that those very bodies have been drawn into environmentally exploitative colonial, capitalist, and military projects, and how both Indian bodies and those environments have been sacrificed. In this chapter, I examine Leslie Marmon Silko's *Almanac of the Dead* to illustrate this paradoxical treatment of the Native American body in dominant environmental thought. Finally, I investigate the bodies of undocumented immigrants as "trash," bodies sacrificed in the momentum of globalization. This dominant disgust toward immigrant bodies as trash masks the ways in which immigrants' bodily labor makes middle-class comfort possible for a vast majority of American citizens. While "shadow labor," as Don Mitchell calls it, is extracted from these bodies as they work in domestic service, slaughterhouses, and construction (to name just a few of the toxic and disfiguring jobs immigrants perform), those bodies are maligned as a threat to nature and nation. Yet those bodies bear the cost of this contradiction in the form of poor treatment of workers, reduced health and access to medical treatment, and, of course, the risking of injury and death in the borderland. With each of these examples, a focus on the corporeal basis of the ways in which these others are constructed reveals a troubling contradiction within environmental thought—that in producing environmentalist bodies, it must create ecological others as well. Although these three examples are illustrative, they are not exhaustive. Environmentalism can be seen as a disabling set of practices and beliefs for any number of individuals or communities, a point that makes critical analysis of environmental discourse all the more urgent, as such discourse increasingly looks to the body as the figurative and literal material from which green subjects will continue to be sculpted.[7]

This book investigates a series of questions about the origins of the tension between mainstream environmentalism and groups it sees as threatening to nature. How does the body come to stand in for ecological harmony? How does concern about the environment make anxieties about a variety of communities of color more palatable than overt racism, even as environmentalism claims to be a socially responsible movement with global reach, invested in issues of interdependence, harmony, and diversity? In what ways does environmentalism—as a description of nature, as a social movement, and as a code of behavioral imperatives—play a role in the exploitation of land and bodies? Along what implicit lines do these environmental codes distinguish between good and bad bodies?

Historical Context: Eugenics, Empire, and Environment

Several contemporary American studies scholars emphasize that the originary myths of American exceptionalism and pastoralism articulated by de Tocqueville, Crevecoeur, and Jefferson, among others, legitimized the displacement and oppression of others, including Native Americans and slaves. For example, Amy Kaplan has argued that American studies needs to foreground rather than deny the "multiple histories of continental and overseas expansion, conquest, conflict, and resistance which have shaped the cultures of the United States and the cultures of those it has dominated within and beyond its geopolitical boundaries" ("Left Alone" 4). But the environment is a key part of this colonial history, a point that few environmentalists like to concede. New Western historians and new American studies scholars have shown that environmental and colonialist practices have been historically intertwined. This analysis of the environmental underpinnings of US colonial history seems necessary if, as ecocritic David Mazel argues, "what we today call environmentalism is generally understood to have had its beginnings in . . . a time and a region that place it directly upon the heels of imperial conquest" (144).[8] The emergence of an environmental movement "on the heels of imperial conquest" suggests a relationship between these projects. For instance, wilderness preservation appropriated land from people whose rights the white majority wanted to deny, promoting an image of America that systematically justified the dispossession of Native Americans and Mexicans from lands across the West. The construction of wilderness parks went hand in hand with imperial expansion. Thus, a significant premise of this book is that American imperialist processes were and continue to be distinctly *environmental*.

Following the logic of imperialist nostalgia, the development of the frontier was accompanied by nostalgia for wilderness, and so cordoning off spaces to conserve was a direct function of settling the frontier. The "construction" of wildernesses throughout the West coincided with the dispossession and displacement of Mexicans, and the confinement of Indians (many of whom had been repeatedly displaced as white settlers moved west) to reservations in the latter half of the nineteenth century was part of the same nation-building project. The latter half of the nineteenth century not only saw the first national parks; it also witnessed unprecedented appropriation of tribal lands, as well as the Treaty of Guadalupe Hidalgo in 1848 and the Gadsden Purchase of 1853, which dramatically shifted the western American landscape and Americans' image of "their" country.

The environment as a "safety valve," as Frederick Jackson Turner called it in 1893, served to replace the role that the frontier had played. When Turner declared the frontier "closed," the independent American spirit fostered by "lighting out for the territory," popularized in the mainstream by Mark Twain and James Fenimore Cooper, for example, was under threat. If the frontier encounter was necessary for the creation of the ideal American, then the close of the frontier meant no more unique American character. With the settlement of the land once considered frontier, the qualities that made Americans unique would have to be artificially produced in a new conception of the frontier—the wilderness. In tandem with urban hygiene reforms and the City Beautiful movement, the creation of wilderness became an essential means of preserving American character. It provided the setting against which the drama of the frontier encounter could be carried out and "progress" could be made.

Only in the context of colonial displacement could the idea of wilderness conservation first begin to take shape. Roderick Neumann, Richard Grove, Diana K. Davis, and David Arnold, for example, have outlined the relationship between European empire and early conservation on a global scale. In the US context, though, this link has only recently been accepted. Environmental historians like William Cronon, Mark Spence, Karl Jacoby, Carolyn Merchant, Stephen Germic, Patricia Limerick, Krista Comer, and Donald Worster, for example, have argued that the wilderness model's insistence that nature be pristine created an image of wilderness as a place "where

man himself is a visitor who does not remain" (as it has been codi-
fied) and rendered wilderness accessible only to the privileged. The
first national park, Yellowstone National Park, institutionalized the
wilderness model in 1872, and the drive for wilderness preservation
then continued until the 1930s under the leadership of Theodore
Roosevelt, Gifford Pinchot, John Muir, and the landscape design
of Frederick Law Olmstead. In Priscilla Ybarra's view, this model
continues to deter people of color from participating in the mainstream environmental movement, as it "erases the ongoing relationship with nature that people of color," such as the Native Americans
and undocumented immigrants I discuss in this book, "maintained
[with the so-called wilderness] for centuries before the establishment
of the United States and westward expansion" (3). It also erases the
legacy of conquest that creating wilderness spaces helped achieve.

Alongside the emerging national park wilderness model, evolutionary theory was deployed to legitimize nativist (as opposed to
Native) ideas, and nature was a justification for social control through
increasingly popularized views of Darwinian thought. Spencer's
interpretation of Darwinian theory naturalized the Anglo-American
race's inevitable superiority in a survival of the fittest. The idea of
nature as wilderness then became a surrogate safety valve for the pressures fomenting in society. Immigration policies between the 1880s
and 1920s increasingly fortified borders and legalized exclusions,
first against the Chinese, but then against other groups, with the
explicit intention of preserving the genetic and cultural purity of the
Anglo population in order to avoid "race suicide." The environment
thus gave troubling social reform policies moral legitimacy in an era
marked by progressive politics and concerns about the political and
economic rights of African Americans, workers, and women.

The invention of wilderness was a reactionary *response*—as opposed
to a *solution*—to these social crises. Progressive Era social reform
movements were often led by individuals such as Theodore Roosevelt and Charles Davenport, for instance, who sought to engineer
an ideal society, socially harmonious and free of social deviants and
groups thought to threaten America's image of itself, which linked
moral purity to whiteness, cleanliness, and reform politics. Darwinian evolutionary theory legitimated white domination, but also
white noblesse oblige in combining welfarist policies, government

regulations, and newly imposed limits on immigration. The nature and purpose of wilderness helped rationalize these policies as appropriate, "progressive," and "natural."

Environmentalism thus emerged in response to these domestic and geopolitical conditions, evolving in tandem with social Darwinism, which portrayed life as a contest for survival. Those who were fit, both individuals and races, "naturally" dominated those who were weaker. Wilderness survival activities showcased America's "inherent" superiority and thereby helped to construct a particular kind of dominant American identity. The nineteenth-century grandfathers of the modern environmental movement, such as Ernst Haeckel and George Perkins Marsh, promoted an image of the ideal American tested in the wilderness, showcasing self-reliance as achievable through an encounter with raw nature. Environmentalism gained support from many whose interests were potentially in conflict, but for whom environmentalism seemed to address their social anxieties: those who were part of the romantic reaction to modernity, such as John Muir; those who wanted to preserve the myth of American exceptionalism, such as Turner; and those who feared the loss of white, Protestant dominance and wanted to prepare Americans for the competition ahead, such as Roosevelt.

Several scholars, such as Jake Kosek and Peter Coates, have identified these connections between Progressive Era environmentalism and early-twentieth-century immigration policies. But few scholars—if any—have yet linked the social Darwinist fear of race suicide to the social construction of disability, much less acknowledged how this construction was underwritten by the much more acceptable goal of conservation. Scholars of disability theory argue that disability is a social construction that emerged during the late nineteenth century, as methods of quantifying and standardizing the human population became strategies of social reform. For the first time, an idea of a "normal," "average," or, sometimes, "ideal," body shaped these projects of health, fitness, self-reliance, productivity, and American progress. Further, in the Progressive Era, disability could be the responsibility, if not fault, of the *individual*. It was during this period that what disability theorists call "the medical model" of disability came to frame disability as a pathology, difference, and threat to the population.

What happens when we map this historical construction of disability alongside the construction of wilderness, and see them not just as metaphorically related or *parallel,* but as mutually constituted, *related* phenomena? My argument is that they converged to support an emerging sense of a fit, pure national identity. As much as "the national mythologies of white settler societies are deeply *spatialized* stories" (Razack 74), they are *corporeal* as well. That is, the wilderness provided the necessary backdrop to the "Rough Rider" image promoted by Roosevelt and his contemporaries. The physically fit, self-sufficient man, capable of living a "strenuous life," was the American ideal, the opposite of which was physical disability.

As Gail Bederman notes, Roosevelt's "strenuous life" was a fantasy of raw masculine identity endangered by a feminizing—and, I add, *disabling*—modern society. If modern urban life was feminizing and disabling, wilderness spaces provided the correct countergeography within which to hone the ideal American male body. Rescuing this masculinity involved mythologizing the past ("wresting the continent from Indians and installing a higher civilization" (Bederman 182)), but also, as Bryant Simon attests, maintaining a fit and healthy body and testing it in the "new frontiers" of Cuba, Panama, and the Philippines. In his support for conservation, Roosevelt headed west to recover his own masculinity, which was, by his and others' definitions, defined as genetically superior and physically fit. As a result, Simon argues, "national glory, wide-open spaces, and powerful bodies were . . . forever linked" (84). Thus, protecting "nature's nation" (a concept famously articulated by Perry Miller) involved deploying "the environment" both *spatially*—through the construction of wilderness areas—and *corporeally*—in the service of sculpting the race and territory into an American national body politic. Without being overtly racist, and backed by the authority of the new science of ecology, environmental views distinguished between those who belonged within America's privileged boundaries and those who threatened its superior nature—understood both as physical wilderness and as the essential identity of the national body politic. Here we begin to see how biopolitics, influenced by ecology, create trans-corporealities by uniting projects of individual bodily disciplines and geopolitics, an insight that challenges distinctions between the personal and the political, the local and the global, the private and the political-economic, the "material self" (as Alaimo calls it) and the planetary.

Given this context, it is not surprising that many of the same figures who were developing the science of ecology and promoting the wilderness movement were the earliest proponents of eugenics. Although it may seem paradoxical that the early tradition of the American ecology wilderness movements—promulgated by Emerson, Thoreau, and Whitman (whose names are associated with values of social acceptance and harmony with nature)—should share views of nature with Ernst Haeckel, George Perkins Marsh, and Roosevelt (all strident advocates of racial and genetic purity), this sharing of ecological and eugenic philosophies suggests that environmentalism's apparently transcendent structure of feeling is firmly grounded in a notion of national purity, a position that requires the construction of ecological others to justify its politics of exclusion.

Early environmentalism's role in meliorating Progressive Era social problems provides a crucial historical perspective for my argument that environmental thought is complicit in, if not responsible for, many of the very social injustices it claims to address. Connections between environmentalism and discourses of fear and policies of social control continue to influence environmentalism today, yet few have analyzed their contemporary implications with regard to how environmentalism becomes a form of social control by othering groups perceived as threats. Environmentalism continues to draw on and perpetuate ideas of nature that reinforce racial and social hierarchies. Thus, white masculinity—and also *able-bodiedness*, as I show in this book—were the barely submerged subtexts of conservation and an emerging environmental politics in the Progressive Era. Thus, a historical framework linking the constructions of disability, wilderness, and a Progressive Era national identity provides a crucial context for my corporeal analyses of how contemporary environmentalism treats its others today, and my effort to outline a more inclusive corporeal ecology.

Theoretical Frameworks

Cultural Theory

The ecological others I examine herein were defined by the early environmental movement in similar ways—as *corporeal* threats in a world of increasing immigration, travel, and urbanization. My emphasis on the shared corporeal histories of these groups is inspired by Priscilla Wald's analysis of this same era in *Contagious: Cultures, Carriers, and the Outbreak Narrative*. Wald argues that anxieties about the healthy body around the turn of the century reflected concerns about increased contact with other people, which new forms of mobility, immigration, and travel exacerbated. The health of the nation became an epidemiological matter. In what follows, I extend Wald's work on the body as carrier, especially her related formulation of the "nation as ecosystem," in order to argue that fears of disabled, diseased, female, immigrant, or racially nonwhite people registered on a corporeal level, in part because the nation was understood in corporeal and ecosystemic—a combination Wald views as epidemiological—terms. That is, imagining the "nation as discrete ecosystem with its own biological as well as social connections" led to projects of "spatial organization" imparted by the "imperative of public health" (23). The Progressive Era conservation and wilderness movements were just as focused on protecting nature from the impacts of a rapidly changing population as they were on protecting nature from the impacts of industrialization. This moment was characterized by more bodies in tighter spaces, creating a new appreciation for public hygiene programs, but also a new appreciation for wide-open spaces and wilderness.

Moreover, I agree with Laura Pulido's assessment that environmentalism is "a form of racism that both underlies and is distinct from institutional and overt racism" ("Rethinking" 17). This assessment helps explain what seems a paradox, noted above: that environmentalism espouses social and ecological harmony, yet it reinforces many social hierarchies. Because environmentalism promotes several goods, including resistance to the devastation of the environment in the names of growth and development, it is easily exonerated of its "bads." Pulido suggests that it actually works in tandem with white privilege. Drawing on George Lipsitz's formulation of the "possessive investment in whiteness," Pulido describes the way white privilege operates. "Most white people do not see themselves as having malicious intentions," she writes, and therefore can "exonerate themselves of all racist tendencies" (15). Environmentalism, like racism, is invested in the fit body. As racism is invested in whiteness, so too is environmentalism invested in the abled body. Environmentalism's moral high ground makes its ableism—and the racist, sexist, and nativist forms this ableism takes—less visible; indeed, they are certainly not institutional or overt. It is precisely its "possessive investment" in *abled-bodiedness* that makes environmentalism's exclusionary tendencies difficult to detect.

Mary Douglas's arguments about purity, pollution, and environmental risk influence my arguments profoundly. Douglas argues that the fact that "the environment" is even on the cultural radar as a problem or risk deserves closer scrutiny from a social-justice perspective. Environmental concerns must be analyzed to see how their framing of issues and proposed solutions reflect, reinforce, or alter "distribution of power in relation" to the environmental problem. If society "produces its own selected view of the natural environment" that "influences its choice of dangers worth attention" (*Risk and Culture* 8), then environmental problems are socially constructed, and knowledge about them is "produced." Further, if people in power "would use risks to nature to get other people to change their ways" (14), then "the environment" is as much a disciplining discourse as it is a material object. My formulation of the ecological other relies on Douglas's argument: those in power are in charge not only of defining the environmental risks, but also of identifying people who are "risks to nature." These definitions are "essentially social rather than scientific" (14). It is with these very social—discursive, historical, and constructed—ways that environmentalism constructs risks posed by ecological others that this book is concerned.

I also enlist Michel Foucault's genealogy of biopower to help explain how a constellation of distinct projects—eugenics, strict anti-immigration policies and sentiments, and conservation—grow out of one imperative: the discipline and improvement of an American population. Foucault's theory exposes connections between seemingly disparate moments of the Progressive Era: the continued fortification of the US–Mexico border, the emergence of the science of ecology, social Darwinism, immigration restriction, the establishment of wilderness parks, and Native American dispossession. I argue that all of these moments are part of one biopolitical ethos that rationalized US attempts to establish identity on two seemingly unrelated scales: the individual body and the national body politic. Following Donna Haraway and Jake Kosek, who have shown how conservation, eugenics, and anti-immigrationism all served the same nation-building agenda, I bring these historical moments together in ways they have not yet been viewed. I argue that these historical moments shaped the construction of multiple subjectivities: the disabled body, the "illegal alien," and the "othered," though still "ecological," Indian. These subjectivities share a common connection to the early environmental movement, a connection that continues to inform the movement today.

Environmental Justice

As environmental justice scholarship shows, this historical tie between nature and nation is partly responsible for mainstream environmentalism's inability to address the issues of social justice surrounding environmental destruction. Environmental justice is concerned with the interconnections between human justice and environmental degradation, and the "places we live, work, pray, and play" as opposed to the empty, pristine spaces of wilderness. Privileging wilderness protection over social justice explains why environmentalism often fails to build coalitions across lines of class, race, gender, and even nation and ability. In this book, I deepen the environmental justice critique of the mainstream even further. Certainly, much mainstream environmental thought ignores certain communities and environments. But it also treats certain human groups as contaminating pure notions of nature and nation and expresses this disgust or fear in corporeal terms. Mainstream environmentalism often views ecological others as unenlightened, ecologically "illegitimate" (in Laura Pulido's words, ("Ecological" 37) threats to nature. Whether breaching expected myths of ecological identity or behaving in ecologically toxic ways, ecological others undermine nature itself. But a corporeal analysis of ecologically illegitimate groups reveals how they are doubly victimized; their *physical,* material bodies often bear the costs of environmental exploitation, and their bodies are *discursively* perceived as threats to national, racial, or corporeal purity, providing a moral rationale for their exclusion and, in some cases, their violent oppression.

A significant environmental justice insight to theorizing the ecological other is its critique of mainstream environmentalism as overemphasizing the domination and exploitation of the natural world at the expense of considering the subjugation of many *human* communities, while ignoring the environments in which under-privileged communities live. One of environmental justice's primary contributions, then, is to insist that the same structural forces that result in the contamination of nature also contaminate its inhabitants' *bodies*. Recognizing that the body is intimately tied to environment, environmental justice charges that the same industries that degrade the environment of both inner cities and reservations, for example, undermine the bodily health and quality of life of their laborers and inhabitants, who routinely are denied access to the spaces where decisions about their bodies and health are made.

Another important environmental justice critique that is crucial to understanding the relationship between social justice and ideas of nature is that mainstream environmentalism constructs environmental problems "as if the human community were uniform, without great differences in culture and experience, without differences in power or access to material influence" (Anthony, qtd. in Chase 352). By including all communities under the category of "human species," deep ecology, for instance, ignores the uneven racial, gendered, and other power structures that shape the relations of different groups to the environment. The universal category "human" creates an "indifference to difference" and makes "multinational corporations and American Indians, members of wealthy countries and those from less powerful groups" (Kollin 139) all equally responsible for the globe's environmental problems. One effect of this "whitewashing" is that differences are overlooked in the name of a universal good, which is protected by an elite class of "eco-managers" authorized to make environmental decisions for all of us (di Chiro, "Beyond" 205). This "new 'green imperialism' thus finds moral cover for itself," such that "whale campaigns" can become "forces contributing to Alaska Native dispossession and displacement" (Kollin 139), for instance.

A related criticism is that mainstream environmentalism privileges a view of nature conceived of as outside the realm of everyday human activity. It values pristine nature "out there," often seeking to identify and preserve "biodiversity hotspots" on a global scale, such as the Amazon rainforest. The attempt to save natural wonders (often from the people who subsist on or near those wonders) follows the wilderness preservation model that has been dominant in the United States. Mainstream environmental groups often advocate preserving lands they deem valuable at the expense of sacrifice zones, such as inner cities and reservations where residents are unable to fight displacement. What distinguishes these two kinds of environments is a question of social justice: whose environment is preserved, and for what purposes? Environmental justice therefore includes environments that are not pristine, such as city centers and abandoned factory sites. As Lawrence Buell argues, the influence of environmental justice on the field of ecocriticism suggests that: "All 'environments' in practice involved fusions of 'natural' and 'constructed' elements. This is evident in the field's increasingly heterogeneous foci, especially its increasing engagements with metropolitan and/or toxified landscapes and with issues of environmental equity" (*Future* viii). Environmental justice has thus drawn attention to "not-in-my-backyard" ideology (known as NIMBY-ism) and environmental racism, which ensure that the most toxic environments are those in which the residents cannot defend their interests. Environmental justice rejects the notion that the inner city is a frightening, toxic "wilderness" whose inhabitants do not care about nature or their own environments (and can therefore be understood as ecologically other to the mainstream). Thus, environmental justice insists that any descriptions, analyses, and solutions to environmental crises be examined in terms of their heroes and villains, and the power structures that shape their relationship to their environments.

Ecocriticism: "Other" Natures

My analyses are interdisciplinary, drawing on literary and cultural studies, geographical theory, and field research. Yet interdisciplinarity characterizes the field of ecocriticism, and so in many ways this is fundamentally a work of ecocriticism. What does ecocriticism do that these other fields do not? Methodologically, this book is ecocritical precisely because I use textual analysis, even as I draw on various fields for the gathering, interpretation, and analysis of texts. The texts I examine in each respective chapter vary and illustrate the interdisciplinary nature of this project. But I analyze these texts—American adventure culture, a case study in Arizona, and a literary text—through a cultural-studies lens that insists that studying discourse can tell us something that other forms of investigation cannot. These textual examples show us that ecological others are constructed by environmental narratives. Narratives not only disseminate information, they create realities, influence economics and politics, and impact the material world itself. Priscilla Wald argues that narratives "promote or mitigate the stigmatizing of individuals, groups, populations, locales (regional and global), behaviors, and lifestyles." Indeed, they so powerfully *matter* that "they change economies" (7). In these senses, then, because they pass as ontologically natural, the material impacts of *environmental* narratives in particular deserve close and critical reading.

This assumption—that discourses matter, regardless of the kind of texts you study—is compelling the field of ecocriticism to be more interdisciplinary and to expand what counts as a text worthy of attention. Early ecocriticism focused on canonical environmental authors who glorified the individual retreat into the pristine space of nature, where the sins of industrialization and anthropocentrism could be redeemed. This pastoral theme pervades much nature writing and ecocritical scholarship. As ecocriticism became more critical of itself, feminist ecocritics, for example, argued that this genre and even the pastoral mode are gendered. Some of these authors enacted what Carolyn Merchant calls "the recovery narrative": wilderness provided a prelapsarian setting to which a man could escape from the toxic (feminine) influences of society, as well as his own complicity in producing this toxicity. Retreating to the wilderness was not just spatial but temporal; one could return to a prelapsarian space of innocence. Krista Comer calls this "the wilderness plot"; environmental texts use wilderness more as a trope or representation of nature than an actual thing itself to move the action and moral message of a text. For example, nature became a masculine space at a moment when urbanization and industrialization led to a "crisis of masculinity." According to Comer, men regained their masculinity through the wilderness plot, a narrative that pervades much of the genre of nature writing, even when the writing is by female authors.

As environmental justice ecocritics have also begun to show, drawing especially on Native American studies and New Western history, this traditional (white, male) nature writing genre ignores the fact that nonwhites lived in and reflected upon the very same landscapes. The wilderness plot is not only gendered but racialized. Beginning in the 1990s, ecocriticism and environmental studies began calling for greater diversity and recognized that the study of the environment and environmental literature had been overwhelmingly dominated by whites and white perspectives. In the 1999 *PMLA* Forum on Literatures of the Environment, contributors noted the Anglo-centricity of ecocriticism. Since then, greater attention has been paid to nonwhite representations of nature, which has not simply increased the number of nonwhite voices but has expanded beyond the genre of nonfiction nature writing and redefined what counts as "environmental" in literature. In other words, "adding more voices" to the canon did not solve the problem. Writings of nonwhite writers and their accounts of nature and their environments did not always resonate with the genre, aesthetics, and politics of traditional environmental literature studies. As a result, what "counted" as an environmental text itself challenged the very terms of the field. Recognizing that a definition of "environment" that includes only wilderness or a limited conception of nature is exclusionary and distorted, environmental literature is beginning to include representations of urban spaces, borderlands, toxic places, the home, the body, landscapes of resistance, and transnational and other views of the environment that account for a broader range of trans-corporealities.

These developments in ecocriticism can be attributed to the influence of environmental justice. Environmental justice ecocritics increasingly address the ways in which disenfranchised groups—communities of color, women, and children, for instance—are disproportionately burdened with the costs of environmental degradation and may even be blamed for it. While the mainstream environmental movement and ecocriticism seek greater input from these communities, the communities themselves are often hesitant to join mainstream environmentalists or to value environmental scholarship, aware that their voices are not being heard, that their definitions of environment do not fit the wilderness model, and that their places of habitation and work are often sacrificed in the name of preserving nature. Sylvia Mayer notes that American environmentalism is "preoccupied with notions of wilderness and wildlife preservation [, which] explains the mistrust black people have harbored toward long-established environmental organizations" (2). Priscilla Ybarra confirms that this exists in Chicano/a studies as well: "Chicano/a studies do not yet relate the natural environment to their priorities in social justice and cultural heritage" (2). The combination of being so long viewed as "closer to nature"—whether in negative terms as "backward" or in positive terms as "noble savages"—and having their social and cultural agendas overridden in the name of the environment has led Native American, African American, and Latino/a communities to distrust environmentalists.

On the one hand, American environmental literature has criticized and rejected urbanization and industrialization, and especially the environmental destruction that accompanied western expansion. At the same time, these views have "fail[ed] to locate people of color anywhere at all in the western drama" (Comer 42) or do so only through the nostalgic tropes of essentialism and a vanished race (of Indians or Mexicans). People of color thus only figure in the western drama as absent, foreign, vanishing, or objects of conquest. Environmental writers consistently ignore this legacy and repeat this erasure of people of color from the wildernesses they describe. For example, Muir and Abbey refer to the presence of nonwhites in the wildernesses of the Sierras and the southwest respectively as "immigrants" or "foreigners," suggesting that nonwhites did not belong in these places. This sense of Anglo entitlement to wilderness fails to acknowledge the historical and literary presence of nonwhites in the natural spaces of the wilderness that these authors were "discovering" and writing about. In this wilderness plot, mainstream environmentalism is a narrative of America's "limitlessness, expansiveness, fresh 'virginity,' optimism, awesomeness, grandeur, a space of forever receding horizons," and a "patriotic landscape powerfully implicated in colonialist rhetorics and ideologies" (Comer 203). Even as American environmental cultural production has been critical in some ways of the ecological consequences of capitalism and expansion, it has also contributed to the frontier and pastoral views of nature that have made these processes possible.

In the chapters that follow, I draw on these environmental justice developments in ecocriticism by analyzing how environmentalism has historically treated a variety of groups as ecologically other on the grounds of race, gender, ability, nationality, and environmental behavior, and argue that it does so on *corporeal* grounds, often at the cost to the *bodies* of ecological others.

Critical Human Geography:
The Promises and Problems of Place

The concepts of "sense of place" and "rootedness" are central to both environmental literary analysis and geographical theory, and my analyses in this book contribute to the debates within these fields about the role of "place" in environmental ethics. Ursula Heise explains that a "wide variety of environmentalist perspectives . . . emphasize a sense of place as a basic prerequisite for environmental awareness and activism" (*Sense of Place* 33). As a result, a hierarchy of senses of place has emerged, which accounts for a certain amount of the exclusion of environmentalism's others: if "place continues to function as one of the most important categories through which American environmentalists articulate what it means to be ecologically aware and ethically responsible today" (29), then place is central to excluding those who are *not* ecologically aware or ethically responsible.

Environmentalist thought often focuses on emplacement, rootedness, and long-term commitment to place as essential to any ethic toward that place. For example, environmental politics and ethics rooted in place seek a return to "the local," as I discussed above. The same is true for ecocriticism, as Lawrence Buell notes, which "has tended to favor literary texts oriented toward comparatively local or regional levels of place-attachment" (*Future* 68). The traditional canon of environmental literature, from *Walden* to Wendell Berry, asserts that an environmental ethic begins with a commitment to one's place. Such an "ethic of proximity" is seen as a spatial foundation for environmentalism. Wendell Berry captures this sentiment: "Without a complex knowledge of one's place, and without the faithfulness to one's place on which such knowledge depends, it is inevitable that the place will be used carelessly, and eventually destroyed" (qtd. in Buell, *Future* 78). This emphasis on the importance of place-attachment, or what human geographer Yi-Fu Tuan calls *topophilia*, has been a foundational tenet within the mainstream environmental movement and a theme of the environmental literature canon.

Indeed, the emphasis on topophilia in environmental politics is perhaps the impetus for the uncritical turn to the body as an ideal way to connect to the environment. In postmodernity, a return to place and its materiality claims to counteract perceived placelessness

and attendant environmental destruction wrought by late capitalism. Indeed, ecocriticism is often dismissed as an unsophisticated
discipline, because it holds onto a naive nostalgia for some mythical
pure nature, while cultural theorists rigorously theorize hyperspatial-
ity and hypermobility, conditions of postmodernity that render the
environmentalist view of place obsolete.

But the fetishization of place has come under critique for a number of reasons. Feminist geographers like Laura Ma Agustín, for
instance, argue that place has been associated with the feminine, as
has home, and that the associated tenets of stability, sedentariness,
and enclosure have generally not been empowering for women. The
nostalgia for a sense of place therefore can be seen as expressing a
masculine impulse for a lost sense of belonging that feminists, post–
women's liberation, are happy to have destabilized. Place-attachment
promotes other kinds of problematic inward-looking orientations. As
Buell notes, "devotees of place-attachment can easily fall into a senti-
mental environmental determinism" (*Future* 66). Place-attachment
can lead to isolationism, NIMBY-ism, environmental determinism,
essentialism, and xenophobia, and often accompanies a nostalgia for
"the country," a pastoral myth, or pure wilderness constructions of
nature that fail to account for their dialectical relationship with other
places. As Raymond Williams argued in *The Country and the City*
(1973), for example, the country for which many environmentalists
are topophilic is inextricably dependent upon the political economy
of the city, despite environmentalists' desire to keep these places
separate. Even as environmental justice movements increasingly
emphasize "the local" and place-essentialism as a political strategy,
attachment to place is just as often about blood-and-soil nativism,
accompanied by denying other places and processes that constitute
any given place. Although place-essentialism has been a necessary
ethic in environmentalism and environmental literature, place-based
environmental ethics are neither inherently liberatory nor inherently
repressive, an argument I will develop more fully in my conclusion.

It is crucial for an environmental justice perspective of bodies
and place to not privilege any one kind of relationship to place over
another. I resist the argument that the nomad, for instance, "represents a subject position that offers an idealized model of movement
based on perpetual displacement" (C. Kaplan 66), as much as I avoid

the notion that "identities are formed through an attachment to a specific site—national, cultural, gender, ethnic, class, sexual, and so on" (25). These two extremes are neither always true nor always liberatory. Both of these arguments assume a definition of place as static. In contrast, Doreen Massey contends that place should not be understood as static or bounded, but rather as a layering of networks of many places, situated spatially in a web of political, economic, and ecological forces. Against the conventional geographical and environmental wisdom that space is abstract, dynamic, and histori-cal, while place is "location, being, dwelling" (Thacker 13), Massey argues that this distinction between space and place corresponds to other troubling dualisms: local/global, real/abstract, specific/uni-versal, female/male, constraint/agency, and even emotion/reason (*For Space* 184). This thinking creates what she calls a "Russian-doll geography of ethics, care and responsibility: from home, to local place, to nation" (186) (this list might as well start with "the body" before "home"), as well as a view that "place is the victim of global-ization" (101), as theories of placelessness often hold. These views, often taken up by environmentalists and nativists alike, commit "spa-tial fetishism, assuming a politics from a geography" (103).

Environmentalism deploys both of these views of place to demon-ize various communities' behavior in the precious and preserved places of wilderness. In contrast, Massey argues that a sense of place does not in itself guarantee environmental correctness. The image of pristine nature discussed earlier can become a "reactionary isola-tionism" in the mainstream environmental "sense of place," to use Massey's language. Rather than accepting sense of place as morally virtuous at all times and in all places, as many ecocritics and envi-ronmental writers do, Massey's power geometry of place accounts for the unevenness of human agency in relation to place. Massey's concept of the power geometry of place better accounts for socio-ecological and political-economic processes.

Massey argues for a "progressive sense of place" that recog-nizes that understandings of place as only fixed or only dynamic are often deployed for reactionary purposes. A progressive sense of place refuses either "global openness" or "local self-containment" ("Power" 178) as the only options available to the geographical imagination. A progressive sense of place in Massey's formulation takes seriously "the relational construction of space" and places as "criss-crossing in the wider power-geometries that constitute both themselves and 'the global'" (101). The conventional notion of a sense of place is ideologically restrictive, and privileges those who have power over their own mobility.

Massey thus asks, "What is it that determines our degrees of mobility, that influences the sense we have of space and place?" (qtd. in Cresswell 64). What kinds of senses of place do migrants, nomads, refugees, or, I would add, people with disabilities, have? How does gender, class, or race influence mobility or ability to stay rooted in a place? Massey's theory of power geometry accommodates these questions of mobility: "Different social groups, and different individuals, are placed in very distinct ways in relation to these flows and interconnections. This point concerns not merely who moves and who doesn't, although that is an important element of it; it is also about power in relation to the flows and the movement" ("Global" 149). Thus, the point is not sense of place, but rather power in relation to place and to one's stasis or movement. Recognizing the power geometry of different peoples' relations to place is one way that geographers contribute a critical, social-justice perspective to environmental criticism. Again, these may not be new insights to ecocritics interested in transnationalism, eco-cosmopolitanism, migration, or diaspora, but I want to emphasize the significance of the body—particularly the disabled body—in this conversation.

One of the primary reasons geography is central to any critical assessment of environmental discourse is that much of the environmental treatment of ecological others is rooted in geographical assumptions—ideologically shaped views of how nature should look (which has implications for what kinds of bodies should be in it), and what counts as an ecological sense of place. Critically examining the discourses of place, space, and landscape in environmental literature from a geographical perspective is therefore central to my investigation of how environmental discourses draw lines—not just figurative, but spatial and corporeal ones as well—between insiders and outsiders. Following David Harvey, I want to be aware of the ways that "spatial and ecological differences are not only *constituted by* but *constitutive of* . . . socio-ecological and political-economic processes" (*Justice* 6). Many ecocritics fail to attend to the ways in which spatial and ecological conditions are products of geographical, political, economic, and social processes, a "way of reading" that I use geography to illuminate.

For example, "landscape" is a contested key term for geographers, and recent theorizations of the term are also central to understanding each chapter's treatment of ecological others. In each of this book's chapters, the texts I analyze treat landscape in a variety of ways and convey spatial implications of delineating and ordering ecological others. Furthermore, I broaden my literary methodology of close readings of texts to include a physical landscape itself as a text that can be "read" in terms of how it draws lines between ecological insiders and outsiders. Combining literary and geographical methods, then, involves reading places, a method that I use to understand a particular place—Organ Pipe Cactus National Monument in Arizona—in chapter 3. The geographical method of critically reading landscapes contributes to my environmental justice understanding of the issues along the US–Mexico border. I take as a beginning premise the views of Denis Cosgrove, Gillian Rose, Don Mitchell, and Krista Comer, who discuss a variety of ways in which landscape and landscape representations carry unacknowledged ideological baggage that often erases the human politics of labor, gender, and power that bear on those landscapes. A critical geographical awareness of representations of place, space, and landscape can materialize the otherwise abstract processes of history, economics, and culture and reveal the broader interpretive networks in which places and landscapes are embedded. Most importantly, though, I am interested in the ways in which geographical theories of landscape help us understand how spaces are made accessible to some people and inaccessible to others. Ultimately, this issue of spatial accessibility has everything to do with bodies.

But the theorists who are doing the most work on linking this insight to corporeality are scholars at the intersection of geography and disability studies, such as Michael Dorn, Rob Imrie, and Brennan Gleeson, who read landscapes for their assumptions about what kinds of bodies belong in them. Representations of landscape vie to normalize competing narratives of place, invoking varying conceptions of corporeality, nature, and nation in these contests. Certain bodies are not meant to belong in certain landscapes, as Timothy Morton provocatively suggests in this important critique of environmental writing:

> One of the defining characteristics of environmental writing
> is how little attention it pays to the fact that only some bod-
> ies have arms and legs; only some bodies are sighted or can
> hear. There is no such thing as the body, if by that we mean
> something unmarked by gender, race, or physical ability. Envi-
> ronmental writing is keen to embrace other species, but not
> always so interested in exploring the environments of "dis-
> abled" members of the human species. (107)

In other words, environmental discourse that promotes the body as a
site of purification, and, correspondingly, the wilderness as the space
of corporeal purification and ecological correctness, ignores bodily
difference among *people*, even as it emphasizes bodily difference
among *species*. This contradiction is revealing, highlighting the links
between spatiality and corporeality in environmental thought, as well
as the need for closer scrutiny of environmentalism's turn to the body.

From this perspective, we might view wilderness landscapes as
designed to be inaccessible because the wilderness model requires
that the retreat to nature be a physical challenge, the implications
of which I develop in chapter 1. Throughout this book, I build on
insights about the constructed landscapes of wilderness in my critique
of the wilderness model, particularly in my analyses of mobility and
access (physical and legal) to the space of the nation. Environmental
conceptions of place and landscape can be deployed for exclusionary
purposes when they create norms about what kinds of behavior in
places and landscapes are ecologically correct. These environmental
"distinctions," to use Bourdieu's term, help define the ecological
other and reify the bounds of "nature's nation." Attention to the
spatial dimensions of environmental texts allows us to begin to recognize the bases for these exclusions, thereby identifying how to
resist and revise them.

Organization of the Book

In chapter 1, "'Maimed Away from Mother Earth': The Disabled
Body in Environmental Thought and Literature," I investigate
the figure of the disabled body in environmental literature and

contemporary US adventure culture. After outlining historical parallels between the wilderness movement, Progressive Era notions of the fit and ideal American body, and the construction of disability as a category, I argue that it is no coincidence that bodily fitness became the sign of natural superiority in the early twentieth century, as wilderness preservation and social reform movements were also gaining force. Scholars working in the field of disability studies show how disability became the category of otherness against which the ideal, productive, and healthy American was defined. But neither environmental nor disability scholars have scrutinized the way in which environmental literature and thought still see the disabled body as alienated from nature and therefore as the consummate ecological other.

This chapter addresses this lacuna by demonstrating how contemporary environmentalism and its attendant recreational practices of outdoor adventure extend early-twentieth-century conceptions of social Darwinism in their focus on "fitness," self-sufficiency, and purity. I argue that if the wilderness encounter tests and hones the fit body, and if alienation from nature is understood as alienation from our own bodies—both notions that originated in Progressive Era environmental thought—then reconnecting with nature means having a fit body. I show how this environmental attachment to the fit body manifests in contemporary American adventure culture, and how the disabled body literally embodies environmental crisis in modern environmental cultural discourse. I examine contemporary expressions of adventure culture, such as advertisements and other outdoor adventure materials, in terms of how they treat and reify the fit body. I also analyze contemporary environmental psychology and philosophy, which look to practices of the body to reconnect to nature. In these examples, technology and modernity have numbed and "blinded" us to the world around us, undermining our ability to craft an embodied environmental ethic.

Further, to illustrate how significant the disabled body is to environmental thought, I examine how the figure of the disabled person informs quintessentially environmental literary texts; in works by Melville, Wallace Stegner, and Edward Abbey, for instance, the disabled body embodies humanity's alienation from nature. In these literary examples, disability serves as a "narrative prosthesis," as

David Mitchell calls it, to make a point about modernity's environmental crisis. These cultural, philosophical, and literary texts all seem to argue the same thing: the crisis of nature is a crisis of the body, and recovering our connection to nature requires not only getting out into it, but disciplining the body away from its reliance on technology and the "crutches" of society. Drawing on the work of disability theorists such as Susan Wendell and Rosemarie Garland-Thomson, Donna Haraway's theory of the cyborg, Deleuze and Guattari's theory of "becoming," and geographers' analyses of "spaces of exclusion" (e.g., Stephen Germic), in addition to my historical analysis of the relationship between conservation and eugenics, I argue that contemporary environmental thought continues to treat the disabled body as a sign of our environmental crisis—it is ecologically other and out of place in nature. I conclude this chapter with a close reading of an exemplary text, Eli Clare's *Exile and Pride,* which I argue outlines a resistant trans-corporeality. Clare's work challenges environmentalism's investment in various forms of oppression, and especially the way environmental discourses treat the disabled body. Clare offers an inclusive corporeal ecology that avoids the problems outlined in the chapter.

In the second chapter, "Ecological Indian or Ecological Other? Environmentalism and the Indigenous Body in Leslie Marmon Silko's *Almanac of the Dead,*" I examine the paradoxical ways in which mainstream environmental thought treats the Native American body. I illustrate this paradox, as well as one Native American literary response to that paradox, in a reading of one of Sherman Alexie's stories and in a more detailed close reading of Leslie Marmon Silko's novel *Almanac of the Dead.* Environmentalism holds Native Americans up as "ecological Indians," to use Shepard Kretch's term, yet simultaneously imposes a standard of ecological purity on Native Americans that fails to address—and thereby perpetuates—the injustices of Native Americans' position within a (post)colonial context of the US nation-state. Thus, I hope to show, the very gesture of glorifying Native Americans in fact, perhaps paradoxically, can serve to reinforce colonial relations. *Almanac of the Dead* is a particularly helpful novel in conveying this paradox and provides an incisive Native American response to it, which also serves to further articulate that this paradox is problematic for Native American identity.

Silko also brings to the fore the importance of the body in understanding this paradox, as the novel illustrates how Native American (and other nonwhite) bodies bear the costs of environmentalism's investment in the abled body.

Historically, of course, Native Americans were not ecological Indians, but rather were seen as impure threats to the national body politic (the figure of the "noble savage" notwithstanding), a form of ecological other that now better describes immigrants in mainstream environmentalism. In chapter 3, "Poetics of Trash: Immigrant Bodies in the Borderland Wilderness," we see how contemporary environmentalist metaphors suggest that certain bodies pollute the national body politic, creating national "insecurity" in a time of heightened global turmoil. Here, I discuss how the historical relationships among immigration, national security, racial purity, and environmental thought are being reproduced in contemporary US politics and literature, which treat the immigrant body as ecologically other. Enlisting geographical methods of analysis to augment my literary, historical, and cultural studies methods, this chapter is based on a case study of Organ Pipe Cactus National Monument on the Mexico–Arizona border. The borderland in and around Organ Pipe is charged, as it is situated along a contested border and is adjacent to the Tohono O'odham Indian Reservation on one side and Barry Goldwater Military Range on another. This ostensibly pure pocket of wilderness cannot maintain its purity, surrounded as it is by lands charged with such indigenous, military, and political history and significance. Thus, it is fitting that in her book on the monument, Carol Ann Bassett writes that Organ Pipe Monument is a "place of edges."

This chapter examines how the environmental consequences of undocumented activity in the desert wildernesses are portrayed in dominant media and environmental rhetoric, which I frame within a broader understanding of the links between environmentalism and the militarization of the border. Anti-immigrant rhetoric about the impact of migrants on the desert landscape constitutes what I call a "poetics of trash," a catalog of wastes and traces—stains on the pristine landscape that make visible the passage of undocumented bodies through the borderland and feed the dominant environmental view that the border is in "crisis." Although that discourse portrays migrants as a biological invasion of "native" (Anglo) land, it is as much about preserving the racial and cultural purity of the national body politic as it is about ecological stability. It distracts attention from the economic and political causes of migration, suggesting the need for defensive measures to "keep them out" and police the borders, rather than human solutions to the economic pressures that cause migration. By presenting and relating the historical, geographical, political, and discursive contexts bearing on this landscape, it is possible to better understand—and thereby imagine solutions to—the humanitarian and environmental crisis along the border.

Ultimately, the aims of this book are threefold: (1) to clarify some causes of the tension between mainstream and environmental justice agendas; (2) to indict environmentalism for its complicity in exacerbating this tension through its continued construction of ecological others, enabled by its historical ties to colonialism (and, by extension, social Darwinism and eugenics); and (3) to revise mainstream environmentalism to acknowledge the interests of those multiple ecological subjectivities whose own environmentalisms may or may not always be evident or align with the mainstream. These revisions contradict the essentialist and static definition of nature as outside of human history and activity, and illustrate the political, historical, and discursive contexts from which nature variously emerges and the varying cultural politics for which it is deployed.

1

"Maimed Away from Mother Earth"

The Disabled Body in Environmental Thought and Literature

NANCY MAIRS DESCRIBES BEING DISABLED in the US West in ways that cast in stark relief the links between colonialism, wilderness, and the fit body about which this book is concerned. She writes about the challenges of being "waist-high" in the West, where values of wide-open spaces, mobility, rugged individualism, and independence reign. Her own life in a wheelchair gives her a critical perspective on these values. She writes, "To be a Western writer, as that term is conventionally understood, you gotta have legs. I mean working—hard-working—ones" (175). Mairs describes feeling excluded by the rugged-individualist myths of the West and articulates that exclusion as a critique of those myths themselves, not just the physical spaces she is attempting to move within: "I have lived now for more than twenty years," she writes, "in a landscape too large for me, and get-ting larger as my physical condition deteriorates, the conventional West—land, lots of land, 'neath the starry skies above—and the conventional responses to it—exploration, exploitation—demand-ing a physical vigor I've never enjoyed" (176). This passage suggests a link between the fit, rugged-individualist body and the colonial practices of expansion. And further, it suggests that perhaps being excluded from the ethos of "exploration" and "exploitation" is a form of resistance to the forms of disablement that those myths and the histories they represent cause.

This chapter develops a corporeal analysis of the "legacy of conquest" in the US West, especially in terms of this legacy's relationship to environmental thought and literature. While scholarship has focused on the social construction of disability and the built environment, as well as on the constructedness of wilderness spaces, no scholarship considers how the social construction of wilderness creates forms of disability. And more, no scholarship takes the next critical step of asking how the social construction of disability and the social construction of wilderness might reinforce each other. How did it come to be that connecting to nature and cultivating an environmental ethic require having a fit body?

Nancy Mairs's experience of disability challenges the myth of the West and offers a relationship to the environment that counters the rugged-individualist ideal. Her experience of exclusion from mainstream society is both a function of disability and a function of society's spatial tropes. One of those tropes is the notion that "*moving* constitutes the western experience*," as Mairs writes. The freedom to move and escape is "essential to the western experience" (180), and, as she illustrates, ineluctably tied to ideas of corporeal fitness. Mairs's critique resonates all the more when we understand it as a reaction to a literary tradition that has received no scholarly attention: the use of the disabled figure as a symbol for humanity's alienation from nature. In this chapter, I investigate this tradition to demonstrate the significance of the fit body to environmental thought, which owes much of its appeal to the western myths and the legacy of conquest I have been discussing thus far.

Moving is a central trope in early environmental writing that glorifies expansionism, as in Thoreau's "Walking," which marries the fantasy of western escape to both colonial expansion and environmental protection in contemporary environmental thought. Movement implies freedom—both physical and spatial—and dominant literary tropes about movement ignore the position of those for whom movement is not voluntary or for whom it is not possible. Thinking geographically through a lens of "movement" allows us to relate questions of disability and migration to themes of access and exclusion. Thus, although the notion that connecting to nature requires movement (either away from the city, through extreme landscapes, or across vast spaces) has roots in early environmental writing, it makes troubling assumptions about bodies and social order that are central to the concerns of this book.

If environmental literature and adventure culture promote the notion that connecting to nature is a corporeal act, an act that requires a complete, whole, preferably fit body, and if environmental and adventure discourses convey the message that modernity, especially technology, has severed our connection to nature, then alienation occurs at the level of the body, since the problem is that modernity's technologies have compromised the body's ability to perceive and thereby appreciate nature. Nature writer Robert Michael Pyle thus calls the environmental crisis the "extinction of experience" in modernity. Hinting that there are evolutionary implications of our inattention to the world around us, this notion asserts that our neglect of experiencing the world leads to our alienation from and therefore mistreatment of nature. It follows that the correct environmentalist response is to reconnect to nature through disciplines and practices that hone the nature-perceiving body. These practices have their roots in the early wilderness movement, a movement that emerged alongside the historical construction of the disabled category. Thus, this chapter argues that the disabled body is the other against which modern environmentalist identity has been formed.

As environmental historians have shown, the modern environmental movement developed in response to various social, economic, and spatial anxieties of the Progressive Era, which led to a series of perceived crises of masculinity, nature, and national identity. Urbanization, unprecedented European and Asian immigration, industrialization, and changing labor, racial, and gender relations all threatened to undermine the images of freedom and masculine ideals of independence that had been central to American identity, and to thwart the progress that became the dominant intellectual and political current of the era. These crises inspired public hygiene reforms, immigration restriction, and environmental protection, among other measures of what Eric Hobsbawm has called the age of reform.

Social reform policies, including immigration restriction, urban reform and design, and early eugenics, as I elaborate below, helped assuage the pressures of immigration and urbanization. These approaches promised to protect both the safety valve of the frontier and the genetic purity of an American race. The need for nature to serve as a "safety valve" defined the early wilderness movement and promoted American exceptionalism. As Susan Kollin observes, "Mainstream environmentalist rhetoric often advances notions of American exceptionalism, masking the nation's expansionist desires in myths of the United States as a benevolent international force, the protector of imperiled landscapes and populations alike" (11). As such, the early environmental movement helped to legitimize Native American and Mexican land dispossession and strict anti-immigration measures from the mid-nineteenth to the early twentieth century.

Nature—as "resource," as "wilderness," and as "safety valve"—was invoked to protect and sustain American character and national identity. So the beginnings of environmental protection did not occur in a vacuum; they were closely linked to these other social reforms of the time. "The first expressions of protectionist sentiment about vanishing woods and wilderness on the part of the dominant settler culture," Lawrence Buell argues, "coincided with the first intensive systematic push toward urban 'sanitary' reform" (*Writing* 8). The urban hygiene efforts of Jane Addams and the preservationism of John Muir were twin parts of the same utopian impulse of American reform.

Under the pretense of preserving a social safety valve, wilderness advocates were thus able to advance socially repressive agendas. The positive image of environmentalism as protecting nature for resources and refuge disguised its exclusions and legitimized social norms in ways that helped preserve the declining power of the Anglo-Protestant elite.[1] Denis Cosgrove thus argues that environmentalism is riddled with "hidden attachments." Wilderness served as "the theater of American empire" ("Habitable Earth" 35) and became a meaningful idea only in the context of environmentalists' racial and social anxieties. "Contemporary appeals to the idea of wilderness," Cosgrove argues, "still retain these hidden attachments" to racism and expansion (36).

These racial, gendered, and classist exclusions of the nineteenth-century wilderness movement emerge in today's adventure culture, which similarly seeks purity, grace, and transcendence through the wilderness encounter. At the heart of outdoor adventure sports is the appeal of personal challenge. The individual—usually male—pits himself against nature and survives. "[W]hether climbing, running, jumping or plunging," Bruce Braun writes, "it is the *encounter* and the *challenge* that matter." Not only do adventure sports provide "the consummate image of courage and skill" ("On the Raggedy Edge" 181), they also offer transcendence and purification. As adventure writer and journalist Jon Krakauer explains, the appeal of mountaineering is its physical discomfort: "I quickly came to understand that climbing Everest was primarily about enduring pain. And in subjecting ourselves to week after week of toil, tedium and suffering, it struck me that most of us were probably seeking, above all else, something like a state of grace" (136). As Krakauer's language attests, adventure culture posits the suffering body as a site of transcendence.

There are links between what makes today's adventure sports appealing and the nineteenth-century enthusiasm for alpine climbing and so-called wilderness cults (R. Nash). The early wilderness movement's view that the wilderness encounter fosters ideal characteristics in the morally pure individual is also central to today's adventure culture's appeal. Adventure culture relies on a "discourse of courage and conquest" to "suture an anxious middle class masculinity" (Braun, "On the Raggedy Edge" 181). The wilderness encounter continues to give those who participate in adventure sports a sense of moral superiority that is tied to white, elite identity. Today's risk culture thus extends environmentalism's historical "racial unconscious," as Braun calls it.

Scholars are thus identifying the race, class, and gender exclusions of early and contemporary environmentalism. They have begun to document environmentalism's relationship to patriarchy, Manifest Destiny, and other ideologies of domination, as well as their links to contemporary environmentalism. Krista Comer captures this critique, as if in dialogue with Mairs: while the "dominant geocultural imaginary emplots normative western spaces in 'open,' free, uncontained terms," these terms "belong to the realm of the official and the public, which unmistakably are gendered male and racialized white." "For who else" besides those gendered male and racialized white, she asks, "exercises the spatial prerogatives implied by 'openness'? To whom belongs a visual ideology of the panoramic?" (27).

But no scholarship has addressed the extent to which environmentalism, the wilderness movement, and this articulation of ideal American identity developed in opposition to a fundamental category of otherness—disability. As the above passage by Krakauer shows, contemporary adventure culture prizes the fit body—able, thin, young, and male—as a means of transcendence. The role of the body in both the Progressive Era, particularly the era's wilderness movement, and in contemporary adventure culture calls for an analysis of the "corporeal unconscious" of adventure culture and US environmentalism more broadly. To the extent that engaging in adventure culture has become a reflection of environmental sensibility, bodies that do not fit this model are deemed unenvironmental. Extending Progressive Era links between the body, social hygiene, and the wilderness encounter, contemporary adventure culture equates physical fitness with environmental correctness, an equation that I disentangle in the arguments that follow.

Disability studies exposes the extent to which adventure culture's investments are not just racial, gendered, elitist, or imperialist, but rather fundamentally hinge on the fit body. It also allows a clearer understanding of risk culture's rejection of technology (symbolic of modernity's corrupting force) by challenging risk culture's focus on unmediated contact between man and nature. Disability studies theorists contend that *every* body's encounter with the physical world is always mediated. They argue that disability is not an ontological category existing outside of social context, but rather that social notions of purity and fitness helped construct disability as a social, political, and cultural category.

In this chapter I attempt to expose what I call the "corporeal unconscious" of environmentalism, which lends risk culture its moral authority, in order to broaden what count as environmentally good ways of being in the physical world. Even if the myth of an inaccessible wilderness lends risk culture its appeal and meaning, environmentalism can be redefined by a different sensibility, one that values an array of bodies and a wider spectrum of positive ways to interact with nature. Thus, in this chapter, I scrutinize today's adventure culture and the environmental movement from which it emerged; environmentalism is responsible for the ideas of fitness and wilderness that shape risk culture, and risk culture masks its corporeal unconscious behind environmentalism's moral legitimacy. In what follows, I disentangle this relationship and offer a more inclusive model of being in the world.

Adventure Culture and the Fit Body

In adventure culture, proving status through challenges and encounters with raw nature is the best way to attain and display physical fitness, thereby achieving what might be termed a "wilderness body ideal." This notion is an extension of Krista Comer's definition of the "wilderness ideal plot," in which wilderness becomes a "space capable of reinvigorating masculine virility while staving off the emasculating tendencies of 'feminine' civilization" (219). Comer reflects the robust scholarship critiquing the gendered implications of the wilderness retreat. Such scholarship attends to the ways in which wilderness parks were a response to a perceived "crisis of masculinity" at the turn of the century; the appeal of a sublime, mountaintop transcendence could be appealing only to men in such a context. Similarly, scholars have argued that the crisis of masculinity is as much a crisis of white bourgeois identity as it is of gender and sexuality. Civilization could be understood only as "feminizing" in the Victorian era, because of its unprecedented immigration, which turned the city into a socially "unhygienic" space. As Adam Rome has noted, cleaning up cities was a "domestic" chore for women like Jane Addams, while retreating from the city to the purifying wilderness was the privilege of the white male elite. The individual white male who escapes to the wilderness is thus a defining trope in wilderness culture and environmentalism—a "risk culture" take on the pastoral tradition.

The body on the cover of the July 2005 edition of *Rock and Ice* magazine exemplifies the wilderness body ideal (see fig. 1). It "testifies" to its audiences (who both "witness" and are "witnesses") that the body is fit through practices of risk in the wilderness. The fit body is, figuratively and literally, external evidence of internal qualities. This cover illustrates the power of images of the body to signal internal moral authority. The corporeality implied in the wilderness plot suggests the need for an analysis of the wilderness body ideal,

Figure 1. "Witness the Fitness." *Rock and Ice* magazine cover, July 2005. Courtesy of *Rock and Ice.*

which embodies virtue, select status, and, importantly, *genetic* superiority. The centrality of the body to the wilderness ideal invokes the historical relationship between social Darwinism and environmentalism on which my argument builds. Braun hints at these connections: "climbing the corporate ladder is akin to climbing a mountain" and is "presented as something innate in the person . . . and also as a property that belongs to the physically superior specimen whose superiority is deserved" ("On the Raggedy Edge" 199). The activities of adventure culture conflate bodily, social, economic, and genetic superiority. In Braun's gloss of this Darwinian argument, the fit body tautologically reflects deserved genetic superiority.

The sports associated with outdoor adventure have taken varying forms since the inception of the appeal of adventure as a recreational activity. Braun explains that although "adventure has a long history in the United States," it has "returned with renewed vigor in the last decades of the twentieth century." Braun locates adventure culture in "the widespread dissemination of images of 'risk taking' in mainstream media and popular culture" ("On the Raggedy Edge" 176),[2] including popular magazines such as *Outside* and *National Geographic Adventurer*. Shows such as *Survivor, Man vs. Wild,* and *Survivorman* claim to teach viewers how to survive extreme conditions, and the documentary *Touching the Void* (2003), which dramatized the harrowing mountaineering excursion of two British climbers that nearly killed them both, are good examples.

In the past, alpine clubs and mountaineering appealed because they promised escape and discovery. Today, the sport of climbing is precisely about risk taking, not first ascents or merely experiencing the sublime. Nettlefold and Stratford contend that the popularity of risk taking marks a shift away from the sublime view of nature, in which nature is awe-inspiring but not dangerous. In the Kantian sublime, nature is simultaneously beautiful and threatening, but the safety of the human figure is always ensured. In contemporary risk culture, by contrast, the "search for jeopardy" is paramount (Williams and Donnelly 4). Difficulty is central to the appeal and status of climbing. In *Bobos in Paradise: The New Upper Class and How They Got There,* political commentator David Brooks sardonically observes the search for jeopardy in adventure sports: "One must put oneself through terrible torment—and this can come either on a cold mountain top or in a malarial rainforest—in order to experience the spiritually uplifting magnificence of brutal nature. One must mutilate the body for environmental transcendence" (210). In this passage, we can see that risk culture jeopardizes the very bodies it champions. Ironically, bodies on the raggedy edge of risk, as Braun puts it, are by definition in danger of disablement, since risk "mutilates the body," yet environmental transcendence requires this corporeal experience. Just being in the outdoors—in the form of gardening or observing nature, for instance—does not offer the element of risk.

Descriptions of adventure culture frequently emphasize physical fitness and value the body but ignore the category of disability against which the adventuring body is defined. They illustrate the logic of what Mitchell and Snyder call the double bind: "While disabled populations are firmly entrenched on the outer margins of social power and cultural value, the disabled body serves as the raw material out of which other socially disempowered communities make themselves visible" (6). In other words, disabled bodies are simultaneously both marginalized and the invisible, raw material from which the normate body, as Rosemarie Garland-Thomson calls it, gains any meaning. The disabled body is made invisible by risk culture's emphasis on fitness, yet risk culture relies on the threat of disability to make its disciplines meaningful. Even Braun's excellent assessment of the racial unconscious of risk culture commits the double bind by overlooking the corporeal implications of Braun's own argument: "Risk culture is seen to have an explicitly ethical dimension, involving a care of self that involves physical and mental tests, and demands an almost ascetic bodily discipline" ("On the Raggedy Edge" 179). For Braun, risk culture "sutures" white, male, elite identity, but despite his reference to the importance of bodily discipline as self-care in this passage, he ignores the *abled* body on which his argument about the *white* body relies. In the theory of the double bind, the disabled body is simultaneously the most *absent*— even in critical assessments of risk culture such as Braun's—and also the most *necessary* for reifying white bourgeois identity.

The double bind is evident in depictions of risk culture today, in which the disabled body's presence is necessary yet invisible. Descriptions of adventure in magazines, survivor shows, and travel literature frequently depict the discomfort, harsh environment, and dangerous challenges the adventurer faces. Many advertisements for adventure technologies use the prospect of endangerment to sell gear. The ability to control risk, however, is a luxury available only to those with resources. Risk becomes appealing only to those who lack risk in daily life. Braun notes: "the freedom to take risks in nature is undoubtedly a white, middle-class privilege" ("On the Raggedy Edge" 178), and signifies economic status. The double bind of risk culture becomes evident because risk in fact threatens disablement. An adventurer who is injured in the wild would become dependent on technological accommodations and support. The imminent possibility of disablement heightens the risk factor of all sports, but particularly outdoor adventure, where there are no trainers, ambulances, or hospitals nearby.

The rare instances of disabled bodies in risk culture capture this irony. An ACR advertisement campaign promotes global positioning systems (GPS) by presenting images of disabled men alongside their narratives of survival. An analysis of the campaign suggests that disabled bodies signify the absolute opposite of the wilderness body ideal. The ACR Electronics personal locator beacon (PLB) advertising campaign turns on the imminence of disability in the outdoors and on the shared assumption that the only place for the disabled body in the wilderness ideal is as an invisible, looming threat. While adventure culture valorizes independence and bodily integrity, it jeopardizes these very traits. The ads therefore reflect the double bind of disability in risk culture.

The first full-page advertisement includes a full-body image of "Dan," standing on artificial legs, alongside text that tells his true story: "Dan got hopelessly lost for five days and eventually lost his legs to frostbite. Sheer willpower helped save his life amid overwhelming odds. It could have been worse. Or it could have been much better if Dan had packed ACR's new TerraFix 406 GPS I/O." Citing "physical prowess and willpower" (qualities Cosgrove linked to fin-de-siècle national character formation), this ad asserts that all that stood between Dan and death was his willpower, but all that stood between him and keeping his legs was a GPS. Avoiding death is testament to the power of will; able-bodiedness is about personal virtue. At the same time, the ad exposes the implicit contradiction of adventure culture: the individual is at risk without the GPS, so the individual is dependent on technological aid to avoid becoming disabled and therefore reliant on aid. Technology helps reduce disability, yet relying on technology is itself something like a disability, as it threatens the self-reliance of the adventurer.

To sell this technology, ACR must address the problem technology poses for the independent, self-reliant adventurer. A second full-page ad in the ACR campaign exemplifies how ACR glosses this contradiction. The ad features Aron Ralston, the climber about whom the film *127 Hours* (2010) is based. In this ad, Aron is rock climbing, although he is accomplishing this feat with an artificial arm. Next to the image of his body is a narrative of his story: "I've been to a place that no one ever wants to visit and I'll never end up there again: Trapped and alone with no way out. With my right arm pinned under a half-ton boulder, I had no way to communicate my position. Five days later I walked out of Utah's Blue John Canyon. I had to leave my arm behind. But I consider it a miracle, not a tragedy: My story has saved lives—it might save yours." That Aron continues to climb, despite the disability that climbing caused him, attests that a "visual rhetoric of disability," as Garland-Thomson calls it, is at work. The image capitalizes on the viewer's expectation that climbers are, by definition, more than able-bodied—the embodiment of fitness. The visual rhetoric at work in this image is one of "wonder" that coaches the viewer to see Aron as a "courageous overcomer" ("Politics" 61).

The ad text continues to describe how important the PLB is for wilderness safety. In much larger print at the top of the page, Aron is quoted: "I still climb solo. Unless you count my PLB." This statement allows us to rest assured that his dismemberment did not cause disability, at least in terms of how disability connotes dependence; Aron "still climb[s] solo." We are also assured that the lightweight and "convenient" PLB will not compromise the independence and purity of the wilderness encounter: "I still climb solo, only now I carry a convenient 12-ounce backup by my side. You should too." The implication here is that, because Aron now requires technological aid (the most obvious of which is his prosthetic arm), his ability to represent the ultimate fit adventurer is jeopardized. His role is to destigmatize the use of technological aid, which merely serves to reveal that there is such stigma among climbers and like-minded outdoor enthusiasts. Furthermore, unlike Dan, Aron's placement in a wilderness setting reveals the extent to which independence is best achieved through wilderness adventure practices, such as rock climbing.

By taking such care to emphasize Aron's independence despite his reliance on his PLB to avoid further disablement, this ad attests to the double bind of risk culture; dismemberment does not stop Aron, but he is proof that the risks are real. The PLB can help avoid disablement, but the status of the adventurer is preserved by reducing the mediating buffer of such technology. We are reassured that Aron's disability does not get in the way of his independence, a point that is emphasized by the dynamic position of Aron's body in the frame; he is literally transcending his environment and climbing out into the text. Aron's exceptional recovery proves the rule that disability is feared because it is fundamentally about dependence—on other people and on technology. By foregrounding people with disabilities to promote reliance on technology, this ad campaign exposes adventure culture's assumption that bodily ability and the virtue it signals can be attained only without the aid of technology—solo.

Like the stories of Erik Weihenmayer, the first blind man to scale Everest, or Rachael Scdoris, the first blind woman to run the Iditarod, Dan's and Aron's narratives are examples of sensationalized "supercrip" stories, as disability theorists call them. Such narratives glorify individual willpower to overcome bodily impairment. Garland-Thomson refers to supercrip stories as a genre that authorizes pity and amazement. Even as they renarrate "tragedy" as "miracle," as in Aron's ACR ad statement, the corresponding responses are normalization, recovery, or cure. Garland-Thomson suggests that the "visual rhetoric" of images of the disabled simultaneously makes disability "visually conspicuous while politically and socially erased" ("Politics of Staring" 56). Because they imply that responsibility for cure lies in the individual, supercrip narratives express the double bind of disability in risk culture. As Garland-Thomson adds, "the disabled body exposes the illusion of autonomy, self-government, and self-determination that underpins the fantasy of absolute able-bodiedness" (46). They thus signal risk culture's attachment to the abled body. Despite their ostensible aim—to show that people with disabilities can do the same things that people without disabilities can do—supercrip stories, which glorify "courageous overcomers," reinforce rather than challenge the dominant values of ableism: independence, the role of individual will in self-cure or self-recovery, and bodily self-reliance.

The prevalence of narratives about supercrips in adventure culture in particular supports my argument that disabled bodies signify not just the opposite of the abled body, but the abled body *in the wild*. People with disabilities who accomplish extreme outdoor feats capture headlines precisely because disabled bodies are understood as incapable of physically demanding activities. What might be called a "disability panic" underpins risk culture. If the wilderness encounter is defined by the fact that it requires more extreme physical fitness than any other activity, then the disabled body literally has no place in the wilderness.[3] In the wilderness myth, the body is pure, solo, left to its own devices, and unmediated by any kind of aid. Its role is to activate jeopardy in the able-bodied as a disablist presence that waits just beyond the next extreme thrill. The perpetual threat of disablement is only heightened by the absent presence of an adventurer who has been disabled by those very activities. However inspiring and heroic, their stories reinforce the audience's membership in the able-bodied wilderness ideal. After all, Aron "still climb[s] solo."

Adventure Culture's Exclusionary Roots

Risk culture's privileging of independence, willpower, bodily fitness, and wilderness borrow much from early environmentalism and from the wilderness movement of the Progressive Era. Examining these roots further exposes the extent to which today's risk culture extends a longer tradition of anxieties about the body, which were directly related to the overlap of social, genetic, spatial, and hygienic concerns of the time. The rapid growth of cities, changing labor relations, an unprecedented influx of immigrants, and concern about the close of the frontier—popularized by Turner's 1893 World's Columbian Exposition "frontier thesis" speech—led to a series of perceived crises of masculinity, nature, and national identity. At the same time, the emerging theory of social evolution, which saw interactions between racial groups as a struggle for survival, provided a national narrative that united "America" (at least white America) against other races and cultures.[4] Because Progressive Era conservationists were beginning to see the environmental costs of modernity, "civilization" could advance only by combining the qualities of progress with man's primal strengths. In this context, returning to "the primitive," "going native," and "getting back to nature" rendered wilderness an attractive setting in which to spend leisure time.

For advocates like Theodore Roosevelt, wilderness was a setting in which the young, virile, American male could practice the "savage" arts of war, hunting, and a raw masculinity. The increasing popularity of Darwinian evolutionary theory coincided with various social crises to help shape the value of wilderness and inform "biologized forms of racism" (Foucault, qtd. in Braun, "On the Raggedy Edge" 121). The loss of the frontier and the "social hygiene" problems associated with urban spaces were in large part responsible for the wilderness movement of the late nineteenth century. Ensuring national "health" meant enclosing wilderness spaces and honing the fit body.[5] Indeed, Progressive Era wilderness ideology *spatialized* national sentiment through the fortification of American borders, expansion of territorial boundaries, and enclosure of land as wilderness against inferior intruders. And the wilderness ideology was *internalized* in the form of disciplines of the body that merged the health and appearance of individual bodies with the health of the national body politic.

Jake Kosek finds that Turner's frontier thesis is "perhaps the most influential origin story of American nationalism [that] grows out of these persistent connections" between "nation, blood, body, and 'wild' nature in America" (132). Turner argued that the confrontation inherent in the frontier encounter—the encounter between civilization and the wild—created a uniquely American character, defined by rugged individualism, "good" Anglo-Saxon genetic stock, and values of democratic governance. Turner's thesis justified Manifest Destiny on teleological, evolutionary grounds: "It appears then that the universal disposition of Americans to emigrate to the western wilderness, in order to enlarge their dominion over inanimate nature, is the actual result of the expansive power which is inherent in them" (Turner, qtd. in Kosek 133). In this logic, European Americans possessed an "inherent power" to expand and dominate nature, which was perceived as inanimate and uninhabited. This rationale also conveniently justified the domination of Native Americans. Conquest and dominance were about racial survival; *not* to expand and dominate would go against Anglo instincts and Darwinian necessity, leading to what Theodore Roosevelt called "race suicide" (Horsman). With the close of the frontier declared in the early 1890s, Turner worried that the American character itself was endangered.

Historians of wilderness in America attribute the origin of the wilderness movement to the desire to preserve American space that resulted from the close of the frontier. For example, William Cronon writes, "It is no accident that the movement to set aside national parks and wilderness areas began to gain real momentum at precisely the time that laments about the passing frontier reached their peak" ("Trouble" 76–77). If the "real" frontier no longer existed, the experience of the frontier encounter could be artificially re-created. Wilderness spaces allowed the elite to foster the superior strengths of American character that the frontier once furnished. Turner's thesis made wilderness preservation essential to American national and genetic viability.

Environmental determinism backed Darwin and Turner; the success of the Anglo-American race required imperial expansion, resting American genetic superiority on territorial appropriation. Progressive Era evolutionists posited evolution not as a matter of natural selection, but as a matter of "survival of the fittest." This notion revised Darwin's thesis to emphasize dominance over natural selection. Further, in the logic of the survival of the fittest, fitness could be understood on the scale of *national* identity, as opposed to the *species,* as Darwin had theorized. Thus, protected territories were not meant for *all* members of the human species, much less for all members of the American nation. Progressive Era social Darwinists would use this new vision of evolutionary theory to justify imperialism, racism, strict anti-immigrant measures, eugenics, and wilderness protection. Along with dramatically increased restrictions on immigration, urban hygiene programs, and the City Beautiful movement, wilderness protection was implemented under the auspices of social reform. As Lawrence Buell argues, "the first expressions of protectionist sentiment about vanishing woods and wilderness on the part of the dominant settler culture . . . coincided with the first intensive systematic push toward urban 'sanitary' reform" (*Writing* 8). Anxiety about urban hygiene manifested simultaneously in the construction of wilderness spaces, as is particularly evident in the career of Frederick Law Olmsted, who both designed Yosemite National Park and promoted green spaces, such as Central Park, in cities. The example of Olmsted shows how discourses of purity/ pollution united social and environmental causes, giving policies of social control scientific, even medical, authority. Race and class prejudices could be justified as reasonable and necessary responses to social "contagion."

Shared concerns about what was happening to urban spaces, manhood, and nature came together in the Progressive Era under the rubric of what Buell calls "toxic discourse" (*Writing* 30). Drawing on both Ulrich Beck's theory of "risk society" and Mary Douglas's theory of "purity," "dirt," and "taboo," toxic discourse "aris[es] both from individual or social panic and from an evidential base in environmental phenomena" (Buell, *Writing* 31). Understood as a response to the fear of toxicity, the wilderness movement can be seen as an attempt to craft a "purification machine," to use Braun's term, that could alleviate the "unnaturalness," "dirtiness," and impurity of an increasing population of racial others in cities. These anxieties helped to justify containment of Native Americans in reservations and enclosure of land in the form of wilderness.[6]

Immigration, eugenics, and environmental protection constituted a three-pronged approach to fears of "National Deterioration" (Kevles 40). Eugenics became a popular and scientific approach to distinguishing between people who belonged within America's privileged boundaries and those who threatened its superiority. Eugenics also helped construct disability as well as race as meaningful categories (Selden). Both racial and ablest fears were seen as arising from genetic threats from the outside (from immigrants), and from genetic faults from within (disability). Detecting "bad" genes within a white population became a domestic policy in its own right, leading to Family Fitness programs and popular media productions linking bad genes to crime, fed by debates about social welfare, contraception, and eugenics. "Eugenics sidestepped the period's intensively enforced racial divisions," Daylanne K. English argues, "precisely because it engaged forms of modern identity other than race" (16).

Eugenicists were concerned about perhaps less visible threats to white genetic superiority from within the white population itself. Genetics became a guise for exclusion and, worse, medical experimentation, along both racial and ableist lines in the name of purity. For example, eugenicists pushed for immigration restriction not to exclude entire national groups, but to deny "entry to individuals and families with poor hereditary history" (Kevles 47). Immigration restriction based on genetics, as opposed to race, used biological arguments against non-Anglo groups, constructing racial inferiority as disability, as Kevles notes: "high scientific authority . . . drew upon expert 'evidence' . . . to proclaim that a large proportion of immigrants bordered on or fell into the 'feebleminded' category and that their continued entrance into the country made . . . for the 'menace of race deterioration'" (94). Eugenics pushed racial agendas, to be sure, but it did so through discourses of genetic "flaws"—disabilities. Immigration restriction provided "positive eugenics"—preventing external sources of impurity—and sterilization provided "negative eugenics"—preventing the reproduction of the genetically defective. By the 1920s, eugenicist sentiments led to the Immigration Act of 1924 and to forced sterilization of thirty-six thousand white and nonwhite Americans, deemed "criminals," "drunkards," "diseased," "feeble-minded," and "disabled" from 1907 to 1941 (Kevles 116). These eugenicist approaches to social reform framed xenophobia as a biological imperative to gain legitimacy.

In such a context, it makes sense that eugenics' early proponents called it "biological housecleaning" (Kevles 114). Ernst Haeckel, the German zoologist, considered to be the founder of modern ecology, was engaged in discussions of eugenics as early as 1868, favoring death for the "unfit" long before eugenics gained public support (Pernick 99). Environmental and eugenics projects reinforced each other: early environmentalists wanted to dictate who belonged on America's precious soil. Echoing an *Almanac* character, Serlo, whom I discuss in chapter 2, the "purity" of American land was linked to the purity of its American genes. Examples of the overlapping interests of eugenics and conservation abound. Walt Whitman, a canonical proto-environmentalist figure, asked, "What has miserable, inefficient Mexico . . . to do . . . with the great mission of peopling the New World with a noble race?" (qtd. in Horsman 235).[7]

As early as the mid-to-late 1800s, "prophet of environmentalism" George Perkins Marsh was drawing on social Darwinian logic to advance both ecological and racial ideals. Marsh exemplified how ideas about the purity of both land and bodies underwrote early environmentalism. Marsh's biographer, David Lowenthal, explains why Marsh is considered a "prophet of environmentalism": "At a time when the United States was moving at breakneck speed to industrialize and develop the national economy by exploiting the wealth of natural resources to the fullest, Marsh's was a lonely voice cautioning against the risk of careless growth" (x). Marsh was prescient in his call for checks to industrialism.

In accounts like Lowenthal's, which reflect the accepted figure of Marsh as proto-environmentalist, Marsh's environmental alarmism hides his racism. But Lowenthal's description fails to address the fact that, to Marsh, New Mexico and California were "inhabited by a mixed population, of habits, opinions, and characters incapable of sympathy or assimilation with our own; a race, whom the experience of an entire generation has proved to be unfitted for self-government, and unprepared to appreciate, sustain, or enjoy free institutions" (Marsh, qtd. in Horsman 182). Marsh's racial views are not included in his environmental legacy. I would argue that this absence is a result not simply of the inability of a contemporary audience to square Marsh's racial and environmental views, or even of the desire to emphasize his environmental contributions over his less savory social views. Rather, such interpretations ignore—even excuse—the complementariness of environmental and racist sentiments. This link is part of a legacy that the contemporary environmental movement still struggles to reconcile. Marsh demonstrates how concerns about environmental protection and concerns about threats to an American racial purity were inextricably linked.

In her classic essay "Teddy Bear Patriarchy" (in *Primate Visions*), Donna Haraway examines how eugenics and conservation overlapped "in philosophy and personnel" (57). Haraway analyzes the synergy between eugenics and conservation through the Museum of Natural History, which was "dedicated to preserving a threatened manhood." While "conservation was a policy to preserve resources, not only for industry, but also for moral formation, for the achievement of manhood" (57), natural history was "medical technology, a hygienic intervention" for a "pathology [that] was a potentially fatal organic sickness of the individual and collective body" (55). Haraway argues that Roosevelt understood conquest of the frontier as proof that white men were evolutionarily superior to Indians, which allowed him to justify both the establishment of wilderness parks in the United States and imperial expansion in the Philippines and Cuba.[8] For Roosevelt, Manifest Destiny became aligned with "holy evolutionary advancement" (Bederman). Roosevelt was echoing Anglo-Saxon leaders from the Mexican War, who espoused a "bellicose racialism" that demanded that Americans "obey our destiny and blood" (William Gilmore Simms, qtd. in Horsman 166).[9] Because of "the dog-eat-dog nature of the relationships between races and between countries," a nation would "fall a prey to an inferior but more energetic neighbor" if it "ceases to extend its sway" (167).

John Higham attests to how nation-building, racism, and social Darwinism fused in this period.

> By picturing all species as both the products and the victims of a desperate, competitive struggle for survival, Darwinism suggested a warning: the daily peril of destruction confronts every species. Thus the evolutionary theory, when fully adopted by race-thinkers, not only impelled them to anchor their national claims to a biological basis; it also provoked anxiety by denying assurance that the basis would endure. (135)

Roosevelt took up these values and saw male virility, violence, and the wilderness encounter as necessary for civilized men to ensure their superiority over other groups. Because "the men of the masterful white American race had an irresistible evolutionary imperative to assert control over any race of inferior men in their midst" (Bederman 197), Roosevelt romanticized the violence of the frontier encounter as proof that white men were evolutionarily superior to Indians, and he justified imperial expansion in the Philippines and Cuba.

Some wilderness historians have seen the connections between conservation and eugenics, but there is less focus on the corporeal nature of this connection. Roosevelt spatialized notions of bodily fitness, social Darwinism, and national identity to the American landscape in the form of national parks and protected areas, but he simultaneously located these values on the individual body. Rescuing masculinity involved "wresting the continent from Indians and installing a higher civilization" (182). But as Bryant Simon attests, it also meant maintaining a fit and healthy body. Health and physical fitness emerged as important priorities in the Progressive Era, and fitness corresponded to nature in two ways: fitness was evolutionary nature at its best, and evolutionary fitness, according to Roosevelt's followers, was best practiced in nature, or wilderness. This "natural man" view of fitness is responsible for the development of mountaineering and alpine clubs (Williams and Donnelly; Nettlefold and Stratford), the Boone and Crockett Club, the Boy Scouts of America, and the emergence of adventure culture as a recreational activity for the leisure class.[10] Once Teddy Roosevelt headed west to recover his own masculinity, Simon argues, "national glory, wide-open spaces, and powerful bodies were . . . forever linked" (84). It is no coincidence that Roosevelt advocated for the purification of the individual body as a justification for preserving wilderness.[11] Gail Bederman argues that, for Roosevelt, outdoor activity—what he called "the strenuous life"— practiced a fantasy of raw masculine identity endangered by the feminizing work of modern society.

Roosevelt, like Haeckel and Marsh, thus exemplifies how the roots of ecology are "tangled up with much of the unsavory racial and eugenic theorizing of the early twentieth century" (Cosgrove, "Habitable Earth" 38). On the surface, then, it would seem a paradox that the very people who founded the tradition of American natural history, ecology, and the wilderness movement—such as Emerson, Thoreau, Whitman, Haeckel, Marsh, and Roosevelt—would also be those who were most strident in their concerns about racial purity. Foucault's theory of biopower helps explain how the seemingly progressive politics of wilderness preservation and the repressive policies of national purity could be part of the same impulse. We can understand Whitman's and Roosevelt's emphasis on the body as gestures of biopower. Foucault explains.

> The emphasis on the body should undoubtedly be linked to the process of growth and establishment of bourgeois hegemony:

> not, however, because of the market value assumed by labor
> capacity, but because of what the "cultivation" of its own body
> could represent politically, economically, and historically for the
> present and the future of the bourgeoisie. Its dominance was
> in part dependent on that cultivation; but it was not simply a
> matter of economy or ideology, it was a "physical" matter as
> well. (125)

The body becomes an apparatus of the state through discourses of
species survival: "Wars are no longer waged in the name of a sovereign
who must be defended; they are waged on behalf of the existence of
everyone; entire populations are mobilized for the purpose of wholesale slaughter in the name of life necessity" (Foucault 137). Biopower
only necessitates genocide "because power is situated and exercised
at the level of life, the species, the race, and the large-scale phenomena of population" (137). Biopower places the burden of species
survival on individual biology and understands survival in terms of
population dynamics: as Rabinow explains it, "the disciplines of the
body and regulations of the population constituted the two poles
around which the organization of power over life was deployed"
(262). Biopower accounts for why, "from the mid-eighteenth century on," dominant classes were occupied with "a 'class' body with
its health, hygiene, descent, and race" (Foucault 124).

   Horsman's description of the era of American expansion supports
Foucault: "The tide of the American population, with no violence or
spirit of conquest, would transform both North and South America"
(Horsman 255). The body of the nation would be crafted to be as
superior and "fit" as possible according to the laws of natural selection. Natural evolution could explain the expansion of the American
population, rendering violence and conquest obsolete, or at least
invisible. Nineteenth-century imperialist rhetoric assumed that "wars
of extermination were not needed," as one 1855 journalist claimed,
"because superior races simply had the commercial power to secure
for themselves the largest share of the means of subsistence" (qtd.
in Horsman 291). The logic confuses causality; superior races gain
power not because they exert domination, but rather they are racially
superior because they have commercial power, and they will continue to acquire commercial power because they have it already. This

statement attests to this logic's Malthusian influence, suggested in the language of "means of subsistence."[12] These historical statements regarding America's natural territorial expansion reflect the logic of biopower in naturalizing genetic domination.

Thomas Malthus's 1798 *An Essay on the Principle of Population* contributed a key logic to this combination. It forwarded what is now accepted wisdom: populations could outgrow their resources and therefore undermine their viability. Malthus wrote, "The power of population is so superior to the power of the earth to produce subsistence for man, that premature death must in some shape or other visit the human race." Darwin's theory of natural selection explicitly rested on Malthus's theory. Darwin acknowledges Malthus in *On the Origin of Species,* in which he explains that his theory "is the doctrine of Malthus applied with manifold force to the whole animal and vegetable kingdoms. . . . Although some species may be now increasing, more or less rapidly, in numbers, all cannot do so, for the world would not hold them" (117). Darwin thus grants scientific authority to what was for Malthus mere observation; this connection is a classic case of mistaking correlation for causality. They both saw a correlation between population growth and resource availability, and naturalized this relationship as causal. But causality fails to account for political and economic structures of resource distribution, from colonialism to capitalism, which contributed as much to a population's access to resources as their numbers. So, while there might exist a correlation between population growth and resource scarcity, Darwin's use of Malthus began a tradition of spatial anxiety about resource "scarcity" discourse that continues today. Turner's frontier thesis and the anxieties it reflected similarly rested on Malthusian logic, which spatialized social anxiety by defining survival as a function of access to resources and space as a safety valve.

Backed by this combination of Darwinian, Malthusian, and Turnerian environmental determinism, the growth of the Anglo-American population necessitated imperial expansion, linking American genetic superiority to territorial appropriation. Turner's thesis justified Manifest Destiny on teleological, evolutionary grounds. Against Darwin and Malthus, though, Progressive Era evolutionists posited evolution not as a matter of natural selection, but as a matter of survival of the fittest; genetic fitness thus became tied to aggression, competition, and dominance. And, also against Darwin's theory,[13] this fitness was understood to apply to a *national,* as opposed to species, scale. "The eugenic principle of selection on the basis of individual biological and mental quality," Kevles writes, "had been submerged in a principle of racial- or ethnic-group selection" (94–95). This contortion of evolutionary theory, which some historians now refer to as sociobiology or "scientific racialism" (Horsman; Gould, *Mismeasure*), thus justified territorial expansion and the securing of resources for the American population as necessary for survival.[14] But these environmental protections were not meant for *all* Americans. Progressive Era social Darwinists would use this new version of evolutionary theory to justify imperialism, racism, strict anti-immigrant measures, eugenics, and wilderness protection.

The scientific racism of the Progressive Era thus did not have just racist and imperialist consequences. Because the ideas disseminated by Malthus, Darwin, and Turner were inflected by environmental determinism, Progressive Era scientific racism had spatial and environmental consequences. Wilderness thus served both as a space in which the American character could be practiced and as a safety valve of space and resources that would make it possible for an American nation—understood in species terms—to be able to thrive. Progressive Era crises became *spatialized* in the form of solidifying American borders, expanding boundaries, and enclosing wilderness, and *internalized,* in the form of "technologies of the body," as Foucault would put it, that elided individual bodies with the national body politic.

Another reason that the body was central to the Progressive Era's response to industrialism was that industrial capitalism's new forms of labor reduced the bodily risks of everyday work for many. City life in particular, Elizabeth Rosen explains, created conditions that made adventure a preferred form of leisure. She locates the roots of contemporary risk culture in the introduction of technology. "With its urbanity," modern civilization "is so safe compared with life centuries ago. More and more, risk [was] filtered out. . . . Our world is largely explored and there are no nasty surprises waiting over the next hill for us. Our technology erases more and more hardship from our lives" (152). Putting one's body through great discomfort became a prescription for attaining transcendence or virtue, because it allowed the privileged to manufacture risk as a form of leisure.

Dean MacCannell adds that the desire to manufacture risk in leisure activities became a feature of bourgeois recreation. Precipitated by the Industrial Revolution, adventure tourism became an example of what MacCannell calls "work displays." The hard physical "work" of outdoor adventure constitutes "leisure" because work itself no longer risks the bourgeois body. "Strangely, we find ourselves in the midst of an age that has turned notions of 'recreation' on its head," Rosen concludes, "when leisure activities have come to include hard-driving and perilous extreme sports and adventure holidays such as rock climbing, sky surfing, and extreme white water rafting" (147). Work displays corrected the moral atrophy associated with bourgeois privilege; they fulfilled a Puritan work ethic through bodily toil. And wilderness was the best place to express this ethic, as environmental historian Paul Sutter argues: "If virtuous labor in nature was no longer the dominant force of American character, structured leisure in an edifying environment promised to fill the void" (291).

It is within this historical context, in which the purity of the body and the nation led to wilderness, eugenics, and imperialism, that the disabled American body gains meaning. Evolutionary theory was deployed for the purposes of disciplining American bodies as much as for the purposes of imperial expansion and wilderness protection. The relationship between the fit body, national identity, and wilderness that emerged in the Progressive Era ensured that unfit bodies were a threat both to national identity and to nature itself. In an era increasingly interested in the rationalization of labor and economic models of efficiency, the disabled body had no place.

Disability was defined by the inability to contribute productively to the capitalist system, to the body politic, and therefore to society. "Nowhere is the disabled figure more troubling to American ideology and history," notes Rosemarie Garland-Thomson, "than in relation to the concept of work," which assumes "abstract principles of self-government, autonomy, and progress" (*Extraordinary* 46). The disabled figure could exist only in a context where self-government, autonomy, and progress were prized. The term *disability* itself implies the failure to meet a standard of *physical* competency, the standards for which were increasingly being defined in the fin-de-siècle industrial capitalist milieu. Only in such a context is it imaginable that the body that cannot perform the actions of "disciplining, optimization

of its capabilities, extortion of its forces, parallel increase of its useful-
ness and its docility, [and] integration into systems of efficient and
economic controls" (Rabinow 261) becomes a liability.

Although historians of disability attribute the construction of disability to the capitalist work ethic, few make the link between the
wilderness movement and disability. By mapping the historical construction of wilderness alongside the historical construction of disability, I am arguing that there is a material, constitutive relationship
between disability and American environmental thought and practice. That is, if the wilderness movement was responsible for imbu-
ing the fit body with values of independence, self-reliance, genetic
superiority, and willpower, and if wilderness was the setting in which
to rehearse these values and reify the fit and healthy body, then the
concepts of wilderness and disability are constitutively constructed.

The Disabled Body in Environmental Thought

This historical relationship between disability and wilderness helps
explain how disability came to stand for alienation from nature in so
much literary and cultural production. It is striking that the disablist
presence is most evident in texts considered proto-environmentalist,
where disability is the category of otherness against which environmentalism is defined. Adventure culture borrows from environmentalism its rejection of modernity as technology. It shares the view
that humans have been disconnected from a simpler, unmediated,
corporeal relationship to the earth. "Ability" is about *not* relying on
technology, society, or others' help; independence is understood at
the level of the body. Environmental literature's anxiety about the
fate of nature gets expressed as an anxiety about the body. The view
that the environmental crisis is really a crisis of the body stems from
the environmentalist aversion to "the machine," which destroyed
nature as resource, nature as a space of retreat and regeneration,
and nature as an organic system in its own right. Because risk culture
borrows environmentalism's aversion to the machine, and because
disability so often symbolizes dependence on machines in environmental literature, examining the roots of this aversion is central to
a disability critique of risk culture. A disability studies critique of

environmental thought best proceeds from an understanding of how values of independence, self-reliance, and environmentalism emerged in opposition to technology.

Some texts that take up environmental themes of the body are central to the American literary canon. A disability studies–informed ecocritical analysis might argue that, for example, Herman Melville's *Moby Dick* portrays Ahab's disability as a punishment for his corrupt, instrumentalist view of nature. Melville captures Ahab's alienation from nature in Ahab's megalomaniacal pursuit of Moby Dick, the white whale. Ahab's corrupted relationship to nature is symbolized by disability—his lost leg. As the captain of a whaling ship, Ahab symbolizes industrialization's extractive relationship to nature. His bodily incompleteness signals his utilitarian orientation to nature, and justice is served by the ironic use of a whale bone for his prosthesis. Using disability as a metaphor, Ralph Waldo Emerson also invoked the image of the "invalid." For Emerson, the invalid was an "icon of bodily vulnerability" against which the self-reliant, ideal "man" should be defined (qtd. in Garland-Thomson, *Extraordinary* 2). In *Angle of Repose,* Wallace Stegner portrays protagonist Lyman Ward's paralysis as symbolic of humanity's malaise, disenchantment, and having been "maimed away from Mother Earth" (Hepworth 17). These texts reflect concerns about the spread of technology, the loss of an Edenic nature, and the impact of these losses on humans. Such losses posed a threat to the notion of a distinct, self-reliant, and yet innocent American national identity. "As modernization proceeded," Garland-Thomson observes, "the disabled figure shouldered in new ways society's anxiety about its inability to retain the status and old meanings of labor in the face of industrialization and increasing economic and social chaos" (*Extraordinary* 47). From an ecocritical perspective, we might add that the disabled body shouldered society's anxieties about the effects of these forces on the human relationship to nature.

The disability-equals-alienation-from-nature trope reemerged powerfully in 1963 in a book that is considered canonical to outdoor enthusiasts. In *Desert Solitaire: A Season in the Wilderness,* author and environmentalist Edward Abbey offers a "polemic against industrial tourism," in which he disparages the machines associated with it: jet skis, motorized boats, RVs, all-terrain vehicles. These machines defeat the purpose of being in the wilderness, making nature *too* accessible and at the same time distancing humans from the "wilderness experience." Machines disrupt the peace of the outdoors and deaden the human body's ability to perceive and respond to nature. Thus, Abbey asks "how to pry the tourists out of their automobiles, out of their back-breaking upholstered mechanized wheelchairs and onto their feet, onto the strange warmth and solidity of Mother Earth again" (64). In other places, Abbey explicitly states that disabled people should not be granted the privilege of being in the wilderness if they cannot access it physically. His desire to keep the disabled body out of the wilderness highlights the centrality of disability to the logic of wilderness in US environmentalism. Modernity as machine has handicapped us by breaking the connection to nature that only our bodies can make. Getting back to nature requires leaving the modern machines behind.

Abbey's wilderness as a place free of technological interference extends the tradition of the pastoral in environmental literature, a tradition Leo Marx explores in *The Machine in the Garden: Technology and the Pastoral Ideal in America*. Marx describes how "the machine" became the antithesis of true "nature": "industrialization, represented by images of machine technology, provides the counterforce in the American archetype of the pastoral design" (26). The pastoral setting creates a modern Eden, where man can "recover from the fall," as Carolyn Merchant calls this impulse in "Reinventing Eden: Western Culture as Recovery Narrative." The pastoral mode stigmatizes the city as toxic and constructs the "garden" as morally purifying. These texts hinge on the symbol of disability as the result of the body's relationship to nature corrupted by the machine.

Current environmental thought builds on this literary tradition. Like Abbey, many contemporary wilderness advocates believe that technologies from automobiles to wristwatches distort the sensual relationship between self and environment. They get in the way of the body's ability to perceive nature. The environmental crisis is portrayed in corporeal terms; an environmental ethic can be achieved only by returning to the intact body. Following human geographers like Yi-Fu Tuan and Edward Casey, environmental thinkers posit the body as the basis on which humans experience the more-than-human world. Casey writes,

My body continually takes me into place. It is at once agent and vehicle, articulator and witness of being-in-place. Although we rarely attend to its exact role, once we do we cannot help but notice its importance. Without . . . our bodies, not only would we be lost in place—actually disoriented and confused—we would have no coherent sense of place itself. Nor could there be any such thing as lived places, i.e., places in which we live and move and have our being. Our living-moving bodies serve to structure and configurate entire scenarios of place. (48)

Here, place, movement, and body are all interconnected, with no critical view about the diversity and assumed definitions of each of these concepts.

Similarly, to craft his environmental ethic, Paul Adams relies on Abbey's assertion that walking is "the one and only mode of locomotion in which a man proceeds entirely on his own, upright, as a human being should be, fully erect rather than sitting on his rear end" (qtd. in Adams 195). It is only by "walking through . . . environment" that "a kind of rhythmic harmonization" can "produce a heightened sensitivity to the environment, as well as a heightened or special sense of self" (193). Adams's contemporary ethic is deeply indebted to the literary tradition I described above: "To climb and descend a hill on foot is therefore to establish a kind of dialogue with the earth, a direct imprinting of place on self; this physical dialogue becomes silent when one moves by merely pressing on a gas pedal. In peripatetic place-experience lies the basis of a special kind of knowledge of the world and one's place in it" (188). This suggests that able-bodiedness is necessary for a healthy human life in the natural world, for a "direct imprinting of place on self." For Adams, the ideal "multisensory" experience is a "peripatetic place-experience."

Contemporary eco-psychology adopts an environmental ethic of corporeal wholeness as well. Eco-psychologist Laura Sewall, for instance, attributes the environmental crisis of our age to a lack of bodily wholeness. Humanity's distance from nature is "muteness" and "cultural blindness." She further writes: "The ecological crisis reflects a crisis in perception; we are not truly seeing, hearing, tasting, or consequently feeling where we are. Our blindness has tremendous implications for the quality of relationship between ourselves and the more-than-human-world" (246). Sewall uses blindness as a meta-phor to argue that we cannot care about the environment, because we do not *perceive* it correctly, fundamentally a corporeal deficiency. Her use of disability is another example of the disablist presence in environmental thought: panic about the environment is really panic about the body. For Sewall, alienation from nature is (and is *like*) a disability. She echoes the general move within environmental philosophy to emphasize a corporeal environmental ethic. After all, as prominent eco-phenomenologist David Abrams poses, "direct sensuous reality . . . remains the sole solid touchstone for an expe-riential world, . . . only in regular contact with the tangible ground and sky can we learn how to orient and to navigate in the multiple dimensions that now claim us" (x). Only contact with "the tangible ground and sky" and moving away from the artificial pleasures and simulacra can bring about the sensuous connection needed for har-mony between humans and their environment.

This environmental philosophy based on corporeal experience is being expressed not only in philosophical discussions; it resonates in popular expressions of risk culture as well, demonstrating its appeal.. *Man vs. Wild* star and host Bear Grylls echoes this move in environ-mental philosophy in *Bear Grylls Born Survivor: Survival Techniques from the Most Dangerous Places on Earth,* in which he articulates the fantasy of an unmediated encounter with wilderness available only through the body.

> It is only when I return to these so-called "wilds" of nature that I find my own spirit comes alive. I begin to feel that rhythm within me, my senses become attuned to what is all around; I start to see in the dark, to distinguish the smells of the forest, to discern the east wind from the westerly. I am simply becoming a man again; becoming how nature made us. These "wilder-nesses" help me lose all those synthetic robes that society has draped over us. (8)

Grylls's emphasis on heightened bodily perception licenses his authenticity. Adventure removes from the body society's "synthetic robes," which above all inhibit sensual connection to the world. But by putting "wilds" and "wildernesses" in quote marks, Grylls exposes a fissure in the wilderness myth; the very spaces that allow him to shed the "robes" of society are themselves socially constructed, even to Grylls. When these spaces reawaken his senses, however, Grylls becomes "a man again," "how nature made us." Paradoxically, then, only a socially constructed wilderness can make Grylls feel natural and fully human; his embodied encounter with "nature" is more important than "real" nature itself.[15]

Grylls shows how wilderness remains the ultimate site for moral purification, and that the purpose of the wilderness encounter does not necessarily foster an environmental ethic. Grylls's language shows that the wilderness encounter has become what Jean Baudrillard would call a "simulacrum" of an environmentalist gesture. That is, it substitutes a performance of unity with nature for any actual ecological sensitivity that the wilderness encounter purports to cultivate. Embodiment does not necessarily guarantee environmentalism; the wilderness encounter comes to serve the fit body more than it serves nature.

A Disability Studies Critique

I have argued that the wilderness body ideal is a hidden attachment of environmental thought and risk culture. The disablist presence in risk culture modernizes the disablist presence of early environmentalism. This view renders some kinds of activities and environments better than others, depending on how well they enhance corporeal connectedness to nature. A disability critique of this position allows—even *advocates*—the centrality of the body as a connection to the physical environment. But it rejects the notion that only certain kinds of physical activities (walking, mountain climbing), and only certain kinds of bodies, permit this connection. A disability studies analysis rejects the use of disability as an overdetermined metaphor for bodily *dis*connection from the physical environment. Disability studies disrupts risk culture's distinctions between abled and disabled and challenges distinctions between purifying or corrupting forms of technological mediation, distinctions that arbitrarily dictate how a body can connect "correctly" with nature.

A disability studies analysis of risk culture's attachment to the wilderness body ideal begins with the notion that disability is a social construction. Disability theorists demonstrate that "disability is as much a symptom of historical and cultural contingencies as it is a physical and psychological reality" (Mitchell and Snyder, xiv). Historically rooted attitudes toward disability construct it as a negative category, as a symbol for an era's fears. This is not to say that disability is entirely a social construction; on the contrary, to acknowledge the ways that "disability is a form of disadvantage which is imposed on top of one's impairment" is not to discount the experienced realities of physical impairment. Rather, acknowledging the construction of disability allows us to see the extent to which it is "caused by a contemporary social organization that takes little or no account of people with impairments" (Tremain 9). Susan Wendell shows how recognizing the construction of disability allows us to look beyond the individual for sources of disablement: "Societies that are physically constructed and socially organized with the unacknowledged assumption that everyone is healthy, non-disabled, young but adult, shaped according to cultural ideals, and, often, male, create a great deal of disability through sheer neglect of what most people need in order to participate fully in them" (39). Wendell suggests that neglect constructs disability; disability is not an ontological reality existing prior to society's views of it and, as a reflection of those views, its design.[16]

Wendell points out that all bodies are in flux, not just those of the disabled. The rigid binary of disabled–nondisabled is a myth: "we are all disabled eventually. Most of us will live part of our lives with bodies that hurt, that move with difficulty or not at all, that deprive us of activities we once took for granted or that others take for granted, bodies that make daily life a physical struggle" (263). Shildrick and Price remind the "healthy majority" that "they are merely temporarily able bodies (TABs)" (106). Disability studies makes us aware that bodies are abled and disabled at the same time, depending on time, place, and task at hand (Nussbaum). Ability is relative to phase of life and to society's structural expectations and physical designs. Accessibility and design are relative to the ableism that informs their construction. Disability, in this sense, is not static; it is dependent on socio-material arrangements that privilege certain kinds of activities and movements, and it is better understood in terms of a "continuum," "where one is disabled in different spheres of life and to different degrees" (Freund 692). This relativist view of disability rejects the notion that disability is a pathology to be avoided or cured in favor of the view that variation of bodily form is natural or normal. It also insists that the problem of disability is located in social structures and contexts rather than in the individual.

The same myth of the individual that makes it easy to ignore the structural causes of disability also makes it easy to stigmatize the dependence of disabled people on technology, a dependence that, I argue, is at the root of their exclusion from adventure culture and environmental thought. Adventure culture's most foundational myth is that the value of the wilderness encounter lies in the fact that the body is going places and doing things that are inaccessible to those who have not disciplined their bodies to be independent. Cosgrove notes, "It is hardly surprising that [hikers and backpackers on the wilderness trails] should be young, fit, and well-off: the arduous physical exercise necessary is unlikely to appeal to the elderly and infirm" ("Habitable Earth" 37). Leo McAvoy adds that "the very elements that make outdoor areas and programs attractive are their undeveloped nature, their ruggedness, the presence of natural forces at work, and the challenge to interact with nature on nature's terms rather than technological human terms," making "outdoor recreation and adventure environments" by their very nature "a challenge for people with disabilities" (26).

But inaccessibility is only one aspect of wilderness that creates barriers for people with disabilities. A more critical spatial analysis reveals that these spaces that dictate movements are reflections of cultural values. Wilderness spaces are no exception, although urban space is given all the attention in disability scholarship. As Peter Freund argues, "Space is important because of the way its organization constructs bodies and offers bodily possibilities and constraints" (694). That is, we need to see space not only as a place where social interaction occurs, but as a material way of structuring that interaction, as well as a manifestation of cultural biases. If we put these theories of "materialist phenomenology," as S. J. Williams calls it (qtd. in Freund 702), in dialogue with discussions about wilderness as a constructed space, we can see how wilderness is constructed with not only the abled body in mind, but as a way of enforcing fitness.

Denis Cosgrove, for instance, argues that "the highly elaborated codes of conduct and dress for these [wilderness] areas can be as rigid

and exclusive in their *moral* message" ("Habitable Earth" 37, my
emphasis) as in their accessibility or expense. Such codes "articulate
an individualistic, muscular, and active vision of bodily health" (37).
That people with disabilities do not like wilderness because their bodies prevent the correct experience of it is an assumption that McAvoy's
research demonstrates fails to recognize risk culture's hidden attachments. Purity, identity, and individualism are associated with independence from technological mediation or the help of others.

> Adventure turns on crossing a great divide between culture and
> wild nature; it is about physical and moral tests that the encoun-
> ter with *unmediated* nature provides (hence adventure travel's
> emphasis on *self-propelled* transportation is not only a nostalgia
> for earlier modes of travel, it is also about stripping away the
> most obvious source of alienation from nature—modern tech-
> nology). (Braun, "On the Raggedy Edge" 194, my emphasis)

The dualisms in this passage—culture/nature, self-propelled/tech-
nology, past/present, movement/stasis—illustrate how the disabled
body embodies the opposite of wilderness. The wilderness encounter
is authentic only if it involves self-propelled transportation. Movement
is vital, and it is as temporal as it is geographical; hence, the nostalgia.
    But the fact that the disabled body often requires technologi-
cal help to perform adventure activities ignores that *abled* bodies
also connect to wilderness in technologically mediated ways. The
wilderness ideal body relies on apparatuses of technological support
to become purified through the wilderness encounter. Braun calls
wilderness a purification machine to expose its artificiality. Technology is central to outdoor adventure culture. Machines are dismissed
as impure, but adventure culture relies on, even fetishizes, its gear.
The success of the adventure equipment industry (REI and Pata-
gonia, for instance) attests to the technological apparatus of risk
culture. Such artificial "extensions" facilitate the wilderness encounter as much as ramps, wheelchairs, walking sticks, Braille signs, and
cut curbs—technologies that are associated with disability. But what
distinguishes trekking poles, hydration systems, GPS units, or cram-
pons—technologies that permit adventurers to encounter wilderness—from the technologies that are associated with the disabled

body? The former are fetishized as gear, while the latter are stigmatized as intrusive or "mediation," as in Abbey's comparison of a car to the wheelchair. What goes unacknowledged in all these critiques of technology-as-alienation is that adventure activities also require "sets of humans, objects, technologies and scripts that contingently produce durability and stability," and "leisure landscapes involving various hybrids that roam the countryside and deploy the kinesthetic sense of movement" (Macnaghten and Urry 8). The kinds of technologies that would make wilderness accessible to people with disabilities are only qualitatively different from the kinds of technologies that make wilderness available to people without disabilities, even if we buy the distinction. All relationships with wilderness are mediated by these objects, technologies, and scripts.

Environmental rhetoric claiming that technology corrupted the garden registers disabled figures as unnatural, symbols of the imperfections we must strive to avoid or overcome. A disability critique of risk culture insists that technologies themselves are not to be seen as inherently good or bad, but as human constructions: "the social world shapes the meanings of technology" (Gibson 15). Drawing on the work of Merleau-Ponty and Deleuze and Guattari, some disability theorists go further, using phenomenology to argue that all bodies are "becoming." That is, all bodies are in a dynamic state of being between organic and other, organic and machine. No body is enclosed, static, or purely organic. This insight undermines the notion of the independent, self-reliant figure the wilderness body ideal champions. It suggests that all bodies, not just ones designated disabled by dominant discourse, are becoming, dynamic, always in a process of being both abled and disabled relative to context, geography, purpose, or habit. Phenomenology emphasizes that our bodies are not independent objects in the world, but rather embedded in the world *through* objects and habits. The relationship between the body and its environment is constitutive. The body's various extensions—clothes, appendages, backpacks, eyeglasses, and chairs, for instance—are technologies that make possible the body's relation to the world.

This argument has important implications for adventure culture. If, as Braun writes, risk culture is about "refusing the disciplinary regimes of modern society and global capitalism, and about pursuing *embodied* rather than *virtual* experiences" ("On the Raggedy Edge" 179, emphasis in original), then the distinction between embodied and virtual is important to the wilderness encounter. But disability studies challenges risk culture's assumption that the human body is natural, while all other objects in the world are unnatural. It suggests instead that the body/world, natural/unnatural distinction is constructed, and could be constructed differently. In "Disability, Connectivity, and Transgressing the Autonomous Body," Barbara Gibson argues: "the 'non-disabled/disabled' division is actually a false one and . . . all of us inhabit different kinds of bodily differences across a range of experience" (188). Based on her interviews with five people who rely on long-term ventilation machines, Gibson concluded that the relationship between the body and machines ought to be conceived as becoming. As Gibson describes one man's relationship to his wheelchair: "the self is uncontained by the material body and spills over into the wheelchair. The chair is more than a symbolic representation of Jack, it *is* Jack, that is becoming-Jack, just as the body lying in bed is also becoming-Jack, and the future reuniting of Jack and the wheelchair will also be a reconfigured becoming-Jack" (194). The notion of the body becoming suggests that "selves are distributive," they are both "confined to individual bodies and simultaneously connected, overlapping with other bodies, nature, and machines" (189). This challenges "prevailing discourses valorizing independence" (187) and posits the relationship between bodies and machines as "connection," "extension," and testament to the "fluidity of the subject." A becoming body is an "assemblage . . . of multiple bodies, machines, animals, places, and energy ad infinitum" (190). Gibson's use of *becoming* shifts the valence from dependency to connectivity and accepts as natural the human body's relationship with machines.

Donna Haraway's theory of the cyborg provides another point of critique. She suggests that "we are all chimera, theorized and fabricated hybrids of machine and organism" (Haraway, qtd. in Gibson 192). In her analysis of the men using ventilators, Gibson refers to Haraway's cyborg figure: "the transfer of energies, the electrified body flowing through power lines connected to the hydroelectric dam, receiving power . . . from the river, from gravity that motivates the river. And energy is exchanged with other bodies that maintain the dam, manufacture the machines, and service the body. The man, the cyborg, refuses to be an individual organism and re-fuses into an individual organism" (191). This description offers a way of understanding the body's relationship to its environment as simultaneously geographical and systemic. That is, the body's movement in physical space connects it to its geography, which in turn connects it to the wider system of the environment itself—in Gibson's example, the dammed river. Her example, perhaps unwittingly, shows how the body is literally a medium between a finite materiality and a larger ecosystem.

But I would suggest that the intention behind the use of this example is more than just idealistic holism. Environmental historian Richard White argues that there are *material* connections between the body and the land. In *The Organic Machine,* he offers the concept of "energy systems" as encompassing natural and human entities and forces. Using the historical event of the damming of the Columbia River as a case study, White argues that technology is not the opposite of human, as so much of the above adventure and environmental discourse holds. He writes, "The mechanical was not the antithesis of nature, but its realization in a new form" (34). Suggesting that "we might want to look for the natural in the dams and the unnatural in the salmon" (xi), White challenges the oversimplified view that dams ("the machine") are intrinsically bad and that pre-dam fishing systems (as they were in the mythical garden) are intrinsically good.

Together, Gibson and White suggest that understanding our organic bodies as interconnected with other animals, machines, and people through energy systems is necessary for an "ethic of openness" to the other (Gibson 195). Rather than facilitating connection to nature, as adventure culture would have it, the myth of the independent body works against the possibility of an ethic of openness—to other people, to animals, and to nature. No body is detached, autonomous, or independent from its geographical, historical, economic, political, and social contexts. Organicism, closeness to nature, ableism, whiteness—the currently valued poles of Western dualisms—are all relative. Most important, attachment to a myth of a static, independent body prohibits connection, curtailing the possibility of an ethic of openness to others. The notion of a body becoming, rather than being, offered by disability theorists reinforces attempts by scholars such as White, Alaimo, and Haraway to argue that upholding dichotomies between nature and humans, organic and machine, actually inhibits an ethic of openness, not just to nature, but to other *people* as well. A disability approach thus casts in stark relief the hypocrisy of the wilderness body ideal's rejection of technology, since, of course, all persons "employ technologies as extensions of the self" (Gibson 14). Abled bodies do not experience nature any more purely than disabled bodies if we view all technologies as mediating and all bodies as becoming. Thus, not only is there no such thing as an unmediated, independent body, but there is also no necessary relationship between such a body and connection to one's surroundings, much less to nature itself.

The fluid relationship between the body and its surroundings has been a focus of disability theorists, as Gibson attests. Disability theorist Michael Dorn reiterates this argument, contending that, "While many of Haraway's readers may have been shocked to realize the extent to which we each operate as cyborgs these days, it could be argued that this assertion would come as no surprise to disabled people, who throughout this century have found themselves wrapped tighter and tighter into the expanding bio-medical industrial complex" (185). Dorn is not content with the flight from the body that is often implied by postmodern feminist theorists such as Haraway, since disabled bodies are the "bodies most embedded in these new space/power diagrams" of modernity (188). Although theories of the cyborg and becoming challenge the notion of the static, independent body in important ways, Dorn goes further in his theorizing of the disabled body, calling for a theory of "geographical maturity" that reverses the moral valence of the disabled body's relationship to its surroundings.

Rather than viewing the disabled body as a corruption of our corporeality and, by extension, our connection to the material world, the notion of geographical maturity positions disability as allowing an enhanced connection to a material world, not because it is ontologically more material than the abled body, but because the world is designed with abled bodies in mind. Geographical maturity is cultivated by navigating architectural spaces constructed by ableist assumptions about the average body. That is, a disabled body "exhibits a mature form of environmental sensitivity by remaining attentive and responsive to changing environmental conditions" (183). Most geographies are not designed for people with disabilities and thus require that much more sensory attention to navigate.

Returning to Mairs's critique of mobility that opened this chapter, Dorn highlights the ableism inherent in the postmodern privileging of the "nomad" (first advanced by Deleuze and Guattari) as a traveler through and among identities, and rather suggests the "creative *spatial dissidence* of disability" can be a "form of being-in-the-world that is never complacent with the state of things, but sensitive and responsive to changing environmental conditions and willing to chart new lines of movement that others might follow" (189, emphasis in original). Rather than insisting that a certain kind of body warrants inclusion in the spatial world or even closeness to nature, Dorn's argument suggests that bodies for whom topographies are not designed offer *better* environmental sensitivity—better understood in his terms as "spatial dissidence"—than the fit ideal and its corresponding orientations toward nature—expansion, conquest, and individualism. In other words, disability studies does not reject the body as an important site of self- or environmental awareness. It merely challenges investments in the fit body.

An examination of risk culture through the lens of disability studies shows how invested adventure culture and environmentalism are in the fit body. Mainstream environmentalism does indeed have a troubling relationship to disability and should continue to be self-critical about its blanket rejection of technology, often implicit in its use of disability as a metaphor for humanity's alienation from nature, and its historical ties to eugenics, national purity, and class and race exclusions. But despite a troubled historical relationship, environmentalists and disability studies theorists share important values, which risk culture's attachment to the fit body unfortunately obscures. Both advocate an increased awareness of place and of the body in place.

And, like many environmentalists, disability theorists argue that society should be more accommodating to varying "pace of life" abilities. Pace of life expectations are in themselves disabling: "expectations of *pace* can make work, recreational, community, and social activities inaccessible" (Wendell 38). A slower pace of life can create the conditions for a greater awareness of nature. In his discussion of the environmental impact of the introduction of the railroad system in America, for example, William Cronon bemoaned what Karl Marx termed "the annihilation of space by time" (*Nature's* 207). In this example, the railroad is not in itself the problem, despite its role as anti-pastoral leitmotif in much US environmental literature. The problem is how speed over distances reduces awareness of localness or place. This *symptom* of the railroad is what disrupted the human–nature relationship. Edward Abbey can be seen as concerned about the spatial consequences of an increased pace of movement: he wrote that "we could . . . multiply the area of our national parks tenfold or a hundredfold . . . simply by banning the private automobile" (69). To Cronon and Abbey, a slower pace of experiencing nature might lead to a more ethical stance with regard to it, since "a man on foot, on horseback or on a bicycle will see more, feel more, enjoy more in one mile than the motorized tourists can in a hundred miles" (67). Addressing the relationship between disability and environmentalism will require that we address this symptom without banishing the machine from the garden.

Thus, despite the fact that risk culture sells itself as key to getting back to nature, risk is not essential to developing a good environmental ethic or appreciation of transcendence. If contemporary environmentalism excludes those who cannot afford or do not have the desire to participate in dangerous outdoor sports, it is reinforcing environmentalism's historical exclusions. When risk culture is linked to environmentalism, its attachment to the abled body makes environmentalism less accessible, restricting the movement's potential for influence. "After all," disabled adventurer Bonnie Lewkowicz writes, echoing the environmental justice call for a greater environmental "ethic of openness," "the more of us there are going out into nature to do these things, the more likely it is that those mountains, rivers, and shorelines will be preserved for all of us for many more years to come" (34). To the extent that the wilderness encounter does foster an environmental ethic, then, making wilderness accessible will have the important result of making environmentalism accessible as well.

Eli Clare: Putting the Deviant Body Back in Nature and Naturalizing the Deviant Body

Environmental writing by people with disabilities serves as a powerful correction to the myths of rugged individualism and fitness that plague American adventure culture and much environmental thought. Clare exposes environmentalism's corporeal, ableist, and sexual investments, and even points to the intersection of all of these forms of oppression. Accounts of experiences in nature and the wilderness by such writers not only refute the ecoliterary trope I outlined above but provide new views of nature that have implications for crafting an embodied environmental ethic that does not insist on corporeal fitness. As a transsexual, queer, disabled writer, Clare (once "she," now "he," as he puts it)[17] challenges the notion that only certain bodies belong in nature and outlines the ways in which environmental thought erases and even abuses impure bodies in the name of nature. Yet he reclaims the self-conscious retreat to wilderness as a form of recovery and resistance, illustrating the possibility that wilderness does not always already have to be a space for the privileged, fit, and pure bodies.

In his memoir, *Exile and Pride: Disability, Queerness, and Liberation*, Clare describes the lived experience of cerebral palsy in ways that challenge the metaphor of disability in environmental thought and literature. Clare takes on the metaphorical "mountain" of societal prejudices against corporeal otherness. His memoir fittingly opens with a chapter titled "The Mountain," which begins with the following passage. The "mountain as metaphor looms large" in the lives of marginalized people, people whose

> bones get crushed in the grind of capitalism, patriarchy, white supremacy. How many of us have struggled up the mountain, measured ourselves against it, failed up there, lived in its shadow? We've hit our heads on glass ceilings, tried to climb the glass ladder, lost fights against assimilation, scrambled toward that phantom called normality. We hear from the summit that the world is grand from up there, that we live down here at the bottom because we are lazy, stupid, weak, and ugly.

This passage expresses Clare's feelings about having cerebral palsy in terms of the challenge of climbing a mountain. The mountain is a fitting metaphor because of the symbolic values that capitalist and adventure culture attach to it: upward mobility, escape, conquest, and vision, which getting to the top entails. And, as I have argued, these values activate adventure culture, rendering Clare's critique of the "glass ceiling" and "glass ladder" applicable to wilderness culture as well. Clare thus engages the idea of the mountain as what might be termed a "master landscape," which stands in for more than mere topography.

But Clare's mountain is not just a metaphor. These musings on the symbol of the mountain emerge from his own experience attempting to climb Mt. Adams. Internalizing these symbols linking the mountain with achievement and physical fitness, Clare attempts to climb Mt. Adams. Clare's emotions about the climb are a mixture of thrill and fear. He chooses the mountain himself and seeks out the personal challenge; he looks "for a big mountain, for a long, hard hike, for a trail that would take us well above treeline" (3). The beginning of the hike is hard, but invigorating, just like a typical adventure narrative. Clare "takes the trail slowly, bringing both feet together, solid on one stone, before leaning into my next step." But soon Clare begins to get "scared as the trail steepens, and steepens again, the rocks not letting up." He "can't think of how I will ever come down this mountain. Fear sets up a rumble right alongside the love in my bones" (4–5). This sublime response hints at the disablist presence operating in the text. The mountain is real too; Clare wants the view from above treeline and he loves mountains. Yet achieving this kind of connection is a struggle, a struggle that Clare argues comes less from being deprived of the view and more from the "internalized supercripdom," "becoming supercrip in my own mind's eye" (3).

In order to explain this internalization of supercripdom and its disabling effects, Clare discusses the distinction between disability and impairment. He quotes Michael Oliver, who argues that impairment is "lacking part of or all of a limb, or having a defective limb, organism or mechanism of the body" (5). Disability, in contrast, is "the disadvantage or restriction of activity caused by a contemporary social organization which takes no or little account of people who have physical [and/or cognitive/developmental/mental] impairments and thus excludes them from the mainstream of society" (6). The material obstacles of built environments are more obvious in the ways they are disabling. But even on the mountain, the symbolic meaning of getting to the top of the mountain is disabling for Clare. These neat categories distinguishing impairment from disability get confused when society's ableist values are internalized.

That is, Clare's internalized ableism is disabling in ways that make it hard for him to distinguish his own limits from the limits that society imposes. Thus, for Clare, the experiences of limitation cause a "frustration [that] knows no neat theoretical divide between disability and impairment" (7). Clare writes that "post-revolution," when the mountain is stripped of these associations glorifying independence, fitness, and transcendence, he will be able to accept his body's limitations as "neither heroic nor tragic" (12), which are the only visual rhetorics available to us, as the example of Aron Ralston above attests. The literal mountain will no longer contribute to his "internalizing supercripdom," reminding him both of his disability and his impairment. Clare's memoir provides a crucial intervention exposing the association between the fit body and the cultural significations of climbing the mountain.

But Clare retains the possibility that the body's connection to nature is a means of transformation and empowerment. He provides a much more inclusive model of connection to nature derived not from an encounter with a master landscape—the mountain—that enables transcendence and visual dominance, but one that locates the value of the experience in the body. Clare replaces the master landscape of the mountain with his body as the vehicle through which nature is engaged. "I will never find home on the mountain," Clare concludes. "Rather," he writes, "home starts here in my body" (9). He goes on to define his body: disabled, violated, white, "marked by Douglas fir and Chinook salmon, south wind whipping the ocean into a fury of waves and surf, . . . by the aching knowledge of environmental destruction, the sad truth of that town founded on the genocide of Native peoples." In these passages, Clare describes what might be considered "impurities" of his body, rejecting the wilderness body ideal's pretenses of topographical and genetic superiority. In fact, he does quite the opposite. By eschewing nostalgia and acknowledging his own ties to Native genocide, Clare finds an environmental justice ethic through his body's relationship to the environment. And, by embracing the very aspects of his body that society rejects, Clare is able to recognize structural injustice that marginalizes both bodies and environments.

Clare's nature is not a space of bourgeois identity performance, where nostalgia, "going native," and conquering mountains takes place. Clare's view of nature is not the transparent eyeball top of the mountain, the quintessentially romantic location of power and perspective. His knowledge of nature starts in his bones—"home." His substitution of the mountain-climb with engagement with nature at the level of the body suggests a shift away from valuing certain kinds of risk landscapes toward a phenomenological emphasis that renders all landscapes worthy to acknowledge and experience, and all bodies capable of participating in those encounters. Clare's description of the relationship between his body and the landscape exposes the corporeal exclusivity of these limited views of how to connect to nature described above and thereby renders a variety of landscapes—not just those that put the body at risk—worthy of corporeal relation.

Precisely because he does not privilege certain kinds of environments over others, and because his cerebral palsy lends him some geographical maturity, to use Michael Dorn's term, we might even see that othered bodies acquire heightened perceptiveness to the relationship between body and environment. They do so not by any inherent closeness to materiality, but by virtue of their exclusion from the built and symbolic landscapes in which they must function. For Clare, the woods provided the relationships and perspective Clare required as a child to escape his abusers and find a sense of self.

> At 13, my most sustaining relations were not in the human world. I collected stones—red, green, gray, rust, white speckled with black, black streaked with silver—and kept them in my pockets, their hard surfaces warming slowly to my body heat. Spent long days at the river learning what I could from the salmon, frogs, and salamanders. Roamed the beaches at high tide and low, starfish, mussels, barnacles clinging to the rocks. Wandered in the hills thick with moss, fern, liverwort, bramble, tree. Only here did I have a sense of my body. Those stones warm in my pockets, I knew them to be the steadiest, only inviolate parts of myself. I wanted to be a hermit, to live alone with my stones and trees, neither a boy nor a girl. (124)

This simultaneous corporeal and environmental awareness, or geographical maturity, is empowering to Clare because it allows him to disentangle himself from the social structures and people that are disabling. Clare, who in adulthood underwent a sex change to be more biologically male, sought escape in nature from parental pressures to "be more feminine." And the woods provided a space where he could recover a sense of his body after being raped by his father and his friends, who exploited and reified Clare's disability and gender vulnerabilities.

If the mode of the pastoral promotes the escape into nature as a retreat from social responsibility, Clare's retreat is the only place where he can escape these externally imposed, disabling myths and abuse. Being in nature—wandering, observing, roaming, collecting stones in his pocket—showed Clare how to view his body not as "merely [a] blank slate upon which the powers-that-be write their lessons" but as "the sensory, mostly non-verbal experience of our hearts and lungs, muscles and tendons" (120). This form of self- and environmental awareness provides a counter to both the risk and eco-psychological narratives that privilege certain kinds of experiences, bodies, and landscapes as the best for getting back to nature and the body. In Clare's revision of the body in nature, he avoids valorizing particular outdoor activities as providing self-knowledge and environmental sensitivity, while still acknowledging the body as central to acquiring these values. He does not need to climb a mountain or put his body at risk to gain these insights. In Clare's view, nature is a place to escape body scripts, not to perform them.[18]

In further counterpoint to the dominant mainstream wilderness model, Clare gains his most valuable environmental ethics not in the wilderness, but in the city. Clare moved to Portland, Oregon, where he acquired a sense of "what was beautiful and extraordinary about the place I grew up in, and what was ugly and heart-breaking" (25). His ability to perceive the simultaneous beauty and ugliness in the mill town of Port Orford required him leaving that space. He also became politicized about the environment, in part because he saw that urban environmentalists oversimplified the tension between the working classes, whose livelihoods relied on environmental destruction, and environmental preservation. As a result of his hybrid form of rural–urban environmentalism, and because of his particular relationship to disability and queerness, Clare recognizes structural injustice. As he says, he questions strict preservationism that ignores "a wide-reaching analysis of capitalism, class structure, and environmental destruction" and "doesn't examine the links among many different kinds of violence and destruction" (62). Suggesting that environmentalists and loggers should direct their frustrations away from each other and to their common oppressor—corporate bullies—Clare comes to understand romantic views of wilderness as counterproductive.

Clare's sensitivity to structural oppression also exhibits the relationship between identity politics and environmental justice about which this book has been concerned.

> I never grew into the white urban reverence of tree spirits and Mother Earth, a reverence often stolen from Native spiritual traditions and changed from a demanding, reciprocal relationship with the world into something naïve and shallow that still places human life and form at its center. Nor did I ever grow comfortable with the metaphor of clearcutting as rape, the specificity of both acts too vivid for me to ever compare or conflate them. But I did come to believe that trees and fish are their own beings, important in and of themselves, and that I—as activist, consumer, and human being among the many beings on this planet—have a deeply complex relationship with them. (25)

This description avoids claims to closeness to nature based on cultural appropriation, conquest, transcendence, nostalgia for a premodern time, or wholesale rejection of society, despite what it has done to him. Although Clare's woods provide escape from society's disabling features, his environmental ethic is one of openness and commitment toward the oppressed, of awareness of shared structural oppression. His wilderness is a place from which he can craft constructive critique of, rather than uniformly reject, society. Because he sees links among different kinds of violence, his environmental ethic is rooted not in a desire for purity, but in social commitment. Further, by portraying the nature where he escapes social oppression as contested and embedded in human politics, he resists defining wilderness as a space devoid of people, politics, and history. In other words, he sees the space of the woods in terms of its power geometry. By doing so, Clare challenges the construction of wilderness and the ideals of individualism, corporeal fitness, and purification accompanying it.

Being in nature in ways suggested by a disability perspective may thus help to dismantle the very myths and tropes that have informed what counts as the wilderness ideal thus far—Emerson's rugged individual, Thoreau's self-reliant man, Manifest Destiny, Roosevelt's strenuous life, and the Darwinian notion of what kinds of bodies are best suited to be in nature, which create a sociobiological geography of exclusion. Contrary to the notion that the disabled body has no place in the wild, a notion that has its roots in the construction of disability as unnatural and adventure activities as reifying the fit body, getting away from society can be considered a subversive act against the society's material and discursive construction of disability.

Conclusion

In the July/August 2008 issue of *Orion,* mere months before the Beijing Olympics, environmental justice activist and writer Rebecca Solnit argued that the Olympics hide nationalism, torture, and abuse behind the mask of corporeal beauty and fitness: "The celebrated athletic bodies exist in some sort of tension with the bodies that are being treated as worthless and disposable" in China, she writes. Solnit then suggests an analogy between this tension and how the United States treats its environments: "Bodies in peak condition performing with everything they've got are an image of freedom, as are pristine landscapes like Yosemite and the Tetons. But the reality of freedom only exists when these phenomena aren't deployed to cover up other bodies that are cringing, starving, bleeding, or dying, other places that are clearcut, strip-mined, and contaminated" (17). From Solnit's environmental justice perspective, wildernesses and fit bodies both cover up the same thing: a nation's sacrificial bodies and environments. The figure of the disabled body activates an impulse for corporeal purity and environmental pristine-ness. It is also the body sacrificed in order to uphold these ideals, just as preserved parks allow for the sacrifice of reservations, inner cities, and industrial zones.

But, as I have shown in this chapter, there is more than mere metaphor at work in Solnit's relationship between sacrifice bodies and landscapes. The material, literal sacrifice of both bodies and landscapes, for which Solnit holds China accountable (a problem I turn to in the Conclusion), is a central theme in Native American literature. The dual sacrifice of landscapes and Native American bodies in colonial history, but also in contemporary military and labor contexts, belies environmentalism's romantic view of the Native American as "ecological Indian." In the next chapter, I investigate environmentalism's paradoxical treatment of Native Americans as simultaneously ecological and ecologically other. In particular, extending this connection to Solnit's observations about the Beijing Olympics, how do bodies of ecological others, as well as the landscapes they inhabit, serve as the very material upon which dominant forces are built? How is this very materiality paradoxically made invisible by environmental discourses that uphold the Native American as ecological noble savage?

2

Ecological Indian or Ecological Other?

Environmentalism and the Indigenous Body in Leslie Marmon Silko's *Almanac of the Dead*

IN MUCH NATIVE AMERICAN LITERATURE, the deteriorating Native American body symbolizes and literally embodies colonial-capitalism's impact on Native Americans. The corporeal costs of colonial-capitalism on Native American communities abound: exposure to nuclear fallout, diabetes, alcoholism, and cancer appear with greater frequency in Native American communities than in the rest of the US population. Colonial-capitalism disables the Native American body. In N. Scott Momaday's *The Way to Rainy Mountain,* for instance, the Kiowa are "bent and blind in the wilderness." In Simon Ortiz's *Fight Back* and *from Sand Creek,* Native American bodies literally support US military operations, both in terms of uranium mining and on the battlefield. Thus, as these examples show, disability becomes powerful shorthand for Native American exploitation. The disabled body renders colonization intelligible to Native American readers and non–Native American readers alike. The physical diminution of the body metonymically conveys experiences of loss of agency, loss of direction, disconnection from the land, and dispossession wrought by colonialism. When tribal *lands* become sacrifice zones of toxic waste, so too do Native American bodies become sacrificed. Given the trope of the disabled body in Native American literature, in this chapter I argue that the body is central to many Native American critiques of mainstream environmentalism's investment in colonialism. These critiques reveal that the Native American holds a paradoxical place in mainstream environmental thought—the ecological Indian is also ecologically other. In what follows, I show that only through an analysis of the body in Native American thought—as I explore in a short story by Sherman Alexie and develop more fully in an analysis of Leslie Marmon Silko's novel *Almanac of the Dead*—can we begin to see this paradox as a "fissure" in dominant environmental thought that can be exploited for purposes of indigenous justice.

Sherman Alexie's Environmental Justice

In the introduction to his collection of short stories *The Lone Ranger and Tonto Fistfight in Heaven,* Sherman Alexie jokingly warns his readers that although he is Indian, the stories will not be about nature: "There might be five or six pine trees and a couple of rivers and streams, one grizzly bear and a lot of dogs, but that's about all the flora and fauna you're going to get" (xxii). Known for dispelling myths about Indians, Alexie is responding to what Shepard Krech has called the "ecological Indian" stereotype,[1] which assumes that Native Americans are inherently environmentalists. To his nonindigenous readers, this move signals a rejection of this myth; just because Alexie is Native American does not mean that his stories will be environmental. Native American communities, however, are disproportionately exposed to the environmental problems of our day, from nuclear waste dumping and uranium mine tailings to disappearing glaciers and rising sea levels. If environmental concerns are critical to Native American communities in particular, as Winona LaDuke, Simon Ortiz, Ward Churchill, and Valerie Kuletz persuasively contend, why would Alexie distance himself from "nature"?

Alexie's move suggests that the white stereotype of the ecological Indian, ironically, has little to do with nature. This seeming paradox, as well as Alexie's impulse to signal this irony, captures the ambivalence many communities of color, including Native Americans, feel toward mainstream environmentalism. This ambivalence and how it is negotiated in environmental identity politics deserves more critical attention. Native communities do have a vested interest in addressing environmental issues, but not because of an essential "closeness to the land" that mainstream environmentalism ascribes them. Reserved tribal lands contain the majority of US natural resources and have been primary sites of nuclear weapons testing and nuclear waste dumping. Native American communities have borne the costs of the state's policies of environmental racism in ways that would suggest a natural alliance between environmentalists and Native Americans.

Despite these realities, mainstream environmentalism has often relied on the symbol of the Indian as an emblem of *healthy* human–nature relations. Thus, the movement obscures indigenous issues and Native American environmental concerns even as it uses the Indian as a symbol for its own agendas. As Alexie would put it, mainstream environmentalism cares more about a symbolic myth of precontact, primitive affinity between Indians and "pine trees," "grizzly bears," and "rivers" than contemporary indigenous environmental issues. And this nostalgic environmental ethic often pits environmentalists against Indian claims and interests, such as self-determination and land rights. Because Native Americans often want to do things with their land that do not fit environmentalist ideas of nature, or their expectations of Native Americans, these groups are more often at odds than not, contrary to the myth of the ecological Indian.

Indeed, nostalgia for an ecological Indian identity impedes mainstream environmentalism's perception of contemporary environmental problems facing Native Americans, which, I want to argue here, are (at least in part) *caused by* the mainstream's attachment to the stereotype Alexie rejects. Native Americans are often characterized as living in more environmentally sustainable ways than are contemporary Euro-Americans, yet they are often oppressed in the name of "pristine" nature. Alexie's rejection of the equation of "Indians" with "nature" can be understood as a reaction to the use of the ecological Indian for agendas that are not those of Native Americans and may even be hostile to their interests. Indeed, mainstream environmentalism puts Native Americans in an impossible position—to support modern environmentalist agendas or be seen as not authentically Native American.

I argue that the use of Indian identity to advance environmental causes is a form of cultural imperialism, what Larry Lohmann has called "green orientalism." That is, the ecological Indian stereotype not only appropriates Native American identity, it imposes forms of identity and representation for non-Indian ends. Like the wilderness movement's geographical erasure of Native Americans through dispossession, this stereotype ignores historical and contemporary realities in favor of white environmentalist sentiments. The stereotype actually *diminishes,* rather than authorizes, Native American agency. As Soenke Zehle observes, the ecological Indian stereotype presses indigenous communities to "appear primarily as repositories of ecospiritual alternatives" (335) and not as ecological actors in their own right. On the surface, the ecological Indian stereotype seems to support both nature and Native American interests. As Zehle adds, it also "lock[s] native peoples in immutable identities." Conflict between Native Americans and environmentalists emerges when indigenous "communities open their land to commercial development, resource extraction, or waste disposal in the pursuit of economic autonomy and self-determination only to be confronted by others who consider such acts a betrayal of their ostensible identity as spiritual ecologists, without knowledge of their desperate need for jobs and income" (335).

In this sense, ecological Indians can just as easily become ecological others—betrayers of non-native environmental sensibilities and of non-native expectations of Native American identity.

One response to the impossible demands of western environmentalism on Native Americans is to reject a connection with nature entirely, as Alexie does, in favor of a contemporary, multidimensional, fluid, often urban, Native American identity. An alternative response is to critique these conflicting stereotypes as yet another form of cultural imperialism—imperialist nostalgia in green garb. For example, Bruce Braun points out that environmentalism's relationship with Native Americans is "deeply ambivalent," stemming from "contradictions within environmental discourse itself" (*Intemperate* 80). He argues that a "discourse of indigeneity" romanticizes Native Americans in their pre-contact form, removing them from "history" and relegating them into "nature" (89) and gives environmentalism its particular "*postcolonial* form" (87, emphasis in original). Braun further argues that relegating indigeneity to the past abstracts Native Americans from any historical context, which means that indigeneity "quickly become[s] a cipher whose content is filled by the environmentalist or the state official, and thus a vehicle for very different political and ecological agendas from those of the people purportedly represented." These "ecopolitics" become the "latest in a long history of neocolonial incorporations," comprising what Braun calls "postcolonial environmentalism," where "indigenous identities are defined and contained within the environmental imaginaries of European environmentalists and the postcolonial nation-state" (81).

These critiques are important because they highlight the ways in which indigeneity is a social construction that is used for nonindigenous ends, because they reveal the ecopolitics of neocolonialism, and because they shed light on the internal contradictions of environmentalism. But, as Tania Murray Li argues, this critical position, as important as it is, runs the risk of treating "representation as a one-sided imposition" (qtd. in Ramos, 360). Native Americans are not empty vessels or "ciphers" with no power over these representations. On the contrary, many indigenous groups have used those expectations and stereotypes for politically productive ends, performing a version of what Spivak calls "strategic essentialism." "Orientalizing themselves," as Jean Jackson has described, is a way to rearticulate, challenge, and re-present environmental issues. Even if they use the identity politics that are ascribed them, and which are more a reflection of white cultural norms than Native American identity, deploying these stereotypes for the purposes of subverting dominant environmental notions and agendas is powerful. As Alcida Ramos argues, "when theoreticians tell us that essentialism is bad politics, what they do is create a theoretical blind spot" (379).

Ramos suggests that displays of identity—both those of white people claiming authenticity by being close to "'real' Indians" and those of "equally avid 'real' Indians"—serve important political and strategic ends for both sides. Indians can "turn their cultural capital into political muscle against undesirable state policies" just as white environmentalists want to use indigenous closeness to the land as political muscle against those state policies (363). "Part nature, part artifact," Ramos concludes, "the Indian provides the nation with a reservoir of arguments that justify" many different positions (367). Larry Lohmann further argues that green orientalism can compel indigenous groups to "act out assigned roles which they can . . . 'twist and subvert' to their advantage" (qtd. in Li 172). Whether these twists and subversions are interpreted as evidence of limited power or as sources of empowerment within a postcolonial context is the subject of much debate. But to dismiss the agency gained by these strategic deployments of indigeneity—by self-orientalizing, so to speak—is to ignore the ways in which discourses of indigeneity are constantly made and remade, in flux, complex, and reflective of power negotiations that are two-way, as well as the ways in which tools such as cultural essentialism and ecological Indianness can subvert the same spirit of colonial othering that spawned them.

Ramos describes how important the ecological Indian stereotype, or "culture" card, was in a resource contest in Brazil:

> In indigenous hands, the culture concept . . . becomes an important tool to mark their differences from majority societies. Once in command of the technology of writing, the Indians use it to their own purposes. The same happens with culture. They have no qualms in instrumentalizing certain cultural features they know will impress the whites, regardless of whether such features are part of their own traditions, are borrowings from other peoples, or are newly created. (369)

The debate between essentialism and constructivism fails to capture the variety of ways that both approaches can be used to achieve a variety of ends—both political and personal, and sometimes both or sometimes one at the expense of the other. These negotiations cannot be theorized in one way—as either an oppressive form of postcolonial environmentalism or a form of strategic essentialism.

Debates over the relative political effectiveness of strategic essentialism for identity politics are beyond the scope of this project, but what I want to draw out here is that mainstream environmentalism's myth of the ecological Indian not only puts Native Americans in an impossible situation—they either perform as ecologically Indian or risk being inauthentic if they seek immediate jobs over long-term forest sustainability, for example—but also fails to account for the ways in which environmentalism itself emerged out of the very colonial history from which it presumes to rescue Native Americans. This additional layer of irony within mainstream environmentalism is often ignored in debates over whether the ecological Indian is a form of strategic essentialism or cultural imperialism. It is this insight that I elaborate in this chapter: environmentalism not only makes impossible demands of Native American identity; these demands are precisely impossible because environmentalism initially served colonialism's agenda of dispossessing Native Americans of territory, land, and access to resources. By pointing out the ways in which environmentalism treats Native Americans as ecologically *other*, in contrast to the Indian as the ideal ecological subject, I hope to show that environmentalism has ties to colonial history that continue to emerge in contemporary environmental debates, which seek to circumscribe Native American sovereignty even as they draw on the representational power of the myth of the ecological Indian.

Revealing these ties helps to explain why Alexie would simultaneously eschew nature and describe Native American environmental injustice in terms that do not conform to conventional nature writing tropes. That is, although Alexie distances his book from nature, and himself from white environmentalist readers, he does address environmental issues in the text. Following the playful mode of the trickster, he says one thing and then does another, drawing our attention to the contradiction he seeks to critique. Rather than writing about his characters' essential connection to "flora and fauna," he discusses the environmental and human health costs of colonialism, capitalism, and racism on the reservation. Alexie's disavowing of nature forces his white readers to rethink mainstream concerns and white expectations of Indians. It allows his later attention to environmental justice issues to revise the mainstream, as it suggests that indigenous communities are capable of articulating their own environmental concerns and identities.

In his short story "Jesus Christ Is Alive and Well on the Spokane Indian Reservation," Alexie simultaneously rejects the ecological Indian trope and hints at Native American environmental concerns in ways that reveal mainstream environmentalism's connections to colonialism. He does this by outlining one way to understand environmental concerns as an indigenous community might define them, as opposed to how a white reader might want to define them for Native Americans. The 1974 World's Fair in Spokane provides the context for Alexie to contrast mainstream environmentalism and environmental justice and evoke the environmentalism–colonialism link. The story hints at why Native American writers and scholars resist close association with environmentalism, even when they address environmental issues in their work.

White visitors to the fair capture Alexie's critique of mainstream environmentalism. They enjoy one of the fair exhibits of a statue of an Indian that, when triggered by the push of a button, voices a clichéd ecological message: "We have to take care of the earth because it is our mother" (129). This message reflects the emerging ecological sensibility of the 1970s environmental movement, which looked to Native Americans as premodern people who coexisted harmoniously with nature. Native American identities were portrayed as inherently environmentalist, embodying a pre-industrial golden age of harmony between humans and nature.

Ironically, though, the myth of the benign ecological Indian—as represented by the statue—could emerge only once Native Americans had been conquered by Anglo-European colonialists. Renato Rosaldo explains this seeming paradox in terms of what he calls "imperialist nostalgia"—a sense of longing and desire for that which is conquered, which the process of conquering paradoxically engenders. Indians were seen as a mortal threat to white civilization, which called for their violent destruction and displacement while imagining the "West" as uninhabited—as a frontier destined for conquest. US expansion had both environmental and human costs, and, as both nature and Indians were viewed as "vanishing," they both became fetishized others. This nostalgia fuses them together as one symbol of a lost way of life. As Susan Kollin describes it, "the colonizer's nostalgia for an authentic Indian belatedly tries to call back a lost world that it had earlier banished." In turn, it is important to recognize that any "return to the authentic 'native' is a return to an origin already invented by the colonizer" (141). Thus, appreciation for a premodern native–land harmony is possible only within the context of conquest of western lands and of Native Americans. In sum, regardless of Native American environmental interests, the symbol of the ecological Indian is a product, not a vestige, of colonialism.

Even as they erase this history of conquest, the World's Fair statue and its message signal this erasure. The statue itself reflects imperialist nostalgia for an ecological Indian myth. It reflects its white audience members' preference for this myth, which is located in the past and therefore better represented by a "dead" statue than a live Indian. Meanwhile, Indians have not vanished, despite the message the statue is meant to convey. In fact, they are living in the land in close proximity to the fair, where the very colonial processes that the fair celebrates—expansion, exceptionalism, settlement, growth—have damaged the land and undermine the local Indian community. Alexie juxtaposes the statue and the fair scene with a real-life Indian and real-time scene: James, an Indian character, comments on the river behind the fair, where he "knows something more" has happened: uranium deposits from mining on Indian land (to make weapons for the US military) have polluted the water. Because it would force them to recognize their complicity in contemporary and historical injustices, the (white) spectators prefer the myth of a vanished "noble savage" and its attendant myth of humanity's harmonious relationship to nature over the real, present environmental issues of the Spokane Indian community. Mainstream environmentalism, which promotes the ecological Indian myth, reinforces colonialism's destruction of Native American sovereignty by making these contemporary environmental injustices invisible to white spectators, whose preference for the dead Indian lulls them into believing that being at one with Mother Earth can possibly be consistent with the legacy of conquest. The spectators do not want to know about the environmental concerns Indians would define for themselves in present time. The artifice of the fair assures their denial about what has really happened to the landscape and the people that the fair presumes to glorify. Looking beyond the statue would involve white culpability and expose the imperialist and military agendas of US expansion, thereby undermining the narrative of progress that the fair commemorates.

This story also underlines another environmental justice criticism of mainstream environmentalism. In its attention to a *global* sense of environmental harmony (as exemplified by the World's Fair and reference to mother earth), it ignores *local* concerns, and how these local and global issues are mutually constituted. The fair celebrates US power and advancement and also portrays mainstream environmentalists as smugly confident of their own good intentions and global vision, while they ignore the polluted land that stays there even after the fair moves on. This contrast between local and global scales of environmental representation has implications for social justice. Some environmental justice scholars criticize mainstream environmentalism for emphasizing the global scale of environmental problems (climate change, biodiversity "hot spots," the depleting ozone layer) at the expense of local concerns, where people without political or economic power experience global problems in local ways daily. That is, environmental justice advocates are more likely to frame environmental issues in terms of health, pollutants, and structural inequality, while mainstream environmentalism is more likely to care about environmental problems they are privileged to avoid experiencing at the phenomenological (corporeal and local) scale, such as climate change. In Alexie's story, for example, James's environmental concern is the local river on the reservation, while the statue is concerned about a global-scaled, imagined space—Mother Earth.

Alexie's contrast between these different representations of Indians, imagined and real, reflects in fictional form the environmental concerns that Native American scholarship addresses: the troubling trope of the vanished Indian, which the statue symbolizes; the authority of traditional ecological knowledges and epistemologies over "expert" ecological science and white nature aesthetics (as James's knowledge of "something more" implies); and the sacrifice of Native American identity and land in the name of protecting Mother Earth, US nation-building, and national security. Alexie's story illustrates the contradictory place of indigeneity in mainstream environmentalism, which puts the preservation of wilderness and wildlife over the preservation of tribal communities, even as it nostalgically uses Indians as symbols of a more ecological past. And Alexie hints that this seeming contradiction is a reflection of the continued imperialist project of Manifest Destiny.

The Ecological Indian/Other:
Leslie Marmon Silko's *Almanac of the Dead*

Leslie Marmon Silko's novel *Almanac of the Dead* further develops this critique of mainstream environmentalism as a contemporary manifestation of colonialism. Environmental concerns pervade the text, yet Silko frequently frames environmentalists as colonialists. Silko uses this contradiction to critique environmentalism and colonialism. In this way *Almanac* does more than simply outline how Native American oppression is tied to environmental destruction, as most readings of the text argue. These readings fail to recognize a much more complex and ambivalent treatment of environmentalism, which operates in the novel as both a pro- and anti–Native American politics in different times and places, dramatizing the strategic essentialism–versus–cultural imperialism debate described above. Given Silko's challenges to the colonialist investments of environmentalism, any reading of the novel as environmental that fails to register Silko's ambivalence ignores the novel's revision to environmentalism. *Almanac* illustrates how environmentalism can both support and thwart social justice, and that environmental discourses accomplish the latter by treating colonialism's others as *ecological* others. Silko's ambivalence toward environmentalism makes sense, given environmentalism's paradoxical treatment of Native Americans, and the novel is a call to identify the ways in which environmentalism is embroiled in the very oppressions it claims to eschew.

This novel also emphasizes the corporeality of ecological others in its critique of mainstream environmentalism as contemporary colonialism. To trace the body in the novel is to trace colonialism's impact on Native Americans, which exposes environmentalism's investments in social control. The following story illustrates the novel's focus on the body as a way to understand the links between environment, colonialism, and social justice: as twin mixed-blood Native Americans Zeta and Lecha are learning about their family history, their Yaqui grandmother, Yoeme, describes her marriage to their grandfather, Guzman, a descendant of Spanish colonialists. The arrangement was strategic: "Why do you think I was married to him? For fun? For love? Hah! To watch, to make sure he kept his side of the agreement." Guzman's side of the agreement was to protect Yoeme's people's land from further appropriation by white people. Yoeme "was married to him" (by arrangement) to help protect her people's land. But despite this position of leverage, Guzman's complicity in colonial projects causes Yoeme to leave him. She describes the moment she left, which was precipitated by a "fight involving big cottonwood trees."

> The fucker Guzman, your grandfather, sure loved trees. They were cottonwoods got as saplings from the banks of the Rio Yaqui. Slaves carried them hundreds of miles. The heat was terrible. All water went to the mules or to the saplings. The slaves were only allowed to press their lips to the wet rags around the tree roots. After they were planted at the mines and even here by this house, there were slaves who did nothing but carry water to those trees. "What beauties!" Guzman used to say. By then they had no more "slaves." They simply had Indians who worked like slaves but got even less than slaves had in the old days. The trees were huge by the time your mother was born. (116)

Confused about the relationship between Guzman's love of trees and the separation of their grandparents, Zeta and Lecha ask, "But why did you fight over the trees?" Yoeme switches directions in her response, speaking no longer about trees: "They had been killing Indians right and left. It was war! It was white men coming to find more silver, to steal more Indian land. It was white men coming with their pieces of paper! To make their big ranches." Yoeme informs Zeta and Lecha of the colonial context of her marriage to Guzman, in which a "war" was causing the slaughter of her people and the theft of their land. As part of her story about the transport and maintenance of the trees themselves, Yoeme's description of the war connects Guzman's love of trees to the conquest of Native Americans and their land. Indeed, as they listen to Yoeme's story, Zeta and Lecha keep getting confused about whether Yoeme left "because of the trees" (116) or because "Guzman hated Indians" (117). Their confusion underscores Yoeme's point: the two reasons are related. Colonial views of the environment were central to colonialism's justification of violence against Native Americans.

Guzman's hatred of Indians and his love of cottonwood trees are intermingled in this story, as attention to materiality—of bodies and of nature—reveals. Colonialism is violence against slaves (black and Indian), against land, and against nature—and these forms of violence are related. Zeta and Lecha's confusion about whether Yoeme left Guzman because of his racism or because of the seemingly trivial, unrelated issue of "trees" suggests that Guzman's imperialism includes both racism and a "love of trees." But Guzman's love of trees is a paradox: his landscape aesthetic, which requires the trees to create a setting in which Guzman feels comfortable and powerful, is not really about nature. Imperialist affection for nature is often characterized precisely by attempts to convert landscapes of colonized lands into the image of the garden that the New World promised. "Virgin land" *requires* colonial settlement to convert it into "the garden." His love of trees and his use of slaves to transport and plant them epitomize colonial landscape aesthetics. Guzman's ambition to impose a more verdant landscape on the existing desert landscape reflects a "green colonial" aesthetic, to use Richard Grove's term; Guzman simultaneously controls and appreciates nature, but only an aesthetic and domesticated version of it that the cottonwood trees, imported from elsewhere, illustrate. Guzman's love of trees is strictly aesthetic and instrumental—what we might term "eco-colonialist." Just as the colonial conceit justifies extracting Native American peoples from their land for utilitarian purposes—slavery and territorial acquisition—so too does eco-colonialism design artificial landscapes in the name of loving nature. In line with the environmental history of colonialism more broadly, Guzman's mastery over his slaves corresponds to his mastery over the landscape.

In contrast to the eco-colonial aesthetic that justifies extracting cottonwood trees from their context in the name of love, Yoeme outlines a view of nature that values the cottonwood trees' role within a broader cultural system. She articulates the Yaqui understanding of the trees' relationship with their environment and her people: "the cottonwood suckles like a baby. Suckles on the mother water running under the ground. A cottonwood will talk to the mother water and tell her what human beings are doing. Then those white men came and they began digging up the cottonwoods and moving them here and there for a terrible purpose" (117). Here, the land, water, and cottonwoods communicate corporeally—like a mother and her baby do through the intimate act of "suckling." A superficial love of trees is in fact hateful when it doesn't take these connections into account. This contrast between green colonialist values and indigenous values allows Silko to distinguish indigenous environmental concerns from those of colonialism and even to outline a dominant environmentalism that *supports* colonial ideologies about landscape

and race. Furthermore, Silko dramatizes this distinction by emphasizing the corporeality not only of the tree–land relationship, but of
the land–Native American relationship. That is, Guzman's planting
of the cottonwood trees does not simply serve the "terrible purpose"
of imposing a colonialist vision on the desert, exploiting slave labor,
and tearing the trees from their place in indigenous cosmology. The
trees serve the "terrible purpose" of the ultimate act of violence—the
lynching of Yoeme's clansmen (118). Silko's description of trees to
lynch Native Americans critiques eco-colonialism on multiple levels.
Guzman's "love of trees" is an aesthetic expression of a distinctly
imperialist irony: the use of "nature"—*literally* in the form of the
cottonwood trees themselves, and *symbolically* in the form of import-
ing a colonial landscape on an incompatible environment—to steal
land, exploit the environment, and remove Indians from the garden
of the New World.

This story thus signals the centrality of the body as the site of
these terrible purposes in *Almanac*. Silko's critique of the paradox
of eco-colonial values registers at the level of the body: it was the
labor of black and Indian slaves' *bodies* that was extracted in order
to impose an artificial landscape on the land. The cottonwoods that
resulted from this *corporeal* labor are in turn used to lynch the bodies
of the slaves that grew and tended them. This double corporeal violence of colonialism is fundamentally related to its treatment of the
land and nature. Silko is able to convey the paradox of colonialism's
violent love of trees only through her description of Indians' *bodies:* like natural resources, they are simultaneously the raw material
from which colonialism was built and on which it enacts conquest.
Just as the bodies of trees are destroyed by being uprooted from
their "mother" land and water (in a so-called act of love), so too is
Yoeme's body—the exotic Native female body—exploited to gain
control over her people, whose bodies are ultimately lynched on the
trees that come to symbolize the dispossession of both the environment and Native Americans by colonialism. Thus, this story distills
Almanac's critique of the link between colonialism and environmentalism, as well as how these forces achieve their ends *materially,*
and sets the stage for the following further trans-corporeal analyses
of the novel.

Environmental Justice in *Almanac:* "The World of the Different"

While primarily a novel about indigenous justice (the return of land to indigenous peoples), environmental justice scholars treat the novel as central to the canon of environmental justice literature, because it also scrutinizes the relationship between indigenous injustice and environmental exploitation. The novel explores the dual oppression of both the environment and Native Americans under colonial-capitalism; one critic captures the environmental justice interest in the novel, arguing that *Almanac* shows how "oppressions and exploitation of people and land are inextricably linked" (Kang 737). But I would suggest that this conventional environmental justice reading of *Almanac* does not sufficiently address the novel's critique of colonial-capitalism, much less environmentalism's investment in colonial-capitalism, and thereby misses its central project of indigenous claims to and understanding of "land." Merely highlighting the ways in which the novel shows parallels between social oppression and environmental degradation—how the oppression of land and people is "inextricably linked"—does not do justice to the novel's environmental justice contribution.

In my view, Bridget O'Meara offers a more accurate reading of the novel. For O'Meara, the novel draws important parallels that allow us to see connections in ways that the dominant order would not have us see: the "history of globalization is inextricable from the histories of colonization and attendant discourses of power and . . . difference, which naturalize the violent exploitation and commodification of land, labor, and the body of the 'Other'" (64). Although this reading allows for a more sweeping definition of environmental justice—as a critical analysis of power—it still leaves conventional views of the environment intact, and ignores how these views are entangled in the very colonial apparatus that causes these multiple forms of oppression. And, most important for the purposes of this book, these conventional environmental justice readings of *Almanac* fail to account for Silko's emphasis on the body as her primary launching point for the novel's attacks on both colonialism and environmentalism.

The central problem in *Almanac* is US colonial appropriation of Native American land. Affirming Edward Said's point that "imperialism is an act of geographical violence," the novel shows that colonialism entails land dispossession, displacement, and forced settlement, as well as enslavement, rape, torture, and murder. Colonialism attempts to erase indigenous language, culture, and religion. Colonialism has criminalized and condemned Native American rituals and oral tradition; it has dismissed Native American views of time, animism, intergenerationality, and the existence of multiple worlds as lacking any basis in reality, and has substituted individualism for communalism. Colonial-capitalism continues to exploit and marginalize Native Americans economically, as well as through legal coercion, sexual abuse, political corruption, and the denial of Indian land claims. And on the occasion that Native American history, oral tradition, and cultural practices are recognized, the novel insists, colonial-capitalism also commodifies them.

Almanac suggests that challenging contemporary colonial-capitalism is a matter of historiography—it requires a retelling of US history. In its insistence on revising dominant narratives of history as well as how history is told, *Almanac* dispels the linear and progressive narrative of western expansion. Like historian Patricia Limerick's call for recognition of America's legacy of conquest and American-studies scholar Amy Kaplan's assessment that imperialism shapes US nationalism and identity, Silko's recasting of US history emphasizes the subjugation of peoples and lands in the name of western civilization. The novel accomplishes this rereading by reframing the "discovery" and subsequent "civilizing" of the Americas by Columbus and European colonialists in terms of the indigenous and African conquest, oppression, slavery, and injustices these processes involved. The legacy of conquest counters the dominant historiography that teleologically naturalizes the settlement of the Americas. *Almanac* provides alternative stories that counter the glorification and inevitability of these founding narratives and expose the social injustices on which they are built.

As in Marx's writings, *Almanac* forecasts revolution as inevitable because the destructive forces of capitalism undermine themselves. For example, Zeta and Lecha's white geologist father, who led miners to uranium deposits, is punished for his role in betraying the land and the indigenous communities who live near the deposits.

He contracts cancer from his exposure to toxic elements. Like the Marxist view of how capitalism will undo itself, his undoing is an inevitable result of his role in the extraction of resources. He

> had been perfectly capable of destroying himself. His ailment had been common among those who had gone into caverns of fissures in the lava formations; the condition had also been seen in persons who had been revived from drowning in a lake or spring with an entrance to the four worlds below this world. . . . The white man had violated the Mother Earth, and he had been stricken with the sensation of a gaping emptiness between his throat and his heart. (121)

His role in facilitating the commodification of Mother Earth caused his ailment. Revolution is not a matter of revenge or vying for power; it is nature's inevitable response to the "greedy destroyers of the land" (156). The deterioration of his body is self-inflicted and inevitable, an analogy for the fate of capitalism in Marxist thought.

One mestizo character, Calabazas, affirms this notion of revolution as retribution: "Guns and knives would not resolve the struggle. He had reminded the people of the prophecies different tribes had. In each version one fact was clear: the world that the whites brought with them would not last. It would be swept away in a giant gust of wind. All they had to do was wait. It would be only a matter of time" (235). It is the white world's inability to sustain itself—not a violent uprising of "guns and knives"—that will be its undoing. The white world is unsustainable, and so it would just be a matter of time before it destroyed itself. The communities most vulnerable to colonial-capitalism—people of color, women, children, people with AIDS, the homeless, and immigrants, for example—are the "despised outcasts of the earth" who will take part in the revolution. The very fact that they are not "part of a single group or organization" is precisely what empowers them (513). Even this description—despised outcasts of the earth—hints at the fact that what unites these groups is what they share with nature—being "othered" by Destroyer discourse and conquest.

This connection between outcasts and the earth can be seen in Silko's portrayal of the signal that the revolution will begin: the emergence of the stone snake from a uranium pit mine in New Mexico. The pit mine is a symbol of the Destroyer's exploitation of the land and people of the Americas, and it is a *uranium* mine, symbolizing the destructive capacity of science, which is responsible for nuclear bombs. The mine is an emblematic landscape because it bore the human and environmental consequences of colonialism: the containment of Native Americans on reservations, the extraction of uranium from Native American land for US military operations, the desacralization of the physical landscape, and the exploitation of Native American labor, which made all of these actions possible. The snake's signal from the pit mine ends the book, but it foretells the revolution: "the snake was looking south, in the direction from which the twin brothers and the people would come" (763). The "twin brothers and the people" will converge in the United States and, from there, reclaim the lands of the Americas.

Dominance is not just economic, political, and geographical violence; violence against vulnerable members of society—children, animals, women, and the disenfranchised—is *sexual*. Characters with political and economic power are almost always also sexually pathological, and they are equally likely to abuse a natural resource, an animal, and any other member of a vulnerable group. For example, a corrupt judge, Arne, takes bribes to ignore environmental and tribal laws and has sex with his basset hounds. Judge Arne thus captures the way *Almanac* draws parallels between environmental concerns (such as "wilderness," but also our "companion species," to echo Haraway), and indigenous injustices. Another character, Bartolomeo, who turns out to be more interested in communism than indigenous justice, sexually exploits a white woman, Alegria, apparently as revenge on capitalist hegemony. By punishing Alegria for his emasculation by colonial-capitalism, Bartolomeo illustrates how racial empowerment can be just as much about sexual power as it is about race. Further, the neo-Nazi character, Serlo, both obsesses about his "*sangre pura*" and loathes all things feminine, and his friends include a wealthy gay entrepreneur who trades in specialty pornography—snuff and rape films, and films of abortions and sex changes. Trigg, a man who traffics in illegally harvested body parts and organs, is incapable of having an orgasm, and he manipulates organ donors to give up their lives by giving them blow-jobs while "the victim relaxe[s] in the chair," "unaware he [is] being murdered" (444). Menardo, the founder of a company that insures other companies against civil unrest, is so paranoid about designs on his own life that he wears a bullet-proof vest while he sleeps; the vest serves as a prophylactic to all sensations, ultimately denying his human sensuality. Ironically, protecting the body diminishes its function. These examples show how *Almanac* makes connections between sexual behavior and corrupt power. As in Foucault's assessment of biopower, sex and blood (as a symbol of both genes and violence) are related in this novel.

But Silko does not simply use sexual corruption as a metaphor for moral corruption. *Almanac* conveys colonial-capitalism in sexual terms to suggest that the Destroyer's insatiable appetite is *simultaneously* violent and sexual. Destroyers are, by definition, "humans who [are] attracted to and excited by death and the sight of blood and suffering. . . . Secretly they were thrilled by the spectacle of death" (475). Death and suffering "excite" and "thrill" Destroyers; in Freudian terms, the sex drive and the death drive are the same. One typical Destroyer character, Max Blue, links his sex and death sensibilities on the grounds that they are both "natural" because they are consequences of evolution: "All death was natural; murder and war were natural; rape and incest were also natural acts. Serial murderers who chewed their signatures on victims' breasts and buttocks and even the baby-fuckers—they were all consequences of human evolution" (353). This tautological explanation for violence echoes sociobiological justifications for colonialism—the victors of colonialism are the genetically superior race because they conquered, while the victims of colonialism are evolutionarily inferior because they were conquered. Drawing parallels between these biopolitical logics, *Almanac* both equates the degree of each set of offences and reveals the self-serving logic underpinning western expansionist historiography. And, in addition to illustrating how evolutionary logic can be deployed to naturalize violence, Max Blue's thoughts convey how Destroyers literally get off on dominance and violence. By equating colonial-capitalist exploitation with sexual dominance and deviance, *Almanac* shows the interconnectedness of patriarchy, anthropocentrism, misogyny, and racism.

Where it fails to follow through on its own commitment to dismantling dominant hegemony, though, is in its treatment of homosexuality, which *Almanac* clumps together with these other forms of "deviance," such as bestiality.[2] The novel frames homosexuals not as another group of "despised outcasts of the earth" who have been deemed "unnatural" and oppressed by the dominant order, or as a maligned group that could be indigenous allies through the logic of their shared oppression (a logic that the novel otherwise supports), but rather as symbols of patriarchy through sexual "unnaturalness." Male homosexuality is not only a sexual perversion; it is an unnatural distaste for women, just another expression of patriarchy. In this sense, *Almanac* reinscribes the same tautology about homosexuality that it criticizes in Max Blue's colonial-capitalist sociobiology, which Silko critiques for using "evolution" to justify social oppression. Surely, drawing on *Almanac's* sweeping distaste for all things masculine, Silko could just as easily have framed heterosexual relations as a *product* of colonial-capitalism, not natural at all, as they involve men.[3] This paradoxical treatment of sociobiology—as both a rhetoric of colonial sociobiology and as heteronormative—undermines the novel's success at challenging the Darwinian logic of biopower, in my view. Nonetheless, Silko's highlighting of the sex/death drive reinforces the centrality of the body to the novel's critique of colonialism. The body is the material of objectification, and the location where objectification's effects are experienced. The novel would have provided a much more powerful critique of Destroyers with a more nuanced treatment of sexuality, but as it stands, Silko's discussions of the body within colonialism allow her to critique colonialism's environmental and patriarchal investments.

In many ways, the novel's emphasis on indigenous land sovereignty suggests that indigeneity and environmentalism are compatible and mutually supportive. The "geographical violence" (to use Edward Said's definition of imperialism) of colonialism did not just undermine indigenous sovereignty; it also entailed environmental destruction. Manifest Destiny entailed indigenous conquest, but also deforestation, railroads, loss of animal populations, and landscape alterations for settlement and farming. Just as *colonialism's* oppression of Native Americans paved the way for *capitalist* oppression of Native Americans, so too does colonialism's environmental destruction extend in the capitalist era, particularly in the form of rapacious destruction of land (and bodies) for development and economic gain. Exploration, discovery, and even mapping licensed the "scientific study" of land, like scientific knowledge of body, which objectified it for purposes of exploitation. We can see the retribution for these actions in the self-destruction of Zeta and Lecha's father, for instance, described above. Treating the environment as a "resource" (giving it "exchange value," in Marxian terms) legitimizes the extraction of minerals, water, wood, and animal products, as well as unregulated polluting as a by-product of these processes. Colonialism and capitalism are therefore interrelated in terms of how they treat Native Americans and the environment of the United States.

Further, this dual impact of colonial-capitalism on indigenous groups and the environment has been *materially* related: expansion and capitalism commodified Native American lands, which led to the containment of Native Americans living on resource-rich lands on reservations. Conquest of lands for the purposes of territorial expansion and resource extraction necessitated the conquest of Native Americans, just as the "civilization" of Native Americans necessitated territorial acquisition. These projects reinforced each other. That is, in order to conquer Native Americans, their ties to the environments in which they lived and in which their identities were embedded had to be cut. And in order to acquire the resources and territories of the Americas, the indigenous populations had to be moved to reservations. Thus, environmental destruction and indigenous conquest were two sides of the same colonial project, a project that capitalism, often through the military industrial complex, extends. The ideological aspects of colonialism—desacralization and commodification of the land, Western cultural and linguistic forms, patriarchy, and historiography, for instance—facilitated this territorial appropriation and environmental destruction.

The novel articulates the social justice implications of colonial-capitalism's environmental costs for indigenous communities, as well as the adverse environmental effects of the dispossession and alienation of Native Americans from their lands. It highlights this indigenous–environmental interdependence and colonial-capitalism's effects on this interdependence through two key themes: (1) the ability to appreciate nuances in people and landscapes as matters of justice, survival, and resistance; and (2) the dual, material exploitation of human bodies and environmental resources. These themes, of course, are related in that they suggest that the body is the medium through which injustice is experienced, understood, and combated.

Reading the Landscape

Silko's critique of colonial-capitalist forms parallels some mainstream environmental values, most specifically environmentalism's attention to questions of "place" and "placelessness" in modern society. But while mainstream environmentalism bemoans the losses of place and human perception of place for strictly environmental purposes—in biocentric terms, that is—Silko, in contrast, critiques loss of place and place perception for environmental *justice* ends. That is, while mainstream environmentalism's fetishizing of place often puts the needs of a place's nature above those of people living in that place, *Almanac*'s treatment of place emphasizes the interdependence of place and social justice. In other words, *Almanac* provides an environmental justice critique of place that is missing in the kinds of mainstream environmental discourses I described in the introduction to this book.

To emphasize the importance of appreciating landscape and recognizing the human–nature interconnection, *Almanac*'s villainous characters are characteristically insensitive to place, unaware of nuances in landscape, disrespectful of the importance of healthy land to later generations, and denying of the human history embedded in the land. For instance, responsibility to land recognizes human dependence on it, whereas Destroyer placeless sensibilities treat land as a commodity. The Destroyer character Judge Arne articulates this contrast: while "Indians grew connected to a place; they would not leave Tucson even after all of Arizona's groundwater was polluted or pumped dry," the Destroyer sensibility, expressed here by the corrupt Judge Arne, "doesn't care"; Arne "would probably not live to see it." Destroyers extract value from land, leave it polluted and desiccated, and then move on. They seek short-term economic gain and power, and are not concerned about future generations' dependence on the land. They are content to "abandon" Tucson and Phoenix "by the hundreds of thousands after all the groundwater had been consumed" (651), leaving Indians to bear the burdens of pollution and scarcity that they did not cause, on lands on which they have been forcibly emplaced. Indigenous place ethics recognizes an intergenerational dependence on resources and the fact that those who depend on the land will bear the consequences of its mistreatment. This connection between responsibility to place and environmental justice is central to the novel.

This indigenous land ethic arises from an indigenous way of perceiving the land. The ability to read landscape is central to Silko's environmental justice view of what distinguishes Destroyer views of place from indigenous views of the relationship between land and human history. The Destroyer inability to appreciate and therefore "read" land translates into disrespect for land and its relationship to human needs, as well as a failure to see human dependence on the land. In one example, an insurance man for a petroleum exploration company in Alaska sees the landscape of exploration as a landscape of "frozen wastes," and believes "there was no life on the tundra, nothing of value except what might be under the crust of snow and earth"—oil, gas, uranium, and gold (159). The insurance man delivers these comments while in an airplane, flying above the tundra. This aerial perspective underscores and produces his utilitarian land ethic; his class and race privilege distance him from place, captured by his perspective from an airplane, since his occupation involves hypermobility and therefore the inability to become responsible to any place. He thus fails to read the landscape as land; he is capable only of interpreting it through the lens of the global search for profit. The Alaska Natives who live on the land and perceive it from the ground perceive something very different; their phenomenological intimacy with the land is in stark contrast to the "ocularcentric" perspective of the insurance man in the airplane. The insurance man's bad ethic is thus epistemological and ideological; just as colonizers' perceptions of the lands they colonized as empty, virgin, or waste made it possible for them to impose their own colonial landscape fantasies, the insurance man's inability to perceive the human–nature interdependence of the tundra value makes him only able to grasp the land's exchange value. Thus, just as imperialism is a geographical act of violence in this sense, capitalism erases place as it commodifies it.

Calabazas provides the best example of the environmental justice implications of these different ways of knowing how to read landscape in *Almanac*. While driving through the desert terrain with his partners, Mosca and Root, Calabazas begins one of his "Indian style" lectures (215). It is a "sarcastic lecture on blindness" "solely caused by stupidity" (201) about the importance of recognizing the differences between things.[4] He says: "I get mad when I hear the word identical. . . . There is no such thing. Nowhere. At no time. All you have to do is stop and think. Stop and take a look. Look at it for what it is. This rock is like it is. Look. Now, come on. Over here. This one is about as big, but not quite. And the rock broke out a chunk like a horse head, but see, this one over here broke out a piece that's more like a washtub" (201). Calabazas's lecture demands that his listeners physically explore the environment with their perceiving bodies. His lecture literally guides listeners between rocks in the landscape, as they learn how to read and thereby know the landscape. His lecture insists that sameness between any two things is a myth, and reveals the implications of this myth.

Also, knowing the land means knowing history: "each location, each place, was a living organism with time running inside it like blood, time that was unique to that place alone" (629). Counter to the Western view of time as abstract and linear and space as bounded, here, time and space are dynamic and materially interconnected; time is like blood running through the body of space. It inheres in place; history is present and it is alive with the spirits of ancestors, and it is en-placed. Thus, through its description of reading landscape, *Almanac* suggests that the individual does not live in a spatial bubble, immune to structural and environmental constraints, just as the individual does not live in a temporal bubble, absolved of responsibility to remember the past or free from moral responsibility for the future.

Almanac portrays the inability to notice nuances in the environment as pathological; it is a sign of "stupidity." This insensitivity or stupidity can be a result of posttraumatic stress, whether the trauma is colonial-capitalism or the loss of a loved one; for example, Seese's loss of her best friend deadens her ability to appreciate place: "Seese could not remember seeing the hills and trees or the ocean after Eric's suicide. . . . Seese had been unable to remember anything except disjointed arrivals and departures in international airports" (53). Trauma disconnects Seese from her environment, causing senses of displacement and alienation, which constantly moving through airports exacerbates. Her position in the airport is key here, as Silko has already indicated a suspicion of people who fly a lot (i.e., the insurance man flying over the tundra in Alaska). Postmodern geographer Edward Relph's theory of placelessness in late capitalist society helps clarify *Almanac*'s critique of the kind of disregard for place that airports engender. Airports are the quintessential non-places, because they are "marked by transience"; the airport is "not only [a] feature of placelessness in [its] own right, but, by making possible the mass movement of people with all their fashions and habits . . . encourage[s] the spread of placelessness well beyond [its] immediate impacts" (Relph, qtd. in Cresswell 45).

Placelessness is caused by being "detached from the local environment," and people who disregard place cannot distinguish anything specific "about the particular locality in which they are located" (Cresswell 43). According to theories of placelessness, capitalism causes placelessness, because it commodifies, homogenizes, and standardizes places in the name of growth and efficiency. Placelessness is felt as a loss of "sense of place" and awareness of the uniqueness of individual places. Placelessness leads to seeing all places as "identical," to use Calabazas's term, thereby allowing for the homogenization, or "McDonaldization," of places. Placelessness is thus not just a signal of the exploitation of a place and its inhabitants; as a "stupid" way of seeing—as an unethical epistemology, in other words—it also makes such exploitation possible.

What is important in *Almanac* is that this ability to perceive the landscape is necessary for *social* justice. The ability to read landscape indicates an ability to recognize human–nature interdependence, but it is also related to the ability to appreciate *people*. That is, not only are landscape and people interdependent, as the insurance man failed to see; how one treats the land is a reflection of one's humanity. Silko connects Calabazas's ability to appreciate landscape to his ability to read people in her depiction of the relationship between Calabazas and Root, a character who is white and disabled. Calabazas's lecture on difference in the landscape seamlessly merges with Root's thoughts on disability, race, and the false ideal of normalcy, which Calabazas subversively recasts as lacking nuance. Immediately following Calabazas's lecture on appreciating differences in the landscape, Root muses about "difference" in humans: "Being around Mexicans and Indians and black people, had not made him feel uncomfortable. Not as his own [white] family had. Because if you weren't born white, you were forced to see differences; or if you weren't born what they called normal, or if you got injured, then you were left to explore the world of the different" (202–3). Being white prevents the ability to see. But, in the view of this dominant perspective, white is "normal." And it is also "abled." This passage suggests parallels between Root's thoughts about his own experience of disability to the experience of racial nonwhiteness, as well as to Calabazas's lecture on landscape, suggesting another parallel between ability, race, and place. Racism and capitalism involve an erasure of history and distinctiveness, the homogenization of land and people, and the subsequent exploitation of both. Placelessness and social oppression are thus linked. In this counter-sociobiological narrative, then, racism, ableism, and inability to read the landscape are related because they fail to account for the value of difference to *both* human justice and environmental health.

Indeed, the key to both social justice and nonexploitative relations between humans and nature is seeing and appreciating difference. One's difference in relation to dominant categories of normal enables "special" perspective of both human and environmental surroundings. For example, Mosca thinks Root's brain damage gives him "special power." Root's "situated knowledge," to use Haraway's term, allows him to grasp these environmental justice themes of the intersections of race, ability, and land. Root realizes that difference enables insight into "the world of the different," and so he is able to perceive environmental racism. For example, his reading of the polluted Santa Cruz River acknowledges the environmental and social costs of capitalist exploitation; when he looks at the river, he "thinks 'sewage treatment' not 'river,'" because "Tucson built its largest sewage treatment plant on the northwest side of the city, next to the river" (189). Root can see something that the "normal" person cannot—that the city committed an act of environmental racism by putting a sewage treatment plant where the inhabitants were least able to protest against it (i.e., "not-in-my-backyard," assuming a white, male subject position). Root's special power is that he can see the ecological and social injustice that produced this landscape underneath the merely visual, aesthetic surface of Santa Cruz River. Root demonstrates that the ability to see the world, which is a function of what the mainstream calls "abnormal" or "disabled," in fact provides special power to read landscape and grasp its ecological and social meaning. This is not to say that the novel suggests that disability itself provides an ontological special power, but rather, being positioned by the mainstream as different, in the margins, enables others to appreciate difference in other people and landscapes. Being able to read the human history in the landscape characterizes an environmental justice epistemology. Counter to the conceit of empiricism, which posits the body as a "sense organ" of scientific objectivity (to use Ulrich Beck's term), what we see is a function of our ideology, our position in power relations, and our identity. All ways of reading the land are situated.

The ability to appreciate difference is not only a matter of environmental justice; it is a matter of survival, as Calabazas sees it. Human survival depends on being attentive to differences in the landscape, but also on human diversity (hence, the "inevitability" and self-destruction of the Destroyers). Calabazas revises the typically oppressive logic of the survival of the fittest to advance an ethic of diversity. Calabazas states: "Survival had depended on differences. Not just the differences in the terrain that gave the desert traveler critical information about traces of water or grass for his animals, but the sheer varieties of plants and bugs and animals" (202). Here, reading differences between features of the terrain is a matter of survival. But survival is also ensured by differences between kinds of biota, between kinds of *species*. In contrast to the way that evolutionary logic has often historically promoted an ethic of "fitness" based on the "purity of the gene pool," and in contrast to how it often appears in the novel as neo-Nazi social Darwinism (as the above example of Max Blue illustrated), Calabazas uses evolutionary logic to argue that *diversity* is what keeps a species alive. The value of diversity—as opposed to values of normalcy, ideal, competition, or purity—underlies the well-being of humans in terms of their relation to one another and to their environments. Echoing recent movements to protect "bio-cultural diversity,"[5] and similar to the need for a diversity of landscapes and the ability to read that diversity, diversity of *people* is necessary for human survival. Thus, the novel promotes an alternative Darwinian notion of interdependence as opposed to evolutionary purity. These forms of diversity are not just parallel; they rely on each other.

Further emphasizing the relationship between social justice and ways of reading, Calabazas tells the story of Geronimo. He weaves his points about rocks and diversity as survival into his version of the story about how Geronimo escaped his captors. "Stupidity" about nuances in landscape and people is not only a function of a bad land ethic. It can also be a source of weakness in those in power to be exploited; hence, its role in their self-destruction. Europeans failed to capture Geronimo because they failed to perceive differences in both features of the landscape and among different Indians. Echoing his earlier lecture on reading rocks in the landscape, Calabazas says that, to Europeans, "a 'rock' was just a 'rock' wherever they found it, despite obvious differences in shape, density, color, or the position of the rock relative to all things around it. . . . the hills and canyons looked the same to them. . . . Strategists for the Yaquis and the Apaches quickly learned to make use of the Europeans' inability to perceive unique details in the landscape." Similarly, Europeans' inability to notice differences among Apache warriors also allowed Geronimo to slip through their grasp. Thus, the Europeans' inability to appreciate difference in humans and in the landscape was the source of their undoing. The Yaquis and Apaches could use it to "exploit the weakness of the whites" (225). These stories about rocks, difference, and Geronimo allow Calabazas to reinforce the environmental justice implications of appreciating landscape, but, most important, they allow him to expose how Destroyers' "stupidity" in this area can be exploited to gain the upper hand.

Almanac's most powerful example of the social-ecological implications of homogenizing place is the story of Leah Blue, the white wife of gangster Max Blue. The Blues move to Tucson from New Jersey against Leah's wishes. But she soon sees a market to exploit there and initiates a career as a real estate developer: "the real estate market in Tucson and southern Arizona was wide open, ripe for development." Leah epitomizes the problems with placelessness. She enacts precisely the white Destroyer approach to land that Calabazas warned against—exploitation as a function of "stupidity" and "blindness." It is exploitative, self-serving, capitalist, and disrespectful to the uniqueness and history of the place and environment of Tucson. To Leah, the desert is a no-place, a wasteland. Leah thinks the area is already so polluted that it deserves no special care, despite ecologists' and Indians' claims otherwise. Echoing Guzman's landscape aesthetic, Leah envisions "huge tracts of desert" "bulldozed into gridworks scraped clean of cactus and lined with palm trees" (359).

Leah wants to create a community called Venice, where people could be surrounded by water. Leah disregards the "authenticity" of this place, as Relph puts it, in her insensitivity to the issues of water scarcity in the Southwest desert. Indeed, "the scarcity of water in Arizona and other Western states was an obstacle" to this kind of development. But Leah is undeterred; she is "accustomed to seeing obstacles removed—rolled or blasted out of her way." She feels no need to build within the limitations of the specific geography of the Arizona desert, since "science will solve the water problem of the West. New technology. They'll *have* to" (374). Leah's technological optimism assumes that technology will clean up the mess of capitalism's destruction and compensate for nature's (perceived) lack. This faith in capitalism and technology assumes that they will solve the environmental problems of her activities. They'll "have to" because the market rewards her exploitation, and therefore the market will take care of the consequences by rewarding technological fixes. That is, Leah's responsibility to the land is displaced onto the market, which in turn will "have to" create another "new technology" to fix the very problems it created. This displacement of responsibility is how capitalists rationalize their contribution to the tragedy of the commons.

Leah's disrespect has epistemological origins. She fails to recognize that her activities will exact costs on the environment because she cannot see any *ecological* value there in the first place. Her vision for the place literally prevents her from *seeing* its ecological value; she fails to see the specific ecology and geography of this particular place. When she digs wells to find water and is sued for transgressing environmental laws, she cannot "understand why the Indians or the environmentalists" bothered to sue. She wonders, "what possible good was this desert anyway? Full of poisonous snakes, sharp rocks, and cactus! Leah knew she was not alone in this feeling of repulsion; most people who saw the cactus and rocky hills for the first time agreed the desert was ugly" (750). Like Guzman's imperialist "love

of trees" that opened this chapter, Leah can see value only in a landscape that is aesthetically beautiful to *her* sensibilities, and sees value
only in installing a "clean" oasis there. Thus, she exhibits placelessness in both her inability to perceive the desert's unique features and
socio-ecological value, and in what Relph terms "Disneyfication"—
her desire to imprint a simulacrum of Venice on the "blank slate" of
this placeless place.

To circumvent the legal limitations to turning the "repulsive"
desert into a simulacrum of Venice, Leah has sex with the "owl-shit
ecologist" to help "head off protests by environmentalists against
her plans for Venice, Arizona" (375). Here, we begin to see that
even the environmentalists are not the environment's best ally. Leah
uses sex as power over the owl-shit ecologist, suggesting that the
ecologist's own environmental ethic is not as strong as his desire for
sex.[6] For this ecologist, desire for sex trumps concern for the environment, and capitalism is sexualized. His focus on one charismatic
species—the owl—privileges one species at the expense of considering a whole habitat or ecosystem, suggesting that an environmental ethic focused on wildlife is fundamentally anthropocentric. If a
single species like the owl is a last vestige of a threatened Eden, then
this brand of environmentalist is interested in "protecting the wild"
rather than living with and in nature. The ecologist may appreciate
the desert as beautiful or as containing an ecologically valuable species, which are certainly better approaches than Leah's, but these
views fail to ensure the protection of the desert, much less the owl.

And the legal system put in place to protect the environment can
also be circumvented; Leah asks Max to "play golf" with Judge Arne
to ask him to "dismiss a [water rights] cross-suit" by "some Nevada
Indians" and make the state of Arizona grant Leah her "deep-well
drilling permits" to find water (376). In these cases, Leah's sexual
bribe and her relationship to Max enable her to override environmental activists, Native American land claims, and even the law.
Indeed, the law's ability to ensure justice is directly proportionate
to its (white) practitioners' ability to resist the lures of capitalism
and exploitation, which is to say it is driven by libido and greed,
according to the novel.

Further, Leah's disregard for an ecosystem's value and limitations exemplifies *Almanac*'s message about placelessness in the

postmodern, late-capitalist society. Venice, Arizona, imposes a simulacrum of Venice, Italy, where water abounds, onto a desert environment where water scarcity is the primary source of social and ecological injustice. The novel repeatedly uses these tensions over water to highlight the environmental justice problems of the Southwest. Given the long history of battles over water "reclamation" and rights in the region, Silko's portrayal of Leah's sense of entitlement to water engages the text in *the* political ecological debate of the Southwest—water rights and scarcity. Similar to Guzman's use of water to feed his cottonwoods and the *americanos'* appropriation of good land "where the water was" after the annexation of Mexico, Leah's water politics epitomize colonial-capitalist avarice. Her technological optimism that science will "fix" the problem of water scarcity, combined with her capitalist ruthlessness that overcomes all obstacles to her vision, expresses the arrogance of postmodern, late-capitalist disregard for place: "Leah saw Mediterranean villas and canals where only cactus and scraggly greasewood grew from gray volcanic gravel" (378). As the capitalist version of Zeta and Lecha's military-geologist father, Leah cannot see anything but a landscape's exchange value, even where a very distinct and "beautiful" habitat exists, as Silko's detailed naming and poetic alliteration reflect.

The Materiality of Bodies and Nature

These place themes correspond to the novel's foregrounding of the body as a location of both exploitation and empowerment. The material quality of bodies, like land, renders them vulnerable to objectification and exploitation for profit. Just as capitalism pollutes landscapes and sacrifices place in order to create markets, it extracts value from the bodies of those without political or economic power. The novel takes the commodification of the body one step further; the very bodies weakened by capitalist exploitation, military operations, and environmental degradation are all the more vulnerable to further exploitation. The colonial-capitalist structure thus twice extracts value from bodies. Like Guzman's slaves planting cottonwood trees, "black slaves had labored to make the United States rich and powerful" (427). Later, because they are less likely to be able

to avoid the draft, black Americans became the foot soldiers in a
"war in Southeast Asia." One character in the novel, Clinton, relates
the victimization of African Americans and the Vietnamese: the war
"had been fabricated as a location and occasion for the slaughter"
not just of Asian communists, but "of the strongest and most prom-
ising young men of black and brown and poor-white communities"
(407–8). By emphasizing that the war "slaughtered" black American men, Clinton reveals the racism on which America's "war" for
"democracy" relies. Like the slaves in Yoeme's story that opened this
chapter, black Americans' bodies are doubly extracted to support
nation-building and maintain the status quo.

The character of Trigg expresses how these processes extend
through capitalism. The bodies of the weak are not useless to capitalism; on the contrary, they present a venture opportunity for Trigg.
Trigg's own disablement (he has a spinal-cord injury) amplifies the
corporeal ironies of his capitalist aims. His ultimate goal—and the
ultimate irony of his character—is to make money from the market
in weakened bodies to find a cure for his own disfigurement. Trigg is
the second disabled character we meet in the novel, but he is distinct
from Root in that his disability makes him vengeful, and, rather
than appreciate "the world of the different," he wants to exploit it.
Both Root's and Trigg's disabilities were caused by accidents in their
adult lives, but while Root's disability gives him a "special power" to
perceive social injustice, Trigg's disability triggers his Destroyer sensibility. He becomes self-engrossed, narcissistic, and obsessed with
sex, death, and extracting value from their combined proliferation.

Perhaps Root and Trigg are juxtaposed because, while Root rede-
fines his disability as an *ability,* Trigg seeks to "cure" his disability.
To do so, Trigg disfigures, disables, and renders lifeless the bodies
of the disempowered to obtain the resources to "fix" and thereby
normalize his own body. This contrast between *integrating* disability
versus treating disability as *pathology* corresponds to what Rosemarie
Garland-Thomson describes as a contrast between empowerment
and oppression. In contrast to Root's story of empowerment through
appreciating the world of the different, Trigg's story is one of pathology, in which he corporeally exploits and exacerbates inequalities of
difference in an attempt to erase his own corporeal otherness. To
do so, he opens a business called Bio-Materials, Inc., which includes

plasma donor centers but becomes a front for a black market in organ theft and trading. He believes "there were millions and millions to be made from treatments for people addicted to alcohol and other drugs" (382). Following the sociobiological, capitalist logic that the individual is responsible for addiction and its consequences, Trigg sees this venture as merely speeding up the inevitable. In contrast, the social model of disability, like Silko's point throughout the novel, insists on the structural causes of addiction—colonialism, racism, ableism, sexism, etc. If we interpret Trigg's venture from this lens of the "social model" of disability, we can see that it serves to extract the value of bodies on both ends of capitalist production.

First, his venture necessitates killing people to harvest parts of their bodies: "Biomaterials, not new antibiotics or drugs, were going to be the bonanza of the twenty-first century. . . . Not just plasma, not just blood! . . . Biomaterials—the industry's 'preferred' term for fetal-brain material, human kidneys, hearts and lungs, corneas for eye transplants, and human skin for burn victims" (398). Blood and plasma can be extracted without killing their donors, but harvesting biomaterials requires killing their donors, which raises the sticky question of who has the power to consent to supplying this new market demand. Those in power whose bodies need repair use their economic power to purchase corporeal wholeness, but do so at the cost of the corporeal wholeness of the poor. Indeed, Trigg "bought a great deal" of the bodies he uses "in Mexico where recent unrest and civil strife had killed hundreds a week. Mexican hearts were lean and strong, but Trigg had found no market for dark cadaver skin" (404). Here, Silko emphasizes the racial dimension of Trigg's business by noting the fragmentation of these bodies. That is, hearts and eyes are desirable because they are not racially marked. But skin—*the* signifier of racial identity—has no value. Ironically, though, the very bodies most "available" to be harvested are, coincidentally, nonwhites. Thus, if economic growth can result from civil unrest, lack of services for homeless, vets, and the diseased, then human rights, racial equality, and human security are inversely related to economic growth. The harvesting of the body parts of the disenfranchised creates a market incentive to institutionalize inequality and perpetuate political unrest. Clinton interprets it all as just another word for slavery, highlighting postmodern late capitalism's relationship to colonialism: "all around them lay human slavery," although "it had been called by other names" (411).

Trigg's success in this market underscores *Almanac*'s message that capitalism feeds not only off the (live) *labor* of bodies, but off the *death* of material bodies themselves. That is, capitalism perpetuates itself by turning bodies weakened by the alienation that its own labor extraction created into sources of capital for those in power. As Trigg's company shows, capitalism can survive only by creating new markets all the time, and by extracting the lives of some bodies to support the lives of others. At one end of the process, then, these bodies' strength is extracted, while on the other end, the same process that weakens bodies by exploitation, war, and inequality turns those same bodies into a new resource. The by-products of warfare and structural injustice—masses of anonymous dead bodies—can feed a different market: the market for disassembled body parts to extend the lives of the wealthy.[7] But of course, this market perpetuates the cycle by supporting the need for warfare or other means to produce anonymous masses of bodies.

In their discussion of the internationally acclaimed display *Bodies . . . The Exhibition,* Hsuan Hsu and Martha Lincoln outline the environmental, social justice, and corporeal implications of the "biomedical utopia" that the exhibit promotes, a "utopia" that resonates with Trigg's project to perfect the human form through his own, and through the erasure of "imperfect" human forms. Hsu and Lincoln's analysis suggests that *Bodies . . . The Exhibition* is a real-life manifestation of Trigg's vision, in that the medical gaze creates a market for dead bodies of the poor; bodies and body parts are worth more dead than alive, in this scenario, as the roaming Chinese bodies that comprise the exhibition "specimens" are procured with questionable "consent." Transnational capitalism, which Silko's rendering of Trigg's organ trade scrutinizes, is dehumanizing at the most fundamental level: it literally kills people. Again, Silko's fictional metaphor is in fact reality, if we take seriously Hsu and Lincoln's analysis, as well as their depiction of medical anthropologist Nancy Scheper-Hughes's research:

> Scheper-Hughes has documented the growth of a black-market commodity chain that connects wealthy "transplant tourists,"

local organ procurers, corrupt medical practitioners, and desperately poor "donors" in the global South. Contextualizing these transactions in a predatory regime of global capitalism and grave social inequalities, Scheper-Hughes establishes that the flow of commodified biomatter typically proceeds "from South to North, from poorer to more affluent bodies, from black and brown bodies to white ones, and from females to males," exacerbating entrenched divisions between these regions and alienating the most structurally dispossessed people in the global order from their own bodies. (70)

This echoes Trigg's interests in body parts. Hsu and Lincoln continue:

Scheper-Hughes terms this pattern of exploitation "the new cannibalism": evidence of a world economy in which human life and its biological supports circulate like any other natural resource. In the "organs market," she states, "Organs and tissue donors—both living and dead—are treated not as people, but as suppliers of the organic medical material needed for research, experimentation, and advanced medical technologies." (75)

Like Trigg's flow of biomaterial from the poor masses of the South, *The Exhibition* "produces a category of beings who are . . . undocumented and physically unidentifiable; tenuously grounded in time and space; disarticulated from claims to productive capacity or agentive status; and rendered beyond the soteriological reach of 'human rights'" (Hsu and Lincoln 25). The market in biomaterial is not a fictional metaphor for the extraction of labor from shadow bodies, victims of political unrest, colonialism, and transnational capitalism. As *Bodies . . . The Exhibition* illustrates, the aestheticization of the dead body through the medical gaze ("edutainment," as the exhibit's creator calls it) exemplifies the "complex materialities," to use Alaimo's words, and gains twice from the exploitation of disenfranchised and invisible populations. Their bodies become a "natural resource" that literally sustains (to extend the notion of "cannibalism" to this reading of Trigg) and even, ironically, *enhances* the bodies of those in power, linking this fetish powerfully to a long history of eugenics and biopolitics, a link I have been arguing ties all the "others" of the chapters of this book.

A parallel to this form of corporeal extraction can be read in the novel's treatment of the way in which the bodies and labor of race horses are extracted for the purposes of amusement: "the more horses that got hurt or just lay down and died, the more money people made" (197). The harvesting, dissecting, and trafficking of bodies allows Silko to show that bodies are the resources capitalism uses to fuel its growth, and that the loss of corporeal integrity is a necessary externality of the capitalist system, the cost of which, like pollution, is borne by the weak.

The alienation of humans from their bodies reaches a whole new level in a world of globalizing markets and wars, and unprecedented movement of people. Just as these phenomena lead to placeless-ness—the "dissociation of culture from place," in Anthony Giddens's words—so too does it lead to the detachment of humans from their own bodies. The "neoliberal" capitalist narrative asserts that human well-being everywhere will be improved when economic growth occurs in some places, like Wall Street. But Silko shows the false logic of thinking that "what was good for businessmen and industrialists [in the United States] was good for Mexico" (492). Capitalist global-ization is just another form of colonialism, which relies on extraction of human and natural resources to support the elite. In this example of trans-corporeality, "savage capitalism," growth for the sake of growth, is inversely related to human equality, and "economic secu-rity" does not necessarily translate to human security. Highlighting how these abstract political economics translate in material, personal ways, Bartolomeo's ex-lover Alegria states: "the system that starved and destroyed human beings for the profit of a few was a system that must fall from the sheer weight of the bodies of the dead" (307). Alegria reframes, in corporeal terms, the Marxist notion that capital-ism's contradictions (the notion that it *requires* the very resources that it diminishes) will undermine it.

Just as body parts become harvestable, *Almanac* shows how bodies and nature alike are vulnerable to colonial-capitalist destruction. For instance, the corporeal dissolving (through cancer) of Lecha and Zeta's father parallels the loss of minerals from the landscape he surveyed as a geologist, a process in which he participated and for which his body suffers. Silko relates Root's ability to read the fluvial landscape of Tucson to his corporeal otherness. The exploitation of both bodies and land disrupts the notion that humans and nature are separable, that one is subject and the other object, and suggests that the connection between bodies and land is not a whimsical indigenous notion, but a stark material reality. The bodies of veterans are made vulnerable by the same napalm that destroyed Vietnamese environments and Vietnamese *people,* and, in a nasty metaphorical twist, those vulnerable bodies become the material for Trigg's biomaterials industry.

The novel parallels bodies and land in another way. Silko critiques the dominant scientific "biologizing" of inequalities, a logic that turns undesirable people into unnatural species. Menardo's insurance company, Universal Insurance, seeks to suppress Indian "squatters" surrounding the coffee plantations around Chiapas by sending "a crop-dusting plane to dump insecticide and herbicide on [them]" (475). This act equates people and plants, because they are similar nuisances (i.e., weeds) and because they are exterminable by the same process. Universal Insurance ignores the reason the "squatters" are there in the first place—colonial-capitalism. The crop dusting approach thus erases history as well as the living environment and its inhabitants. The consequences of these failures are both socially and ecologically unjust and, ultimately, unsustainable; Silko's narrative makes her readers understand that managing biotic life for the sake of the safety of elites will backfire. Using nature as an authority and echoing Rachel Carson's critique of DDT, Silko shows that, just as herbicide and pesticide paradoxically disrupt the very ecosystems in which coffee plantations grow and which they are deployed to protect, so too will attempting to erase people from the land defeat its purpose. Biodiversity—not monoculture—is needed to promote growth. *Almanac* frames these efforts as part of the cause of the revolution; Destroyers will have brought on their own undoing through misguided, sociobiologically justified practices like this, executed in the name of nature.

Almanac's Critique of Environmentalism

In all of these ways, *Almanac* advances an environmental justice position: appreciating the "world of the different," as Root and

Calabazas do, has social justice *and* environmental implications. My reading thus far has developed this interpretation, which nonetheless still falls short of a full appreciation of the intersection of environmental and social justice issues in the text, as well as the revolutionary potential of Silko's work. A full appreciation of the novel's environmental justice contribution requires closer scrutiny of its powerful critique of environmentalism. Despite land being the central concern throughout the novel, Silko treats environmentalism with ambivalence, suspicion, and, at times, outright rejection. As I illustrate below, Silko's treatment of environmentalists is more critical than collaborative; she is more interested in exposing environmentalists' investments in racism and colonialism than in building coalitions with them. As Alex Hunt observes, "Silko is clear that the wilderness preservationists . . . are not the ideal allies of indigenous people in their concern for the earth" ("Radical" 269). To assume that because the novel is so centrally about land and Native Americans that it is fundamentally environmentalist overlooks the many ways in which Silko attacks environmentalists (especially "wilderness preservationists"), ways that are informed by her perspective that environmentalism has not transcended its colonial legacy.

At times, indigenous land ethics seem to align with environmentalism's efforts to protect nature. And environmentalism often looks to a Native American land ethic as a model for how to treat the environment. This appropriation of Native American views results from the notion that Native Americans are inherently environmental—that they are "ecological Indians." But Silko challenges the ways in which white mainstream environmentalism appropriates Native American land ethics for its own purposes and draws attention to the ways in which environmentalism is just as likely to work *against* indigenous interests as it is to work for them. The owl-shit ecologist who overlooks environmental regulations in exchange for sex with Leah Blue provides one of several examples that show how environmentalists are sometimes more interested in protecting white (and often male) dominance than in protecting nature.

The conventional environmental justice reading of the novel equates "defending nature" with defending indigeneity. But Silko's treatment of this fraught relationship between indigenous and environmental cultural politics suggests that "defending nature" is an excuse used by dominant groups to marginalize and further oppress those it labels others. It is precisely because "the environment" is often used *against* indigeneity (and further marginalizes vulnerable groups) that these conventional readings fail. Silko sheds light on a constellation of environmentalism's exclusions, which are not limited to Native Americans. Although it seems paradoxical that *Almanac* would criticize environmentalism, given all of the ways that it promotes the interests of "Mother Earth" and the land, I would argue that it is precisely this paradox that makes the novel such an important example of the direction environmental justice scholarship must move.

Silko portrays indigenous attitudes toward environmentalism as ambivalent and cautious, and the indigenous attachment to the land she promotes is not necessarily environmentalist, even in environmental *justice* terms. Although white, Western attitudes toward nature are often contrasted with indigenous views of land, characterizing the indigenous ethic as "environmentalist" misses an important tension between these positions and ignores the ways in which environmentalism—as a political movement and as a way of understanding the world—has often *supported* colonial-capitalist oppression of indigenous and other vulnerable groups. Although the environment and environmentalists will play a critical role in the revolution the novel portends, Silko offers a series of stories and characters that illustrate how environmentalism often legitimizes colonial-capitalist interests and constructions of the world.

Put simply, putting "earth first," as the radical wilderness preservationist group Earth First! would have it, is not the same as Silko's motto of "land first." Her perspective is similar to the distinction that Ramachandra Guha and Juan Martinez-Alier make between an "environmentalism of the poor" and "First World environmentalism." Although their efforts may sometimes overlap, Silko contrasts indigenous issues (land rights, self-determination, community, and the historical connection of Indians to the land) with the conventional environmental issues: wilderness protection, recreation, a strictly aesthetic appreciation of nature, protection of endangered species, and nostalgic attachment to a preindustrial, "pastoral" world. For example, First World environmentalism can be characterized by an "obsession with preserving biodiversity [that] ignores the poverty and suffering of the poor and marginalized, and willfully obscures the history of colonization and its related social and environmental consequences" (Adamson, *American Indian Literature* 170). When environmental goals conflict along these lines of privilege afforded by colonialism, mainstream environmentalism often enlists stereotypes of "ecological Indians" to coerce "defending nature," enacting a form of modern eco-imperialism. Attending to these moments in the text thus reveals ways in which ecological others—Native Americans, but also women and nonwhites—are constructed.

One striking example of the novel's stance toward mainstream environmentalists occurs at the novel's end, at the International Holistic Healers Convention in Tucson. There we learn that environmentalists will play a crucial role in revolution, as the convention brings together revolutionary characters from various previous narratives and from various parts of the Americas. And the indigenous groups at the convention accept the assistance of environmentalists, as they share a similar, anti-capitalist rhetoric. The purpose of the international convention, "called by natural and indigenous healers," appears to be, above all, environmental: people are convening "to discuss earth's crisis" (718).

No wonder, then, that a group of "eco-warriors," called Green Vengeance, are featured guests. The Barefoot Hopi, one of the Indian revolutionaries, aligns with the eco-warriors. Like the real-life group Environmental Liberation Front, or ELF, Green Vengeance presents a video of acts of destruction committed by the eco-warriors against iconic infrastructural monuments to capitalism and environmental degradation, the most symbolic of which is Glen Canyon Dam. The video celebrates six eco-warriors who "gave their lives to free the mighty Colorado [River]" as an act of "war" against the "biosphere tycoons who were rapidly depleting rare species of plants, birds, and animals so the richest people on earth could bail out of the pollution and revolutions" (728). The eco-warriors "were determined to destroy all interstate high-voltage transmission lines, power generating plants, and hydroelectric dams across the United States" (729).

The Barefoot Hopi speaks about what indigenous groups share with the eco-warriors, whom dominant society often terms "terrorists." Again, Silko reframes the debate by challenging the dominant discourse about what constitutes terrorism: "eco-warriors have been accused of terrorism in the cause of saving Mother Earth. So I want to talk a little about terrorism first. Poisoning our water with radioactive wastes, poisoning our air with military weapons' wastes—those are acts of terrorism!" (734). Despite evidence that a Green Vengeance–indigenous alliance is emerging at the convention, Silko makes it clear that the motives of Green Vengeance are quite different from those of the indigenous communities. Both may want a complete overhaul of the capitalist system, to reframe the government as terrorists, and to value the land for purposes other than profit, but their alliance can be only tactical. Silko insists on the power of the indigenous groups to choose the terms of their activism, explicitly against environmentalists' terms. True, the Hopi's promise that "a force was gathering that would counter the destruction of the earth" (734) accurately describes the revolution, but the "affluent young whites, fearful of a poisoned planet" function to help the Hopi to "raise a great deal of money," as "Green Vengeance had a great deal of wealth behind their eco-warrior campaigns" (726). The Barefoot Hopi's promise of "all human beings belong[ing] to the earth forever" is portrayed by Silko as rhetoric deployed to persuade environmentalists to finance revolution on *indigenous* terms.

In the midst of the seemingly postracial convention (as it seems to its white participants), where people of all colors are ostensibly coming together in defense of the earth, Silko reminds us that this one-earth, one-people fantasy makes it easy for whites to ignore the ways in which racism persists, and particularly, the ways in which racism takes "environmentalist" forms. Silko exposes the contradictions of white environmentalists funding indigenous struggles: "even in a dirt-water town that hated brown people as Tucson did, the Barefoot Hopi already had people fumbling for their checkbooks, and he was only getting warmed up" (734). Whites see the alliance as ideological; environmentalists think they share an ethic with indigenous groups because both reject capitalist objectification and exploitation of nature. But in the minds of Zeta and the Hopi, environmentalists are privileged whites whose assumptions can be exploited to gain *financial* support. By articulating the monetary, utilitarian agenda behind the Hopi's lofty rhetoric of racial unity and planetary holism, Silko reveals the underlying schism between indigenous and environmentalist views of nature. This scene also offers a powerful critique of the environmentalists' entanglement in the very capitalist systems they profess to hate. After all, anyone who has a great deal of money has benefited from the privilege of whiteness within the racist hierarchies of colonial-capitalism. The scene reveals how indigenous groups use the stereotype of the ecological Indian to their own advantage.

Similarly, throughout the novel, vulnerable groups "perform" mainstream environmental sensibilities to gain white support. Silko describes the coalition-building strategy of the Mexican revolutionary Angelita, who adjusts her appeal for support according to her audience's stereotype of Indians: "If Angelita was talking to the Germans or Hollywood activists, she said the Indians were fighting multinational corporations who killed rain forests; if she was talking to the Japanese or US military, then the Indians were fighting communism" (513–14). This statement suggests that "the Germans" and "Hollywood activists" are in positions of power by virtue of their colonial legacy, but each group has environmentalist sensibilities that can be exploited to support indigenous ends. Their environmentalism is a form of imperialist nostalgia and sentimentalism toward indigenous people. But, as Angelita knows, these environmentalists are more interested in subverting capitalism and saving rain forests than in supporting indigenous sovereignty. Assuming the "ecological Indian" identity is tactical, as opposed to an essential quality, the indigenous revolution might be environmental, but "saving the rain forests" is not the *indigenous* vision of what it means to be "environmental."

Angelita's performative tactics also show that environmentalists' alliances with indigenous communities are paternalistic and privilege a white vision of environmentalism over the actual environmental concerns of indigenous people. Marxism and environmentalism might have some things in common with indigenous claims, but this passage suggests that Silko sees their differences as equally, if not more, important, and finds Marxists and environmentalists hypocritical when they are willing to support indigenous communities only when the communities fit environmentalists' stereotypes. The passage compares environmentalism to communism in that they both appropriate indigenous ideas for their own ends; they are both forms of "white man's politics."

In another passage, Silko mocks the whites who perform goddess- and tree-worship by narrating their gestures as superficial and even ridiculous: "freshly cut evergreen trees were tenderly arranged in a circle by white men wearing robes; it looked as if tree worship was making a comeback in northern Europe." Here, tree worship is a simulacrum of connecting to nature; the *performance* (to extend Judith Butler's theory) of nature-worship matters more than the trees themselves, as they have been cut down and torn from their roots for the ceremony. This scene recalls Guzman's removal of the cottonwood trees for his landscape design; the novel's theme of trees being removed at their roots to serve the so-called nature- loving sensibilities of those in power makes a compelling connection between colonial landscape sensibilities and contemporary environ- mental rituals. In both cases, "love of trees" paradoxically inspires unecological behavior. Silko exposes the hypocrisy of mainstream environmentalists: their efforts to connect to nature are narcissistic, and not necessarily about nature at all. In another example, "white men from California" (the state that is often associated with New Age appropriation of Native American traditions) dress themselves in "expensive new buckskins, beads, and feathers" and rename them- selves "Thunder-Roll" and "Buffalo Horn." Here, Silko seems to be hinting that elite white men "going native" is more a reflection of how alienated they are in their capitalist lives than of their support of indigenous identity. Despite their attempt to be seen as envi- ronmentalists and their support of Native Americans, these men's appropriation of Native garb achieves neither.

In both these scenes at the convention, Silko emphasizes the hypocrisy of environmentalists, as well as their naïveté. Indigenous venders exploit white imperial nostalgia: "Money was changing hands rapidly; fifties and hundreds seemed to drop effortlessly from the white hands into the brown and black hands" (719). Once, slav- ery and colonialism extracted resources of land and labor from the "brown and black hands" and enforced cultural assimilation and conversion. Now the direction of flows is reversed; whites put money back in those brown and black hands and perform what they take to be indigenous traditions, as brown and black people will perform simulacra of the very identities the whites conquered. The ironies of imperial nostalgia abound in these scenes. But Silko uses irony here to show that the concern for indigenous cultures and traditions amounts to commodification and not to genuine support for claims indigenous people themselves would make. In return, the indigenous participants at the convention capitalize on their own commodification by using white money to support revolution against them.

Silko's aligning of Germans and environmentalists in the above reading of Angelita's environmental performance hints at environmentalism's ties to Nazi ideologies of pure blood and soil. These ties to "eco-fascism," as Janet Biehl and Peter Staudenmaier call it, provide a key context for Silko's critique of environmentalism's legacy of social control. As in the German context, environmentalist attachments to notions of purity and pristineness in the US context have been enlisted to support other projects of purity, such as purifying the (male) body, the (industrialized) city, or the (white, Anglo-Saxon Protestant) nation. The character that best captures *Almanac*'s message that the attachment to purity can be socially repressive is the African American militant Clinton. With insights gained from his education in Black studies, Clinton conducts consciousness-raising radio broadcasts in which he informs his listeners about the history of blacks in Africa and African American oppression in the Americas and connects Native American and African American histories in an effort to unite these distinct racial groups who share a similar history of oppression and slavery. As he campaigns for racial justice, Clinton explicitly implicates environmentalism in the oppression of people of color. In the following passage, he thinks about how deep ecologists and "defenders of the Earth" often view nonwhite groups as "pollution."

> Clinton did not trust the so-called "defenders of Planet Earth." Something about their choice of words had made Clinton uneasy. Clinton was suspicious whenever he heard the word *pollution*. Human beings had been exterminated strictly for "health" purposes by Europeans too often. Lately Clinton had seen ads purchased by so-called "deep ecologists." The ads blamed earth's pollution not on industrial wastes—hydrocarbons and radiation—but on overpopulation. It was no coincidence the Green Party originated in Germany. "Too many people" meant "too many *brown-skinned* people." . . .

"Deep ecologists" invariably ended their magazine ads with
"Stop immigration!" and "Close the borders!" Clinton had
to chuckle. The Europeans had managed to dirty up the good
land and good water around the world in less than five hundred
years. Now the despoilers wanted the last bits of living earth for
themselves alone. (415)

The environmentalist position that the earth has been brought to the
brink of disaster by overpopulation is neo-Malthusian, and Clinton
pinpoints environmentalists because their response is to blame the
poor, the nonwhite, and immigrants. Those who seek to defend
America's "limited" resources on the so-called sinking ark of the
planet argue for closing borders and keeping the nation's population in check, as Clinton points out. This requires demonizing
immigrants as "aliens" and treating them as ecologically other in
part because they are seen as a drain on America's finite resources,
but also because they are viewed as excessively fertile and too selfish
or unenlightened to understand the environmental consequences of
their own reproduction. Fertility becomes another form of environmental "pollution."

Controlling reproduction and immigration to preserve America's
resources is not just a modern environmentalist goal; appropriat-
ing resources and land by controlling the fertility of Indians was
central to the colonialist project. Throughout the first half of the
twentieth century, "Indian women were the targets of an aggres-
sive government-funded mass sterilization program as part of the
effort to take over resource-rich Indian lands" (Unger 45). These
neo-Malthusian connections between population control and land
persist. Overpopulation in other parts of the globe (those largely
inhabited by nonwhites) puts pressure on America's borders, while
the fertility of nonwhites inside the borders of the United States
must be controlled to ensure that only white people have access to
America's limited resources.

Clinton's reference to the "extermination" of human beings "by
Europeans" for "health purposes" immediately suggests Hitler's
genocide, not only of Jews but of the gypsies, the disabled, and
others defined by the Nazi regime as imperfect. It also suggests the
same logic of racial hygiene used by eugenicists who would control

population genetics to breed "good citizens" for the American national body. The link between Nazi nationalism, eugenics, and environmental values is well documented by Janet Biehl and Peter Staudenmaier in *Ecofascism: Lessons from the German Experience.* Biehl and Staudenmaier describe how ecofascist ideology deploys the "environment" for social control: "For a people seeking to assert themselves against an outside intruder, an 'ecologized' *Heimat* [homeland] in which they are biologically embedded can become a useful tool not only against imperialism but against immigration, foreigners, and 'overpopulation.' Elaborate justifications for opposing Third World immigration . . . draw on 'ecological' arguments against 'overpopulation'" (35). The 1973 "Ecological Manifesto" of Germany's National Democratic Party "invoked the 'laws of nature' to justify a hierarchically structured, 'organic order that would govern social relationships.'" This manifesto inveighed against "the environment polluted and poisoned by a humanity that lives increasingly isolated in a degraded mass" (qtd. in Biehl and Staudenmaier 40). Ecofascism exemplifies Foucault's theory of biopower in that it supported policies of eugenics and immigration control, thereby expressing the two "prongs" of biopower—the individual body and the nation-as-species population. Ecofascist ideologies of biopower serve elite interests by ensuring the purity of genes and the purity of the imagined space of the nation. Clinton's thoughts about pollution and race similarly identify the relationship between purity and controlling fertility, closing borders, and eugenics.

Here as elsewhere, Silko draws on US history. In the late nineteenth and early twentieth centuries, US leaders drew on nationalist and environmental arguments to justify social engineering on this basis. Welfare went hand in hand with hygiene; immigrants too easily became dependent on handouts from the state, and their fertility threatened white domination. As Mary Douglas has documented, environmentalist discourses of purity and pollution were "harnessed" in the nineteenth century as part of "men's attempts to force one another into good citizenship," and the "laws of nature" were "dragged in" to sanction a moral code of racial superiority. Douglas thus echoes Clinton's critique: "certain moral values are upheld and certain social rules defined by *beliefs in dangerous contagion*" (*Purity and Danger* 3, my emphasis), making Clinton's and

Foucault's recognition of the genocidal undertones of environmentalist discourses about hygiene, pollution, and population historically accurate as well as relevant to contemporary battles in US politics.[8]

Focusing on the effects of overpopulation on limited resources ignores the historical causes of environmental destruction, such as "the rapacious resource depletion of colonies by imperial powers, the forced introduction of monoculture and plantation agriculture in the tropics, displacing subsistence and indigenous agriculture, . . . and the distortion of household structure by colonial wage systems" (Seager 215). The fact that resources are limited is less a function of overpopulation than it is a function of historical and structural injustices. Clinton makes these connections: "the despoilers had managed to dirty up the good land and good water" themselves. "Defending the earth" against overpopulation becomes an excuse for extending colonial practices of oppression, legitimizing the control of immigration and limiting—or, in extreme cases, manipulating the reproduction of others—to ensure good "resource management." The colonial-capitalist Destroyers may become defenders of the earth when they realize the damage that they have caused, but they are still more likely to deflect blame elsewhere and claim the moral high ground, as Clinton knows. Clinton's thoughts encapsulate *Almanac*'s critique of the links between environmentalism, population control, and colonialism.

On the surface, it seems a paradox that despoilers of the earth could so easily portray themselves as defenders of the earth, but again, this slippage is precisely the contribution of *Almanac* to environmental justice that I want to emphasize. *Almanac* suggests that this transformation can take place without seeming a contradiction because the despoilers use the environment as a rhetorical device to support the colonial-capitalist status quo. Environmental discourses of "laws of nature" and "purity and pollution" legitimize coercive measures to force others into so-called good citizenship, that is, into lives that do not challenge the system. These modern, environmentally inflected extensions of colonial power target groups that were the subjects of colonialism and whose anti-environmental behaviors make them unworthy of citizenship in the modern state. Clinton's ruminations reveal how environmentalism can turn colonial others into ecological others as colonialism becomes capitalism.

This spatial dimension of environmental protection, which expresses fear of environmental degradation as fear of crowding and loss of "living room," disguises racism and xenophobia as ecological sensitivity, but Clinton sees through it. Through these neo-Malthusian metonymic slippages, brown-skinned people become pollution; like others who spoil the pristine wilderness and threaten resources, they are constructed as ecological others. The anxiety projected by groups who make this argument is corporeal; the visceral "feel" of overpopulation—too many *bodies* in too small a *space*—makes it easy to gain support for rejecting immigrants and for programs of population control to address problems that stem from poverty and colonialism. Anxiety about space is really anxiety about race and class. As Frederic Jameson argues, losing what Hitler called "living room," or *lebensraum*, is the fear of "losing comfort and a set of privileges which we tend increasingly to think of in spatial terms: privacy, empty rooms, silence, walling other people out, protection against crowds and other bodies" (qtd. in Heise 75). And, as I argued in the previous chapter, in the US context, this fear is also about the loss of the "wide-open spaces" of the vistas and landscapes of the American West. *Almanac* is thus concerned with the relationship between space and social control, and thus, more specifically, wilderness and eugenics.

With his obsessions about purity of blood and land, his research on eugenics, and his interest in the "rapture of the wide-open spaces" (545), the character Serlo epitomizes the modern eco-imperialist of Clinton's imagination. Serlo modernizes colonialism, particularly through eugenics and capturing resources for use by the few. He is the logical extension of colonial environmental sensibilities taken to the extreme. He is not the eco-warrior, anti-capitalist expression of mainstream environmentalism, but rather the "biosphere tycoon" version, against which eco-warriors organize. But his sensibilities are, nonetheless, rooted in distinctly colonial *environmentalist* values— fear of pollution, loss of space ("elbow room"), and racial purity.

Serlo's disgust for inferior races arises from his vision of how nature should work and what it should look like. Serlo is white and independently wealthy. He invests in his own "research" projects to manipulate human genetics and construct artificial biospheres so that those with "*sangre pura*" (pure blood) can avoid the coming revolution. Indeed, the imminence of the revolution provides the excuse Serlo needs to press forward on his projects to engineer his ideal social-ecological conditions. Serlo's two-pronged response to the social unrest of the world—genetic and spatial—is congruent with Foucault's biopower, the most potent form of power in the modern world. Serlo's "utopic" vision requires both eugenics and the control of resources, nature, and even the biosphere through constructing "alternative earth units," a vision not that far removed from the goals of many environmentalists.

Serlo allows Silko to scrutinize the role of environmental ideas and discourses in the colonial-capitalist apparatus. Serlo's obsession with purity and pollution is both hygienic and genetic—related to daily practices of the body and to genes—and he believes his own genes reflect "the importance of lineage" (541). Serlo owns a *finca* (farm) in Mexico, where he hosts other friends of sangre pura, namely, Beaufrey (the gay purveyor of black-market pornographic films, mentioned above). At the finca, Serlo works on his plans to create a research center and an institute to refine genes and create "alternative earth units." The finca "was to become a stronghold for those of *sangre pura* as unrest and revolutions continued to sweep through" (541). Beaufrey and Serlo see themselves as being "entirely different beings, on a far higher plane, inconceivable to commoners." To them, aristocratic descent means being above the law and entitled to judge others. They believed "the words *unavailable* and *forbidden* did not apply" to them (535).

But unlike Beaufrey, who acknowledges that "riches meant little if the cities were burning and anarchy reigned" (542), Serlo thinks his pure blood not only exonerates him from any blame in perpetuating the conditions that are causing the unrest, but also licenses him to transcend it entirely. Like many environmentalists today, Serlo has an apocalyptic view of environmental implosion, but he sees this as the fault of the "degenerative masses" and believes his wealth and superiority give him the right and the means to escape. While the masses are suffering "below" on earth, he and a "select few would continue as they always had, gliding in luxury and ease across the polished decks of steel and glass islands where they looked down on earth as they once gazed down on Rome or Mexico City from luxury penthouses, still sipping cocktails." Serlo's alternative earth units will be "loaded with the last of the earth's uncontaminated soil, water, and oxygen" and be populated by people with uncontaminated blood. They will "be launched by immense rockets into high orbits around the earth where sunlight would sustain plants to supply oxygen, as well as food" (542).

Serlo takes no responsibility for creating the problems he seeks to escape, and he has full confidence that his earth units will be "capable of remaining cut off from earth for years if necessary" (543). Joni Adamson argues that Serlo's desire to "remove the last of the earth's clean air and water, leaving the planet a virtual prison for people of color," is an extension of the power relations that have allowed "European countries and the United States [to extract] natural resources from the homelands of indigenous people for more than five hundred years" (*American Indian Literature* 172). But I would argue that Adamson does not go far enough in her critique of what Serlo represents. Her interpretation of Serlo's resource imperialism misses the environmentalist underpinnings of Serlo's fantasies of appropriation and escape. Land appropriation and escape have roots in the notion of the "pastoral," a notion that also played a significant role in shaping modern environmentalism.

Serlo's ties to environmentalism are best understood in light of Raymond Williams's formulation of the links between imperialism and the environmentalist pastoral trope. Serlo's fantasy of escape is typical of the capitalist-imperialist "pastoral," as Williams famously described it in *The Country and the City*. Williams contends that capitalism and imperialism have created the discourse of division between "the country" and "the city." They have constructed the unspoiled country as the polar opposite of the polluted city in order to escape the unlivable environment they themselves created through capitalist exploitation. As Williams writes, the appeal of the country is not an innocent response to crises of the city; rather, when we "limit ourselves to their contrast," we commit the sins of the imperialist pastoral fantasy. We must "go on to see the interrelations [between city and country] and through these the real shape of the underlying crisis" (297). In other words, the country did not exist prior to the city, like some prelapsarian notion of Eden before man's fall. Capitalist-imperialists feel entitled to escape from the mess of the city (which is nearly the entire planet in *Almanac*) and retreat to a protected, pristine country. In this narrative, it is the elites who are entitled to escape and to remain ignorant of their own role in creating cities that make the country both necessary and desirable. Williams's analysis demonstrates that the country is just as much a product of modern society as the city. It is not, as the pastoral myth suggests, a place where the last remaining unspoiled nature remains, and where only the privileged few can secure access. Serlo's pastoral fantasies are expressed in his protected finca and his alternative earth units, which, in Williams's formulation, fail to account for Serlo's own complicity in the problems he hopes to escape. Through Serlo, Silko critiques this elite sense of entitlement to a pure environment (escaping to the country) that characterizes much mainstream environmentalism. Serlo's earth units enact the delusion of the pastoral Williams describes.

Silko's critique of Serlo's earth units can be seen by contrast with the choice she makes for the location of the revolution's origin—the uranium pit mine in New Mexico. The despoiled pit mine provides a counternarrative to the dominant environmental construction of ideal landscapes as pristine places where no evidence of human history is allowed to exist. If these places are "nature" and mines are "sacrifice zones," then Silko's choice of the pit mine as the originating site of the revolution represents not only a rejection of colonial-capitalist exploitation but also a rejection of the wilderness model put forth by mainstream environmentalists, of which the alternative earth units represent the logical extreme.

Silko further critiques Serlo's eco-imperialism by comparing the privileged gaze from Serlo's earth units to the penthouse perspectives of contemporary elites "in Mexico City and Rome." Serlo's "men of *sangre pura*" look down on the laborers below from the clean, polished, and protected "islands" above, the very existence of which fuel the unrest below, as the islands extract all of the best resources from the earth for the comfort of the elites. Serlo is Williams's capitalist-imperialist, refusing to recognize that the problems of the earth *stem from* his destructive acts, which create the need for a pastoral escape. Serlo's approach to the environment is to seek technological fixes rather than address its root causes. Like all the other colonial-capitalists in the novel, Serlo does not see the interrelation of his fantasies and the discomforts he feels entitled to escape.

Serlo's desire for a dominant "transparent eyeball" perspective of the earth mirrors how the pastoral impulse is enacted in the representation of earth from the perspective of space, a representation embodied in the visual of "spaceship earth." This global vision of the planet was popularized in the 1960s when the Apollo Space Program first photographed earth from space. Although some have argued that this image greatly promoted concern for the environment, as people could see the planet as a whole and understand its limits, the position of power implicit in its distanced gaze can also be seen as a perspective of domination and control, as viewers cannot see the messy details of human activity and institutions, like the nation-state and capitalism, on earth. As Giovanna di Chiro warns, the image of spaceship earth is a neoliberal environmental fantasy of a "global commons" controlled by an "international class of enviro-experts" ("Beyond" 206). Both Serlo's distanced gaze and his technological approach suggest ways in which Silko critiques environmentalism through him.

The spaceship earth perspective that the elites enjoy from Serlo's earth units suggests another line of critique, especially when viewed in light of the insurance man described above. Like the insurance man's view of the tundra from the perspective of an airplane, the image of spaceship earth privileges the visual as the primary mode of representing nature. This visual emphasis, or "ocularcentrism," is central to the process of objectifying landscape, as geographer Gillian Rose argues. For Rose, the "imperialist gaze" is also male; it feminizes landscape by treating it as an object of consumption or domination through the sense of vision. Silko explicitly articulates this point from a Native American perspective in *Yellow Woman*.

> So long as human consciousness remains within the hills, canyons, cliffs, and the plants, clouds, and sky, the term *landscape*, as it has entered the English language, is misleading. "A portion of territory the eye can comprehend in a single view" does not correctly describe the relationship between the human being and his or her surroundings. This assumes the viewer is somehow *outside* or *separate from* the territory she or he surveys. Viewers are as much a part of the landscape as the boulders they stand on. (27)

Consistent with her focus on the body in *Almanac*, here Silko is attuned to the potential imperialist problems of privileging the visual. It is no surprise, then, that she portrays Serlo's orientation to nature in terms of the visual. He too sees land as a two-dimensional snapshot to be viewed—that is, "landscape"—which makes him the embodiment of Calabazas's observations about white ways of perceiving landscape, described above. This distanced viewpoint is part of the same imperialist orientation that makes whites unable to detect nuances in landscapes. Yet the pastoral fantasy of ethical and geographical escape requires this distancing move. *Almanac* suggests that this fantasy is impossible and environmentally culpable. Further, the distancing move will ultimately be as undermining of white power as it is enabling.

Serlo's earth units are a reflection of his underlying mainstream environmentalist ideologies, because cordoning off pristine nature is a fundamental premise of wilderness protection. To designate some land worthy of preservation and other land sacrificial, as Serlo's finca and earth units do, goes against the indigenous view that seemingly disparate environments are in fact interdependent and rely on each other. Silko's treatment of Serlo's earth units dismantles "those Euro-American scientific and philosophic discourses on which mainstream environmentalists base their argument for creating wilderness preserves where some species are viewed as 'contaminants' and targeted for removal, but other species are viewed as 'endangered' and targeted for protection" (Adamson, *American Indian Literature* 169). Silko's critique of the earth units is similar to her critique of the owl-shit ecologist; both create hierarchies of places or species to protect. This is the essence of the wilderness model, which divides environments and species worthy of protection along lines backed by science, but in which cultural and social hierarchies inhere. Although the earth units are fictional, contemporary environmentalism shares in their appeal and logic. Wilderness zones, NIMBY environmentalism, and structures like the Eden Project and Biosphere 2 are all examples of the separatist, pastoral (environmentalist) logic behind Serlo's earth units that Silko scrutinizes.

Serlo's eco-imperialism is not limited to this pastoral, resource-sequestering fantasy of escape and power. It is crucial to read Serlo's environmental values alongside his eugenics projects in order to

understand how Silko "draws direct comparisons between biological warfare and the policies of environmental racism" (Tillet 159).
Serlo's obsession with eugenics extends a theme of *Almanac* that
we saw in Silko's depiction of Clinton's suspicion of environmentalists, who conflate genetic and environmental pollutions. Silko's
rendering of Serlo underscores the link between environmentalist
and eugenicist sensibilities, a link that activates the construction of
ecological others. Serlo reiterates the Foucauldian notion that purity
of *nature* and purity of *genes* are the two prongs of biopower. Serlo
is as fastidious about the purity of genes as he is about the purity of
the earth units' environment. Drawing on the evolutionary ideological logic of racial hygiene, Serlo insists that the survival of the fittest
is not about social justice; Serlo believes that the Nazi agenda he
is perpetuating "was concerned with survival, not justice" (546).
In the "strict biological order to the natural world," he continues,
"only *sangre pura* sufficed to command instinctive obedience from
the masses" (549).

Linking her description of Serlo to Clinton's wariness about
hygiene and pollution, Silko depicts Serlo's environmental and
eugenicist logics through a discourse of purity. That he is "ahead
of his time with his fetishes of purity and cleanliness" (547) informs
his views of nature and of human genes. His obsession with purity
is so excessive that he refuses to partake in sexual intercourse. Fear
of contagion associated with intercourse leads him to believe that
penetration is "silly, unnecessary, and rotten with disease" (546).
Rather, he follows in his grandfather's pursuit of collecting his and
other superior semen in extensive sperm banks from which "superior
human beings would be developed" (547). Using knowledge he has
gained from studying at "private institutes for eugenics research" in
Europe, Serlo pursues his own eugenic agenda: eliminating the racial
threats to pure blood.

In Serlo's view of genetic purity, though, women do not exist.
Women are dirty and contaminating, and so Serlo's eugenicist
agenda involves eliminating women from the reproductive process. Serlo's research "had obtained reports from research scientists
working to develop an artificial uterus because women were often
not reliable or responsible enough to give the 'superfetuses' their
best chance at developing into superbabies" (547). Serlo's view

of women's irresponsibility echoes US eugenicist thinking, which paternalistically insisted that women were "mothers of the nation." For US eugenicists, the path to racial dominance or race suicide was the woman's to take. Serlo's agenda of "proper genetic balance" takes no chances; it removes women entirely from the equation. Their messiness and irresponsibility are evolutionarily unnecessary, even dangerous.

Serlo further erases women from the eugenicist project by eliminating the need for sexual intercourse altogether. Just as he wants to sequester only the purest parts of earth in his earth units, Serlo envisions a human society of only men of *sangre pura*. In this sense, the earth, women, and "degenerative masses" are similarly unhygienic, environmentally polluting, and genetically contaminating.[9] They are equally messy and require artificial measures of purification. Serlo's aligning of nonwhite, female, and nature as the others against which the dominant order defines itself reflects the importance of nature to social control. Through Serlo, Silko shows how environmental elitism relates to the dual ideologies of ethnic cleansing and misogyny.

Conclusion

Just as Alexie's depiction of the World's Fair in Spokane allows him to make connections between environmental and indigenous injustice, even as he rejects mainstream environmentalism for its investment in colonialism, Silko's description of a collection of "despised outcasts" allows her to make connections between different oppressions, and redefine environmental justice in opposition to mainstream environmentalism. On the one hand, environmentalists sometimes contribute to the indigenous effort to "take back the land." But Silko is clear about the fact that their own view of how to treat that land is sometimes in conflict with indigenous views. Environmentalists may be anticapitalist in some ways, but residual colonialist aesthetics and privileges are just as likely to undermine their alliance with indigenous groups. As long as indigenous reversal of colonialism is the task at hand, these groups share more than they differ, which makes their alliance more strategic than automatic or natural, like the way environmentalists in the novel naively perceive it.

Silko's portrayal of environmentalists allows her to reveal how they participate in constructing ecological others even as they find a role in the indigenous revolution. It is in her description of the strained role of environmentalism in the indigenous revolution, as well as the indigenous leaders' strategic use of the stereotype that they are ecological Indians, that Silko establishes the terms of indigenous environmental justice. As *Almanac* demonstrates, Native Americans occupy a paradoxical place in environmental thought; they are simultaneously ecological Indians and other, a paradox that renders their exclusion that much more difficult to see. But, as *Almanac* reveals, it is precisely this paradox that creates the possibility for a distinctly Native American vision of environmental justice in contrast—even opposition—to mainstream environmentalism. Following through on the tensions that Alexie only hints at, *Almanac* establishes connections between colonialism, environmentalism, and social control, and it does so by scrutinizing an underlying ideology of the pure body. Environmental notions of purity and pollution, as exemplified in the above analysis of Clinton, inform the "corporeal unconscious" of colonial-capitalism; physical bodies themselves are doubly othered. They are the material from which power is derived, and they shape the logic by which boundaries of exclusion are drawn.

3

The Poetics of Trash

Immigrant Bodies in the Borderland Wilderness

THE RELATIONSHIPS BETWEEN spatial and corporeal violence, as well as between access and exclusion, that I describe in the previous two chapters is perhaps most clearly at stake in a contemporary case study of the US–Mexico border. Discourses of national purity and pollution infuse debates about national security and dictate how to manage the border, as popular media treat the border as hermetically sealing the United States from the "tides" of racial others—so-called economic immigrants, environmental refugees, and other "ecologically incorrect third worlders" (Adamson, "Encounter" 169)—threatening to corrupt the nation.

Contemporary border narratives extend the spatial tropes of colonial expansion in the US West. As Razack contends, since the 1990s a new national story, an extension of previous colonialist versions, has emerged: "The land, once empty and later populated by hardy settlers, is now besieged and crowded by Third World refugees and migrants." This chapter examines the most current expression of the national story—the US–Mexico border as a barrier protecting nature's nation. Following Razack, I argue that the current dominant geographical imagination is "clearly traceable in the story of origins told in anti-immigration rhetoric, operating as metaphor but also enabling material practices such as the increased policing of the border and of bodies of colour" (75). As Razack suggests, then, anti-immigration rhetoric evinces the spatial stories of the nation and has material geographical and corporeal impacts.

In this chapter I draw on Razack's insight to examine anti-immigration rhetoric for its spatial tropes of the nation. But I add to Razack's thesis an analysis of the way the *environment* is invoked to make anti-immigration not just a national security imperative, but an ecological one. That is, immigrants are trespassing protected ecosystems and wildernesses, not just national boundaries. They are thereby not just threats to the nation and to American "blood and soil," but threats to a very modern view of the "nation-as-ecosystem" (Wald 23). I argue that it is because popular discourse about immigration frames the nation as ecosystem that immigrants can become ecological others. The notion of the ecological other that I am forwarding in this book allows us to recognize how discourses of nature, nation, security, and ecology continue to form a "culture of US imperialism," as Amy Kaplan succinctly described in "'Left Alone with America': The Absence of Empire in the Study of American Culture." The environmental debate surrounding immigration in Organ Pipe contributes to the ongoing formation of this culture of US imperialism. Taking as a premise Kaplan's argument that "the borderlands link the study of ethnicity and immigration inextricably to the study of international relations and empire" (16–17), understanding immigrants as ecologically other highlights the role of environmentalism in this ongoing colonial project.

I also want to add that the dominant anti-immigration discourse draws on the kinds of wilderness adventure sensibilities of exclusion and elitism I describe in chapter 1. That is, the perception that the wilderness along the US–Mexico border must be preserved as both a safety valve for the nation and a playground for its able-bodied elite informs immigration policy there, so much so that the price of access to the United States is risk of death or disablement. These questions of access, exclusion, and corporeal risk are central to humanitarian efforts along the border but are rarely raised in public or scholarly debates about environmental protection and immigration policy.

The Environmental Impact of Immigration
in Organ Pipe Monument

With more immigrants seeking entry into the United States than since the first decade of the twentieth century, it is no surprise that undocumented immigration has increasingly dominated public debate.[1] Recently, though, concerns about the ecological impacts of immigration on the borderland environment have become part of these debates. In 2004, for instance, the National Parks Conservation Association ranked Organ Pipe Cactus National Monument, one of Arizona's treasured borderland natural areas, in "America's top ten endangered parks," due to the "more than 200,000 undocumented border crossings each year [that] cause serious damage to the park's plants, animals, and historic artifacts" (Himot 32).

Eighty-five percent of Arizona's border with Mexico is protected as parks, refuges, monuments, and natural areas. Nestled within a military range and Tohono O'odham tribal land, these preserved areas operate within a patchwork of vying stakes—tribal, military, security, environmental, private, corporate, and cultural—that entangle the Arizona borderland in what Sharon Stevens has called a "socioecological web," "where every strand reverberates in response to the movement of any other strand, as with passing breezes or insects on spider webs" (2). The Arizona–Mexico borderland is such a web, and how we talk and think about the environmental impact of immigration reverberates there. Media, environmentalists, rangers, politicians, and nativist groups such as the Minutemen have begun to capitalize on the shock value of migrant damage to the environment, for political purposes. The fear of immigrants—or worse, terrorists—coming into the United States gets fueled by evidence that their presence is damaging the delicate desert environment of the Southwest. Anti-immigration and national security alarmists readily make use of the environment to shape their case against immigrants and rally support.

In this chapter, I examine the rhetoric of environmental alarmism surrounding the Arizona borderland wilderness, focusing on Organ Pipe Cactus National Monument as a case study because it illustrates how the borderland is being contested in this particular historical moment. The rhetoric surrounding Organ Pipe Monument helps frame the immigration debate and has a direct impact on the policies and laws that impinge on this landscape. Mary Pat Brady's definition of landscape helps clarify my use of Organ Pipe Monument as a lens through which to view the role of the environment in the debate. Brady offers a critical definition of landscape, as opposed to the way that landscape has been used as a visual tool of conquest, as in Silko's formulation I cited in chapter 2. Landscape is "not a simplistic depiction of scenery," as Silko critiqued, which can be used to enframe or exclude different social groups, "but rather the conscious construction of a perspective," Brady writes. It is "a *way of seeing* a region that, in concert with policies, laws, and institutions, *physically makes the land*, produces the landscape materially and sustains it ideologically" (17, my emphasis). Echoing my argument from chapter 2 that ways of seeing are epistemological and ideological, Brady's critical definition emphasizes that landscape representations construct "ways of seeing" that help to "physically make the land." In other words, epistemologies of landscapes have material impacts on those landscapes, especially in terms of naturalizing who belongs in them and who does not, as I outlined in chapter 2.

Krista Comer also shows the process by which wilderness areas, for instance, are landscapes that, "when mapped by human minds, not only reflect human social organization but, as representational systems, participate in both the construction and maintenance of every kind of racial, gender, class, sexual, regional, and nationalist relationship imaginable" (12). In other words, landscapes are never "natural," not even ones that are represented as natural (such as wilderness parks), and those spaces support power relationships and social structures. Like the notion of place, the ideological assumptions underlying the notion of landscape can operate to support or to resist the status quo. Comer notes that "one group of landscape representations might further . . . heroic white history," whereas another group of representations might "question that dominant history, reveal its internal contradictions," and offer very different "conceptualization[s] of 'landscape' and human relationships to one another and to nonhuman nature" (12). A wilderness landscape, despite drawing attention to itself as natural, is embedded in geographical, social, and historical processes, and "assumes certain social characteristics once it is administered by the state or redesigned for visitors and tourists" (Thacker 17).

Similarly, Gillian Rose adds, "landscape is a form of representation and not an empirical object" ("Looking" 195). This view of landscape as representation, not object, helps to correct the ways that landscape has been used as a tool of conquest. Thus, my hope is that the kind of landscape-based investigation in this chapter can serve as an epistemological counter to the kind of green Orientalism that *Almanac* attacked. By examining "the conscious construction of a perspective, a way of seeing" Organ Pipe Monument, this chapter demonstrates how environmental language about the Monument "produce[s] the landscape materially and sustain[s] it ideologically." The landscape of Organ Pipe Monument is not only a product of policies, laws, and institutions but is constructed by the stories that circulate about it. The story of the landscape of Organ Pipe represents its endangerment by immigrants and smugglers as an ecological issue. In a post–9/11 context, "the environment"—as both representation and the land itself—is a key player in national security debates.

This kind of landscape- or place-based analysis is crucial to understanding debates about environment and security in the borderland. Place grounds the context in which it is embedded; that is, following Brady, its materiality expresses the ideologies that sustain it and the perspectives that produce it. Joni Adamson further suggests that such a focus on "place" allows the literary critic to "move at times from a large-scale pattern or theory to a specific place" and to ask "how differences in ecological, cultural, economic, political, and social conditions get produced and how those differences manifest themselves differently in specific places" (*American Indian Literature* 83–84). By focusing on a specific place, I integrate both field methods and literary analysis, following Adamson's and other critical geographers' Foucauldian view of the interrelation of space, language, and power. That is, I analyze Organ Pipe in order to "be insistently aware of how space can be made to hide consequences from us, how relations of power and discipline are inscribed in the apparently innocent spatiality of social life, how human geographies become filled with politics and ideology" (Soja, qtd. in Villa 1). The discourse surrounding Organ Pipe Monument exposes these relations of power and discipline, and dictates which social groups and which environments are worthy of protection, and which should be sacrificed.

My approach in this chapter thus reflects a methodological shift in the book. As in the other chapters, I examine cultural and literary texts and use theoretical insights from a range of fields, including environmental justice ecocriticism, environmental history, and geography. But in this chapter I also integrate field research methods to augment the textual and theoretical insights from these fields. I visited Organ Pipe Monument to read the landscape there, to understand how the park presents itself to visitors and how the spaces of the park and the border articulate the tensions I describe above. I also talked to rangers, the park superintendent, tourists, environmental activists, and humanitarians working on these issues, to register how stakeholders perceive and portray these problems. I present these field place-based findings alongside textual and theoretical analyses, and attempt to understand the story of this landscape in this historical moment by means of both what is phenomenologically accessible and what is not—what the landscape is and is *not* telling us—as well as within the context of the arguments I have been building thus far in the book. That is, the landscape of Organ Pipe itself communicates who belongs and who does not, and shows how "power is expressed in the monopolization of space and the relegation of weaker groups in society to less desirable environments" (Germic 115). These integrated methods allow me to illustrate how attempts to protect the borderland space there as natural conflict with the realities of the global economy and tensions about disparate cultural meanings of—ways of seeing—the land. Thus, this chapter's methods of integrating textual and field analyses model these theorists' argument—that discourse and land are mutually constitutively constructed.

I hope to show that the greening of the case against immigrants puts immigrants and the landscapes through which they migrate at even greater risk than the dominant narrative suggests. By integrating discursive and landscape-based investigations of Organ Pipe, I make connections between bodies and landscapes, as the competing ways of seeing the border have everything to do with the sacrifice of certain bodies and ecosystems for the protection of others. The green anti-immigrant case makes it easy to harbor racist sentiment, because it is backed by science, while "green hate" directed at immigrants fuels disgust of their bodies, as well as makes it easy to ignore the ways that immigrant bodies are sacrificed by both their exclusion from the spaces of the borderland and the corporeal privileges of a fair labor system. Thus, green anti-immigrationism underwrites strict national security measures as well as exclusionary labor laws, which ultimately do more damage to the ecosystem of the border and to immigrants, even as these measures and laws assure Americans that their border is "secure" and ensures that their goods remain cheap. The integrity of immigrants' bodies and of borderland wildernesses is the price paid for Americans' sense of consumer and geographical security. Green anti-immigrant discourse merely updates environmentalism's troubling historical investment in anti-immigrant, racist, and colonialist projects, and exposes the conflicting demands America has always made of "its" nature.

Organ Pipe Monument: Big Empty or Wilderness Fortress?

Organ Pipe Monument occupies a central place in the environmental imagination of the US West, which makes the monument's "endangerment" of special concern to those who write and act in support of the place. Five hundred square miles of desert, Organ Pipe was designated a national monument by Roosevelt in 1937, and an International Biosphere Preserve in 1976; and, in 1978, it earned official wilderness status. Quitobaquito Springs, located just on the border in the monument, is a magnet for native wildlife and the source of water for Organ Pipe's 227 species of resident, migrant, and vagrant birds (Nabhan, "Land" 85).

Edward Abbey's name for Organ Pipe was the "Big Empty," although due to the springs the park is teeming with animals and plants that do not typically survive desert conditions. Environmental journalist Carol Ann Bassett calls Organ Pipe a "place of edges" for its unique geography and topography. The wilderness area encompasses intersecting ecoregions and climates. The landscape inspired the likes of Aldo Leopold, Edward Abbey, and Gary Paul Nabhan to recognize its unique environmental features in their writing, and it has been immortalized by naturalists and nature writers over the past century. Like other larger and more well-known wilderness parks in the United States, Organ Pipe has become a symbol of American natural heritage. But it is a place of edges for more than its biological and geographical diversity. Perched on the edge of the United States itself, Organ Pipe has been, until recently, delineated from Mexico by a barbed wire fence marking the international border.

As a result, recent national security and immigration policies are putting the park at risk. How does a national monument, which is mandated to protect nature along a border that is quickly being transformed into a "mini war zone" (Kloor 11), negotiate competing demands of national security, visitor safety and satisfaction, and environmental protection? Because undocumented activity in remote parts of the border—especially places like Organ Pipe—has been on the rise since the 1990s, and because national security measures have amplified in the post–9/11 climate, Homeland Security gained approval to build a network of fences and barriers along the entire US–Mexico border. By 2005, it began this process, and by 2007, Organ Pipe had built its own vehicle barrier along its border with Mexico. The combination of increased anti-immigration sentiment, the War on Terror, and immigration policies that are moving undocumented activity into increasingly remote parts of the borderland is creating a "perfect storm" of conditions working against environmental protection and the human welfare of migrants there. This context suggests that critical examination of the discourses of risk, the movement of bodies, and the meanings of the borderland landscape is necessary if we are to craft socially just environmentalist futures.

The environmental costs of immigration are not lost on environmentalists. Beginning around 2000, environmental groups, media, websites, and writers began to convey alarmism about the ecological impact of immigration. The alarmism expresses fear and disgust about the endangerment of this treasured landscape, which is bearing the cost of its border location. A visit to Organ Pipe Monument illustrates how this message is conveyed, and how the Park Service translates the border crisis to visitors. Instead of pictures of the rare flora and fauna Abbey and Nabhan have documented, the most dominant sign in the display case at Organ Pipe's visitor center is an image of trash, surrounded by text describing the national security problem of undocumented activity. The caption of the dominant picture of trash reads: "Organ Pipe Cactus is an attractive place—and not just for scenery. Every year thousands of people are attracted to this remote location to illegally enter the United States. We want you to enjoy your visit to Organ Pipe Cactus National Monument, but it is important for you to be aware of your surroundings." As this text states, some of the very features of the landscape that make it attractive to nature-seekers—its remote location and diverse topography—ironically also make the park appealing to border crossers. But, as I discuss in chapter 1, wilderness excludes just as many as it includes; if wilderness is a national birthright, as the National Park rhetoric insists, then undocumented immigrants are particularly out of place there. Indeed, visitors are made aware of the park's problem with undocumented activity even before they get to the visitor center; they must cross a border patrol checkpoint before they enter the park along Highway 85 from the north. Homeland Security vehicles outnumber civilian vehicles on this road, which is the sole access into the park. The park exists in the middle of what Leslie Marmon Silko has called a Border Patrol state (*Yellow Woman* 114). Sign-posting at all hiking trails bears stickers declaring "trail closed" and explaining what to do in case of an encounter with an immigrant or a smuggler.

In fact, the majority of the park's public access is closed. For reasons of visitor safety, the park no longer offers the natural experience that once drew tourists and naturalists, and inspired environmental writers. Park officials report frustration at having to use limited resources to deal with immigration, smuggling, clean-up, and visitor safety, not conservation, a fact that is not surprising when you learn that the number of undocumented crossings into Organ Pipe Monument is a hundred times the number of registered visitors ("Stompin'" 7). The park has thus become a Border Patrol state, a mini war zone, or a wilderness fortress, to use Mike Davis's language. Yi-Fu Tuan might have called it a "landscape of fear," where the physical space itself communicates to visitors to be on the defensive. The wilderness there has become the buffer between the imagined community of America and those who ostensibly do not belong inside its borders.

Toxic Discourse and Pure Nature

It is significant that the dominant image that conveys this message to visitors is a photograph of trash. Trash is a central discursive trope along the border, constituting what might be termed a "poetics of trash" that shocks visitors, fascinates journalists, and activates public involvement. Just as trash captures Organ Pipe's "problem" at the entrance to the visitor center, it symbolizes the immigration problem in public discourse. I want to argue that it is through the poetics of trash that the environmental argument against immigration gains force. The poetics of trash provoke alarmism about immigration by framing it as dirty, ecologically irresponsible, and morally impure, and it stirs up anti-immigrant sentiment. It dehumanizes, even animalizes, immigrants and ignores the broader, perhaps less viscerally disturbing, sources of the environmental and humanitarian crisis occurring along the border. By cataloging the waste and human traces of undocumented activity, and by passing racism as environmentalism, it aids the dangerous project of "divorcing racism from anti-immigrant sentiment" (Pulido, "Race" 156). Furthermore, the poetics of trash emphasize the corporeal basis for anti-immigrant disgust and construct ecological others in ways that fail to account for immigrants' position in relation to US empire.

The emergence of the environment in this debate functions according to David Mazel's theory that American literary environmentalism, of which the poetics of trash regarding Organ Pipe is a prime example, is a form of "domestic Orientalism." That is, environmentalism's role in the immigration debate should be seen not as a "conceptually 'pure' and unproblematic *resistance* to power," but rather as a "mode for *exercising* power" (144) and delineating between "us" and "them" through the affect of disgust. I want to suggest that the environmental discourse about immigration in Organ Pipe others immigrants, and to argue that we ought to be aware of the "real territories and lives that the environment displaces and for which it is invoked as a representation" (144). Environmentalism has long been wrapped up in projects of colonial conquest and land enclosures; it is no coincidence that it followed "directly upon the heels of imperial conquest" (144). The case of immigration today provides an example of how its "legacy of conquest" continues to render immigrants the ecological other to an imagined community of white (implicitly environmentally enlightened) Americans.

One way that the poetics of trash gets articulated is through the ecological metaphor of "natural" versus "invasive" narrating of human activity in the borderland. Drawing on metaphors of natural disaster, invasion, and deluge, this language depicts the environment, not the immigrant, as the victim. The desert ecosystem is being "trampled to death" by a "tidal wave" of "illegal aliens" evading the law. One article captures the image: "Tide of Humanity Tramples on Organ Pipe Cactus National Monument" (B. Coates). Such rhetoric metaphorically likens immigrants to pollution, contamination, natural disaster, flood, tide, plague, or a "swarm" of overly fertile people of color rupturing "fortress America."[2]

In the rhetoric of biological invasion, immigrants are an invasive species endangering native habitat, as in a 2004 *Hispanic* magazine article titled "National Park 'Endangered' by Migrants." The author's use of quotation marks around the word *endangered* signals its metaphorical purpose; the word denotes a status by which we designate plant and animal species, but here it posits migrants as the invasive species and thus the landscape of Organ Pipe "native," natural, static, and victimized. By invoking ecological language, such rhetoric "demonize[s] invading aliens—at times weaving exotic plants and abject alterities into a common field of moral panic" (Moore, Pandian, and Kosek 29). And, by conflating invasive species and immigrants (the "abject alterities" in this context), the metaphor naturalizes the exclusion of both. Reading immigration in these ecological terms naturalizes fear of invasion on scientific—as opposed to cultural, political, moral or ethical—grounds. It "rel[ies] on the questionable assumption that social systems are indeed in some way homologous to ecological ones," Ursula Heise observes, and the problem with this logic is that "it lends itself so easily to the 'naturalization' of" what really should be seen as "historically, socially, and culturally contingent" contexts ("Ecocriticism" 15). Indeed, this ecological metaphor fails to account for why immigrants are in the delicate wilderness in the first place and deflects blame for environmental damage away from any historical, political, legal, or geopolitical structures, which I will examine below.

This discourse of ecological purity is further enhanced by discourses of hygienic purity that activate environmentalist disgust. Trash is not only ecologically damaging, but aesthetically and hygienically troubling. The sheer amount of trash disposed along the migration journey is indeed alarming: adventure writer Tim Cahill estimated the amount is eight pounds per person (91). The ecological impact of so much trash and traffic is visible to visitors everywhere in the borderlands. Trash and traces invite a visceral response of disgust. Indeed, what response does Cahill's inclusion of the weight of trash per immigrant seek to elicit in his readers if not disgust? And the trash is impossible to regulate, making the rhetoric surrounding migrant damage to Organ Pipe's wilderness appear justified. An article in the *Sierra Times* typifies this response: "The flow of these illegal 'invaders' will continue, and the trash will never cease" (Dare). In depicting immigration as a "flow" and immigrants as simultaneously illegal, invasive, and dirty, this statement renders immigrants ecologically, legally, and hygienically threatening.

In the above statement, Dare also deliberately employs the ecological analogy of "invasive species," indicated by her use of quotation marks. This language suggests that immigrants, like a weed or invasive species, are out of control and environmentally irresponsible; in environmental terms, their littering reaches offensive levels. And they are tied to the trash they leave behind, metonymically becoming trash—unworthy and impure. The language of invasive species is equated here with impurity and dirt, heightening the sense that undocumented activity is dirty because it is, above all, unnatural. Historian Peter Coates traces the use of this metaphor through the past century in America, revealing that it is a common trope in environmental discourse, what Coates calls "the eco-racism of American nativism" (187). Passing racial anxiety as fear of pollution or interspecies conflict works so well because it uses the scientific authority of biological metaphor to obscure its racist implications.

Through this rhetoric, immigrants become an infection in the body of America. Indeed, in much of this discourse, the land is described as an organic being, which has the dual effect of humanizing the nation and demonizing immigrants. In describing post–9/11 Organ Pipe, the poetics of trash narrate this territorial rupture as biological invasion. Immigrants "scar" the land's body by rupturing the "seal" of the national body politic: the border. As geographers Juanita Sundberg and Bonnie Kaserman submit, when "environmental consequences of unauthorized border-crossings are narrated . . . through metaphors for the human body" (15), the natural body of the nation becomes unnatural or diseased. The rhetoric of biological invasion as a threat to native land is as much an argument about protecting the purity of the national body politic as it is about securing ecological stability.[3]

In addition to the dehumanizing effects of this ecological rhetoric, tracking waste is a kind of patrol tourism in the borderland that animalizes immigrants and smugglers. Shoe treads, tire tracks, shrines, burlap, beer cans, and fire circles, for example, all indicate how many of what kind of people—hunters, hikers, Border Patrol, migrants, or smugglers—are doing what, where. Tracking trash has become a new form of tourism that combines "community service" and spectatorship. It distances the trackers from the tracked and placates citizens (many of whom participate in the tracking) into believing that they are doing their part for national security. Worst of all, though, it dehumanizes migrants by animalizing them (a slippage made all the more easy when undocumented immigrants are painted with the same brush as illegal drug traffickers), making disgust at the desperation of others morally acceptable. This rhetoric emphasizes the organicism of the land at the expense of conveying the embodied humanity of immigrants.

Combining characterizations of immigrants as environmentally and hygienically threatening exemplifies what Jake Kosek has described as a discourse of "purity and pollution" about immigrants in America. Kosek's theory elaborates Mary Douglas's analysis of "purity and danger" to explain discourses of environmental racism. "Fears of contagion," Kosek writes, "were expressed by environmental leaders from Muir to Roosevelt to Pinchot and others," who "all saw immigration restriction as vital to the protection of nature's purity" (142). Even Edward Abbey, whose attachment to the borderland wilderness is well documented, argued against immigration on the grounds that "we still hope for an open, spacious, uncrowded, and beautiful—yes beautiful!—society for another" (qtd. in Kosek 142). Trash and hygiene are central to Abbey's sense of "beauty," as are concerns of population and, recalling from chapter 1 his comments about disabled bodies, fit bodies. Abbey went so far as to say that "the alternative, in the squalor, cruelty and corruption of Latin America, is plain for all to see" (qtd. in Kosek 142). That Abbey should despise immigrants as much as he despised people with disabilities is no coincidence, as I've been arguing; in his writing, we can see the centrality of the clean, fit, white, American body to the environmentalist ideal of wilderness space. Abbey's view explains how environmental and racial anxieties come together in the poetics of trash, which is clearly a tradition of environmental discourse. This anxiety about immigration among environmentalists is not new, and discourses of purity and pollution about immigrants "reflect a long-standing conception of a pure nature threatened by various forms of racial difference" (Kosek 143). These discourses "work to preclude [immigrants] from inclusion in the body politic as rights-claiming individuals" (Sundberg and Kaserman 5), confirming Mary Pat Brady's observation that "narratives of place become shorthand references for racial narratives" (16). In the case of Organ Pipe, the narrative of immigrant assault on the beloved monument conveys anxieties about racial purity, national security, and cultural integrity.

The poetics of trash uses ecological sensitivity to create disgust about migrants in terms of the perceived ecological purity of Organ Pipe. These discourses of environmental purity invite the response of disgust, a response that deserves closer inspection. Abbey's concern that immigration would assault the "beauty" of the desert exemplifies how disgust serves to draw boundaries between "us" and "them." In *The Poetics and Politics of Transgression*, Peter Stallybrass and Allon White examine the concept of disgust in terms of how the bourgeoisie historically reinforced such boundaries. They define "bourgeois disgust": "The bourgeois subject continuously defined and re-defined itself through the exclusion of what it marked out as 'low'—as dirty, repulsive, noisy, contaminating. Yet that very act of exclusion was constitutive of its identity. The low was internalized under the sign of negation and disgust" (191). Immigrants in the protected border landscape are coded similarly—as "dirty," "repulsive," and "contaminating." Through the poetics of trash, what might be termed "environmentalist disgust" about the ecological impact of immigration reinforces "insider," dominant identity. It also commits a similar low–high exclusion that is, not coincidentally, reflected in the physical geography of the border, where that which exists "south of the border" is dirty, repulsive, noisy, and contaminating. Just as Laura Kipnis argued about feminist disgust at pornography (that class disgust eschews lower-body functions in favor of upper-body or cerebral skills), arguments that rely on alarmism and disgust to preserve the flora and fauna *north* of the border are not innocent, but rather rely on the affective power of disgust to justify containment of immigrants from the *south* as toxic. The analogy of the body that Stallybrass, White, and Kipnis offer here is not just a metaphor, though; real bodies bear the costs of these corporeal and geographical parallels. Disgust is easily enlisted in the name of beauty and purity to justify exclusionary and disabling legal, political, and economic measures, from neoliberal structural adjustment programs to lack of health coverage for undocumented immigrants; immigrants risk life and limb crossing the border to come to the United States to risk life and limb at work.

Another article exemplifies the way environmentalist disgust arbitrarily distinguishes between good and bad kinds of ecological behavior. It warns that Organ Pipe is "being trampled to death" (Watson), a phrase that echoes the language commonly used to describe what white, American tourists have done to Yosemite, which was seen as "being loved to death." In this formulation, what migrants do is "trampling" and "endangering," while what (white) tourists do is "love." This racism revealed by this binary between "trampling" and "love" further extends the relationship between adventure culture, empire, and eugenics I outline in chapter 1. As Sundberg argues about this rhetorical shift, the distinction between trampling and loving is less about the ecological impact of these respective actions than it is about *who* is exerting the impact. Similarly, border patrol tearing up wilderness in SUVs is more acceptable to many environmentalists than undocumented bodies moving through it. This distinction delegitimizes immigrant ecological behavior, rendering immigrants anti-ecological and therefore not worthy of inclusion in the national body. It also reifies a racially white nation and equates this white identity with the purity of American nature.

This trampling-versus-love juxtaposition limits our definition of environmentally good behavior to the model of national park recreation, which confines environmentalism to highly regulated outdoor activities in designated wilderness areas during leisure time. Environmental justice scholars are increasingly challenging this model for its class, race, and gender biases. Environments worthy of protection and enjoyment should not be limited to national parks and designated wilderness areas, but rather the environments in which people "live, pray, love, and play." As Robert Figueroa contends, "mainstream environmentalism . . . is not about protecting where its constituents live but protecting a natural setting and its nonhuman inhabitants" (177). Alarmist discourse about Organ Pipe belies the fact that protected spaces are privileged over the "sacrifice zones" of the environments where human communities of whites, Mexicans, mestizos, and Native Americans live in the borderland.

Immigrants are disgusting or "ecologically illegitimate," to use Laura Pulido's term, because they are assumed to "not care about protecting their environments" ("Ecological" 37), but also, I would argue, because their illegitimacy is a function of their nomadism. That is, the invisibility of immigrant movement through the borderland amplifies anxiety about contamination. In this sense, immigrants represent the "thirdworldification," as Paul Farmer calls it, of the globe, in which the "Third World leaks" into the United States (qtd. in Wald 45). Because migrants *move through* the desert wilderness, immigrants are presumed not to care about protecting it. That is, their desperation to reach safety prohibits any kind of environmental or aesthetic appreciation of the nature they are trampling. Such values—treading lightly, leaving no trace, and limiting traces of human presence in the wilderness—seem a world away from the context of immigration. Of course, their ecological insensitivity has more to do with their condition of illegality than with their environmental ethic or lack thereof, which the alarmist discourse often fails to acknowledge. That is, the poetics of trash ignores the causes of immigration, the causes of its illegality, the factors that "contributed to the construction of the geographical idea of the Third World," and the ways in which "the politics of colonialism and decolonization produced contemporary conditions" for immigration (Wald 47). In addition, because much environmental thought holds that environmental awareness is a function of place-connection—the logic that the only way to care about a place is to be in it for a long time—it views as morally suspect *movement through* place.

Only people who have dwelled in a place for a significant amount of time can understand and therefore take care of that place. In this ethic, migrants are ecologically suspect by virtue of their movement. If "localism [is] a foundation of environmental thought and ethics" (Heise, "Ecocriticism" 4), then immigrants are by definition ecological others, because they cannot fit any place-centered conception of ecological legitimacy. Citing Rob Nixon in his editor's note in the Winter 2007 issue of *ISLE,* Scott Slovic commented on how this environmental disgust pervades even the work of ecocritics, who "repeatedly run the risk of allowing their 'ethics of place' to cross over into 'hostility toward displaced people'" (v). Fetishizing place-rootedness implicitly renders the *dis*placed ecologically illegitimate. Tying environmental stewardship to place-rootedness serves to position people who move—migrants, nomads, and refugees, for example—as ecologically other because they are migratory. The privileging of place often occurs at the expense of people who move, and is particularly damaging to those who move against their will, because it ignores the geopolitical conditions of their movement.[4]

Priscilla Wald's work on the cultural meanings of contagious diseases provides an excellent parallel to my thesis about the ecological threat of immigrants *as people who move*. In her account of the "outbreak narrative" in US cultural history, Wald argues that fears about contagious diseases dramatize "the danger of human contact in an interconnected world" (4). The fears associated with a "shrinking," globalizing world activate narratives about the spread of diseases, which become associated with people carrying them. Wald argues that fear of the spread of disease conceives the global economy as an ecology (7), fostering "medicalized nativism" that "stigmatiz[es] immigrant groups . . . by their association with communicable disease," and which, importantly, associates disease with "dangerous practices and beliefs that allegedly mark intrinsic cultural difference" (8). The cultural differences that make immigrants epidemiologically other similarly make them ecologically other. That is, their movement signifies their position of disempowerment with relation to the global economy, and their "trashing" of the land becomes a reflection of cultural difference; in other words, the logic goes, "they just don't care about nature the way we do."

And trash makes visible the invisible movement of people through the borderland, marking "the increasing connections of the inhabitants of the global village as both biological and social," "broadcast together in an ever more elaborate network of human existence" (Wald 26). Like disease trails, trash makes "the unseen world appear" and "tell[s] the often hidden story of who has been where and when, and of what they did there," thereby charting "social interactions that are often not otherwise visible" (37). Trash thus "paints the pathways of interdependence" between Mexico and the United States with the brush of environmentalist disgust that "can help overturn or rein-force governing authority" (17). Following Wald's argument, then, we can understand the poetics of trash as a reflection of anxiety about shifting forms of human contact in a new global economic order, in which protecting the ecosystem becomes a matter of "quarantining" the nation (27).

Devon Peña provides an alternative model to the environmentalist fetishization of place. He contends that place moves with migrants in the form of "transnational place-making" or "auto-topography" (2007). In these conceptions, mobility does not necessarily under-mine the important ties among community, identity, and place. Retaining these ties relies not on staying in one place, but rather on a process of place-making. Understanding place not as static, but rather as a process, then, Peña rejects neither the importance of place to subject-making nor the power geometry of migration.

These notions reject the idea that because immigrants have left their places of origin, they are necessarily either fragmented in their identities or blank palettes on which to inscribe American place-culture. Bringing places with oneself is a form of self-determination in the context of global flows of humans. It supports a definition of place that is not about "some long internalized history but the fact that it is constructed out of a particular constellation of social relations, meeting and weaving together at a particular locus" (Massey, "Power Geometry" 154). This "extroverted" or "trans-national" notion of place acknowledges place as a process, rather than a myth for which we can feel nostalgic. It allows place-making in spite of displacement and dislocation to ensure cultural survival. It also challenges the premise of the environmental fetishization of place by suggesting that multiple places can contribute to sense of place. Mobility or lack thereof is not in itself an indicator for self-determination or environmental stewardship.

The "Narrative Razing" of Organ Pipe Monument

In *Organ Pipe: Life on the Edge,* journalist Carol Ann Bassett exhibits the panic some environmentalists continue to feel about the way movement implies immigrants have no ties to the land they roam across. And Bassett provides an example of how the poetics of trash construct the ecological other in ways that can work only by erasing the human history of the border landscape. The poetics of trash not only invokes environmentalist disgust but also prohibits historical perspective about the presence of immigrants in the landscape.

> The constant foot traffic has carved more than a hundred miles of illegal trails throughout the park. Cars, trucks, bicycles, handcarts, and SUVs have left tracks in what was once a quiet wilderness. The constant passage of people and vehicles has affected endangered species such as the pygmy owl. . . . Contemporary sleeping circles have been built near ancient ones, and new rock cairns on ancient trails confuse hikers. Mesquite trees have been cut with machetes for firewood. Campfires have been lit and abandoned. Rare plants such as the night-blooming cereus have been dug up and stolen for their medicinal properties. . . . Bibles, rattlesnake antivenin bottles, plastic water jugs, and food cans litter the ground by the ton along with human feces. (76)

This passage exemplifies how a conscientious, informed, compassionate account of immigration can be complicated by "language and images that tell competing stories" (Wald 32). This catalog appears on the surface to be a straightforward, objective report of Bassett's observations. But, as David Spurr argues, cataloging all that is within view is anything but innocent: cataloging in this way is an example of a rhetorical mode "that comes into play with the establishment and maintenance of colonial authority" (3). Spurr continues, "There is nothing especially conscious or intentional in their use; they are part of the landscape in which relations of power manifest themselves" (3). In other words, as I elaborate below, Bassett's rhetorical modes operate for purposes of representation that, perhaps even against her own politics, support the status quo.

Bassett's litany of wilderness etiquette transgressions—sleeping, moving, and going to the bathroom in undesignated places, subsisting on protected flora, and littering—is neither innocent nor natural, but rather translates disgust as ecological sensitivity. As with the discourse examined above, the lack of historical and geopolitical context for these transgressions obfuscates its racial undertones. By detailing the traces immigrants and smugglers leave behind in terms of their ecological damage, Bassett exemplifies how this environmentalist panic about mobility inflects the poetics of trash and thereby further emboldens environmentalist disgust. If too close a focus on place, such as Bassett's description of Organ Pipe, "is insufficient to understand broader social and ecological processes occurring at scales that cannot be directly experienced and that are therefore outside of phenomenological reach" (Harvey, qtd. in Adamson, *American Indian Literature* 71), then Bassett fetishizes the local at the expense of the broader historical and political picture.

In doing so, she reveals disparate ways of seeing the landscape of Organ Pipe. Rather than imagining the position of the immigrant in the landscape, this catalog assumes and thereby privileges the point of view of the white, American nature-lover-cum-tourist. For example, campfires are often lit by "give-ups," signaling their need to be rescued, but Bassett's language here suggests that migrant campfires endanger the environment for frivolous reasons: they have been "abandoned." Immigrants' movement precludes ecological sensitivity and renders them "ecological thugs" (Peña 200) through the rhetoric of abandonment. This rhetoric suggests that immigrants have agency over their ability to come or go. The rhetoric of abandonment makes it easy to ignore the conditions under which a group leaves its land, and to blame the abandoning group. Narrating departure as "abandonment" cedes entitlement to land based on the logic that the abandoning group failed to care for its land, a logic that played a significant role in Anglo enclosures of tribal lands. The word *abandoned* is charged and has troubling connotations in colonial history. Careless use of it serves to extend this history by forgetting it.

Bassett's alarmism about immigrant impact further fails to account for a wider historical picture in her reference to immigrants "stealing" night-blooming cereus. Bassett's language implies that migrants' use of the rare night-blooming cereus is reckless, enhancing immigrants' status as ecological thugs. This insinuation ignores the vexed context of indigenous resource access in Arizona wildernesses. Prohibiting indigenous access to desert plants was central to the colonization of tribal communities in the Sonora Desert. Before Organ Pipe was a monument, O'odham peoples manipulated the primary source of water there, Quitobaquito Springs, to increase water flow and divert it for plant and animal productivity (Nabhan, "Destruction" 291). They planted and harvested plants there for food, medicinal, and ceremonial purposes, and also practiced irrigation there (291). It was the establishment of Organ Pipe as a monument that criminalized harvesting and led to the usurpation of O'odham water rights. The enclosure of the springs as part of the wilderness made traditional activities "illegal." Demonizing the use of plants in Organ Pipe for medicinal and other survival purposes not only diminishes the physical danger immigrants experience in this landscape but echoes the logic of the National Park Service (NPS) in excluding O'odham peoples and their traces from this land for the sake of cordoning off so-called pristine nature.

Consistent with the National Park Service's history of dispossession that I discuss in chapter 1, as well as the power of a green colonial aesthetic to displace people I describe throughout the chapters, the real ecological thug in the case of Organ Pipe was the NPS, which left an even greater stamp on the landscape than immigrants or smugglers leave today. Upon securing all rights to the land and water in Organ Pipe, the NPS engaged in a "cultural cleansing" of the landscape. "Seeing like a state" here, to use James C. Scott's words, NPS bulldozed sprawling wetlands to create a "Midwestern-style fishing pond," bulldozed and removed remaining O'odham buildings—as well as fields, orchards, and archaeological sites—harbored racist sentiment toward the O'odham, and otherwise "brought about the greatest loss of biological and cultural diversity" (Felger, qtd. in Nabhan, "Destruction" 292) there. In erasing evidence of O'odham presence in the landscape to create a "pristine" wilderness, the NPS imprinted Organ Pipe with a distinctly modern aesthetic of emptiness, revealing the constructedness of wilderness on multiple levels. The NPS completed in material terms what nineteenth-century explorers, surveyors, and miners had set the stage for in their "narrative razing" of Arizona, as Brady terms it, in which the land was narrated as "full of empty" and available for the taking (Brady 17–18).

Conservation acted as an excuse for racial containment during the origins of Organ Pipe, and in the past century conservation and national security efforts have increasingly exacerbated tensions between the park and surrounding stakeholders. As Dan Karalus argues, "ridding the monument of cattle and other intruders aided conservation and preservation goals, but often contended with the efforts of settlers, miners, and natives to maintain cultural and economic traditions in the area" (4). And the park's use of "fencing and signs performed similar functions" of environmental and national security, but they "posed threats to the traditions of some groups while largely helping monument officials offer a pleasing experience to tourists and define Organ Pipe as an environmentally valuable area and later as wilderness" (4).

Karalus's historical analysis of the park's history of creating fences and borders to manage unwanted human and nonhuman "invaders" shows that the park's history is characterized by boundary management—an important point, given my focus here on the environmental bases for corporeal exclusion. The focus on borders and fences to manage who and what can enter the park has been part of the park's explicit mandate from its inception; what has changed over time is the nature of the perceived outside threat. "Threats" ranged over time from tribal hunters (who, in fact, were hunting on their traditional grounds) to cattle to immigrants. Contemporary discourse extends this history of constructing threats and limiting access, continuing the erasure of different peoples in the landscape. By promoting the only value of the park as providing a "pleasing experience to tourists" and as an "environmentally valuable area" or "wilderness," the NPS made nonrecreational uses of wilderness unnatural, illegal, and unenvironmental. The park continues to be constructed as exclusionary through the continued narrative razing of the borderland's biocultural history.

Yet Nabhan argues that this so-called conservation plan was not in the best interest of the environment. Rather, the best environmental plan for Organ Pipe is not one that applies a wilderness or national park model to ecological management, such as "leaving no trace," but one that conceives of Organ Pipe as a "cultural landscape," since "ethnobotanically and nutritionally, traditional cultural management practices of the O'odham have kept their oases rich in wild green leafy vegetables, herbal medicinal plants, and edible fruits." Indeed, "there are strong linkages between human health, biodiversity, protection of endemics, and an indigenous sense of place." Thus, a better conservation plan would involve the O'odham asserting "their reinstated rights to forage and irrigate, burn and prune, eat and drink from the oasis habitat complex" of Quitobaquito ("Destruction" 294).

But mainstream environmentalists reject any contemporary expression of the cultural landscape model, even as they romanticize the presence of "ancient dwellers" as a part of the landscape's *historical* appeal, a consumable aesthetic. Bassett's romanticization of the ancient dwellers of Organ Pipe typifies this contradiction. She acknowledges that ancient dwellers once lived there but skips over a whole era of human use of the area. The landscape prior to Organ Pipe's establishment as a national monument was anything but pristine, Dan Karalus argues. Not only did "the Hiaced O'odham occup[y] or travel through the region thousands of years ago, hunting game, carving trails through the desert sands, and harvesting wild plants," but

> Spanish explorers and Jesuit and Franciscan missionaries trekked through Organ Pipe's desert scenery into the 1700s. In 1849, hundreds of Mexicans braved the El Camino del Diablo through what is now monument land on their way to California in search of gold. Countless graves, cattle skulls, and sheep skeletons offer testimony to the harshness of the Devil's Highway. . . . Small silver and silica mining operations, as well as cattle ranching, marked the period until the creation of Organ Pipe, including the Gray family who occupied a ranch within park boundaries until the 1970s. (5)

This history of the various impacts and movements of various groups—from ranchers and indigenous groups to missionaries and Mexicans—suggests that a more recent human history in this landscape exists. This history undermines Bassett's romantic view of the ancients here. Her ellipsis simultaneously invokes nostalgia for ancient, vanished dwellers and erases this more recent history, a history that undermines the basis of the conservationism she is espousing.

Her ellipsis ignores these activities, but even worse, it ignores the fact that the park was in fact cleared of Mexican and indigenous populations more recently in order to become a wilderness. The region of Arizona in which Organ Pipe is situated was appropriated through political manipulation, coercion, enclosure, violence, and discursive erasure. By portraying the Sonoran region as available, empty, and resource-rich, and its inhabitants as small, vulnerable, and scarce, journalists, mining engineers, soldiers, and surveyors justified and facilitated US conquest (Brady 21). O'odham peoples were dispossessed of their land and confined to reservations, while Mexicans were coerced and manipulated into leaving their northern territory. The tribe's traditional lands were split in 1853 when the United States bought southern Arizona from Mexico in the Gadsden Purchase, which created the present border (Dougherty 10), and left two-thirds of tribal lands in the United States and the rest in Mexico. Adamson affirms the "emptying" of this land to create a "quiet wilderness": "these lands could only be represented as 'empty' or devoid of human culture only after the Desert People [the tribes that make up the Tohono O'odham] had been expelled from the places they had inhabited for centuries" (*American Indian Literature* 16). The US policy toward the Tohono O'odham was "one of subjugation, segregation, and 'civilizing the Indians'" (Weir and Azary 49), which led to the official designation of a Tohono O'odham reservation in 1937. The 1934 Indian Reorganization Act ensured freedom of movement and territorial rights for tribal members (Nagel 7).

Thus, in the mid-thirties, several shifts in tribal and land policies took place in this region. Because very few of the O'odham members signed the official list of tribal members that could guarantee their claim to access, many "could not live on the reservation" and, importantly, "were not afforded tribal privileges because they were not enrolled" as Tohono O'odham (Nagel 7). Furthermore, even though US citizenship status is required to move freely across the border in Tohono O'odham land, many Tohono O'odham members were not granted citizenship or failed to sign up for it because that, by definition, acknowledges US sovereignty. The problem of establishing US citizenship and tribal identity continues to support de facto exclusion from these lands. This exclusion has only intensified since 1986, with changes in immigration and drug enforcement laws along the seventy-five miles of Tohono O'odham borderland, and 2001, which launched a series of national security measures after 9/11.

And Karalus's research shows that even as recently as the 1970s, the park and the government, backed by environmentalists, continued to work to exclude Tohono O'odham rights in the park. With the help of Stuart Udall, the park purchased the landholdings and grazing rights of the Tohono O'odham, and in order "to remove Tohono O'odham cattle from the monument," Karalus writes, "park officials began negotiations toward a land exchange as early as 1979, proposing to give the Nation the land where they currently maintain grazing rights in exchange for a representative portion of land more valuable and accessible to the park." Karalus argues that these efforts were pushed through with the support of environmentalists, who were beginning "to focus on external threats to national parks and monuments" (17).

This context of citizenship, dispossession, and exclusion is excluded in environmental alarmism about what is occurring in the border wildernesses now. Adamson confirms: "Because their lands have been split by political boundaries, appropriated for resource exploitation, and cordoned off for national wilderness areas and military bombing ranges, modern Tohono O'odham understand that the roots of poverty, injustice, and environmental degradation lie at the heart of Western culture's favorite story about itself" (*American Indian Literature* 21). In the twentieth century, Organ Pipe was designated a park in large part due to this legacy of conquest.

Lack of appreciation for its legacy adds to the tension between the Tohono O'odham nation, immigration advocates, managers of federal land such as Organ Pipe, and the Border Patrol. In addition, the Mexican legacy in Arizona further complicates the question of who belongs in this land. Mexicans who had lived in what would become borderland were "'alienized' and proletarianized" by "a combination of capitalist market forces combined with a new system of taxation that imposed taxes on land, rather than on the products of land," resulting in widespread dispossession (Nevins 108). Green anti-immigrant discourse does not account for this history of dispossession of land along the US–Mexico border, even as it uses an imagined history of that land to fortify American identity.

The lack of historical context for migrants' transgressions in Organ Pipe ignores the colonial history of this landscape and the ecological benefits of human impact there. By ignoring this human history, Bassett creates an ecological moral hierarchy. Echoing the "trampling"-versus-"love" binary above, her disapproval of immigrant activity unwittingly renders certain kinds of activity in wilderness more natural than others, and certain kinds of people "better" for nature than others. In contrast to migrants, what hikers do in Organ Pipe is environmentally correct. Meanwhile, the nostalgic view of ancient dwellers' impact on the land absolves them from environmental sin, despite the fact that, as even Bassett acknowledges, they built sleeping circles and left trails.

This stance is an example of what Shari Huhndorf, in her analysis of Native American discourse, calls a "fissure" in white identity; nostalgia for "ancient" dwellers pushes prior human inhabitation further back in history than is true, absolves imperialist guilt, and makes it easy for colonizers to ignore their own complicity in dispossession. Drawing on Huhndorf's formulation, I argue that this fissure exposes environmentalism's ideological ties to colonialism. It exposes the contradiction in arguing against immigration on environmental grounds while ignoring the human history of dispossession of land along the US–Mexico border. This contradiction of nostalgia for and erasure of indigenous history is another example of imperialist nostalgia. Nostalgic stories about the land that erase history implicitly blame prior inhabitants for abandoning their own land, render them ecological thugs, and justify imperialist entitlement to the land. Even if they do not explicitly target immigrants, these stories ironically posit the immigrant—as opposed to the naturalist, tourist, ranger, or border official—as the ecological other in the border landscape.

Even if we agree that ancient dwellers and hikers are more environmentally sensitive than immigrants and smugglers, these narratives make *them* the cause of a problem for which they are a symptom. Although it is undoubtedly unintentional, Bassett's and other environmentalists' rhetorics "biologize inequality" (Wald 47); that is, they serve as "discourses of race and nature [that] provide resources to express truths, forge identities, and justify inequalities" (Moore, Pandian, and Kosek 1) and thus too easily lead to exclusionary ideologies and harsh practices.

"Nation-as-Ecosystem":
The Ecological Argument for Nativism

Alarmism about ecological impact that is irresponsible about its social implications makes the green argument against immigration particularly useful to more extreme nativist groups. These groups appropriate the environmental argument to make a case against immigration in the name of protecting American national identity, which has historically been closely tied to American wilderness. As I describe in the introduction, national parks do not simply protect wilderness for its own sake. Rather, national parks are established with the explicit mandate to represent and preserve American heritage. The logic of preserving American identity by preserving land is foundational to the history of wilderness preservation in the United States. National parks have long been associated with nature *and* national identity, as protectors of "nature's nation," a formulation that assumes "wilderness has been the basic ingredient of American culture" (R. Nash xi). This close tie between wilderness and American identity relies on an ideology of racial exclusion. National parks are, as Stephen Germic calls them, "geographies of exclusion" that "not only define, constitute, and segregate social groups, but function to 'purify' a national(ist) self" (2). As "geographies of exclusion," national parks are "produced" alongside the forging and purifying of an imagined community of the American nation. Ascribing an abstract national identity onto nature commits what Lawrence Buell calls the "America-as-nature reduction" (*Environmental* 15). In this reduction, America's natural heritage metonymically becomes its identity. That is, if America is the Edenic garden of the New World, as Leo Marx has argued, immigration that threatens nature also threatens the nation.

A nativist group aptly called Desert Invasion exemplifies how this reduction gets expressed in the current post-9/11 climate. It declares on its internet home page: "our fragile National Monuments, National Wildlife Refuges, National Parks, and National Forests along the US southern border are being annihilated . . . by illegal aliens [and] are quickly being turned into National Sacrifice Areas." Repeated use of the descriptor "National," as Sundberg and Kaserman observe, cues an association between American identity and wilderness, and does so specifically in terms of Organ Pipe.[5] Further, by using the metaphor of "annihilation" to describe what is happening to the border landscape, Desert Invasion combines fears of biological "invasion" with nuclear annihilation to warn of ecological threats from the outside. This cold war rhetoric, once marshaled for liberatory purposes by Rachel Carson in *Silent Spring* to expose the environmental and health consequences of DDT fallout, is here turned against Carson's project of resistance from below. That is, if Carson was deploying nuclear war as a metaphor for DDT to alarm and empower the public, Desert Invasion uses it here to consolidate the white, American hegemony.

More rhetorical irony is implicit in Desert Invasion's use of the notion of a sacrifice zone. To environmental justice advocates, the term denotes tribal lands impacted by nuclear testing that turned them into sacrifice zones, and where tribal members are sacrifice people (Peña 200). Acoma Pueblo writer Simon Ortiz uses these terms to express the way environmental racism simultaneously sacrifices some land and some people in order to protect elite interests. Organ Pipe Monument is a classic example of this theory; wilderness areas such as the monument are preserved at the cost of other lands, such as the rest of the border environment and Indian reservations. In the environmental justice logic, then, Organ Pipe cannot be considered a sacrifice zone, because it by definition a protected wilderness. Rather, the majority of the environment of the border, damaged by militarization and industrialization invading from the North, is sacrificed precisely in order to protect places like Organ Pipe. Thus, when nativists employ the term "national sacrifice zone" to refer to a protected wilderness area and "annihilation" to refer to what immigrants are doing to nature, they turn rhetorical tools of the environmental justice movement against the ends of both environmental and social justice.

Desert Invasion is only one example of how the environmental alarmism about the protected border wildernesses is being harnessed for exclusionary purposes. This alarmism ignores the human toll of the border crossings and the environmental problems in *un*protected border areas. Admittedly, such groups are more reactionary than journalists like Bassett, but my argument is that the environmentalist disgust about immigrant activity in the wilderness easily leads to racial anxiety at best, or worse, to more explicitly xenophobic measures. This slippage is only enabled by the fact that environmentalism often misrepresents or ignores the borderland's human history, a history that would unsettle tourist entitlement to the border wilderness if made more explicit in national park literature and nature writing.

Organ Pipe Monument's Geopolitical Context

The focus on trash in green discourse about the borderland wildernesses is also dangerous because it establishes the moral inferiority of migrants and the unnaturalness of their presence in the borderland. What is missing in the discourse about the ecological impact of immigration is this wider view, an awareness that places like Organ Pipe are inherently dynamic and unstable, and are entangled in "socioecological webs." How did designated wildernesses become attractive in the first place? Any place-based analysis of Organ Pipe that seeks to understand the tension between ecology, security, and immigration in the United States must begin to contextualize not only the human history of the landscape, but also the broader geopolitical context of the border today.

The current geopolitical context of the border crisis is something of a perfect storm. This context does not evoke the same level of affect as the disgust people feel when they see trash in what appears to be an otherwise ecologically pure environment. Since the 1990s, migrants and smugglers began crossing the border in increasingly remote areas as a result of a Clinton-administration immigration policy, the Southwest Border Enforcement Strategy. This strategy, including Operation Gatekeeper, beefed up infrastructure at urban border crossings, such as San Diego and El Paso, directing the flow of smuggling and immigration into more remote areas. The harsh landscape of the borderland desert was explicitly deployed in a policy of "prevention through deterrence" against immigration. One Border Patrol officer admitted as much in 1996: "eventually, we would like to see all of [the migrants] in the desert" ("Shifting"). The harsh desert makes passage much more difficult. As Adamson contends, "the Border Patrol's strategy . . . wields the environment itself as a weapon in the battle to stop illegal migration into the US"

("Encounter" 234). Thus, the physical landscape itself is deployed against immigrants in the name of national security. The Immigration and Naturalization Service deliberately "instrumentalized the natural environment as a tool of border enforcement" (Sundberg 1).

Environmental alarmism about the border mostly ignores the ecological impact of border security, despite the disproportionate damage it causes relative to undocumented activity. The militarization of the border includes remote video surveillance systems, infrared night scopes, stadium lighting, motion-detecting sensors, and landscape-altering infrastructure such as fencing, roads, and land-infills. Border Patrol uses SUVs, humvees, Black Hawk helicopters, unmanned aerial vehicles, planes, and boats to secure the border (Sundberg 11). Border patrol vehicles, floodlights, roads, and fences do far more permanent damage than the trash migrants leave behind. Combined with the explicit use of "natural barriers such as rivers, mountains, and the harsh terrain of the desert" (11), these measures suggest that border enforcement's damage to the environment is not just incidental to its strategy but is central to it. For the policies to work, the environment *must* be damaged. The green discourse shaping public and policy debates about immigration ignores the fact that both the borderland environment and the 10 percent of all migrants who die in it are victims of these policies,[6] policies that put far more pressure on the borderland environment than failing to "tread lightly" ever could.

National security is thus in direct conflict with environmental security, a conflict that is exacerbated by the 2005 passage of the Real ID Act. In addition to authorizing funds for the wars in Afghanistan and Iraq, the act includes a provision allowing Homeland Security "the ability to waive laws necessary to complete border fences and roads to improve national security." Homeland Security has used the Real ID Act to waive the National Environmental Protection Act, the Endangered Species Act, the Clean Water Act, the Coastal Zone Management Act, and other laws that have been critical to protecting the environment (Segee and Neeley 32–33). The mere threat of Homeland Security's power to use the Real ID Act licenses the state to disregard the environmental impacts of its border security measures. For example, on the eve of Martin Luther King Day of 2007, secretary of homeland security Michael Chertoff invoked the act to waive all environmental laws, to permit the building of a thirty-seven-mile fence in Arizona. In November 2007 just the threat of Chertoff's possible use of the act facilitated state appropriation of wilderness from the Cabeza Prieta Wildlife Refuge in Arizona to build border fencing.

In addition to the ecological impact of border enforcement and infrastructure, and the explicit policy of using the natural landscape as a deterrent, the Real ID Act authorizes environmental destruction in the name of the War on Terror. Thus, the nineties Southwest Initiative, post-9/11 ramped-up infrastructure, and the Real ID Act all explicitly sacrifice environmental protection in the name of security. While alarmism about environmental damage along the border defines immigrants and smugglers as the problem, the environmental costs of these federal policies and laws go overlooked. As long as "the environment" is deployed to support national security, the material environment itself will bear the costs of its own misrepresentation.

Adding salt to these wounds is that these immigration and national security measures are just Band-Aid solutions to the strong push-and-pull causes of immigration. The 1994 ratification of NAFTA "help[ed] to bring about the social and economic transformations that generate migrants" (Andreas 608). In other words, these policies helped *cause* the conditions for increased immigration. Further, labor in Mexico and Latin America is underpaid and unprotected. Demand for cheap labor in factories, construction, and services, as well as the traditional demand for seasonal agricultural labor, has resulted from the relatively strong growth of the US economy over the past decade. Working in the United States is economically attractive and serves as an "escape valve" for Mexico, which is moving out of agriculture, in part because Mexico cannot compete with imports of (often subsidized) US agricultural products. Mexico exports its unemployment problem to the United States, and remittances back to Mexico are a key source of Mexican income: $16 billion was sent to Mexico in 2004, over $20 billion in 2006 (A. Lowenthal), and $23.98 billion in 2007, although the downturn in the American economy has stemmed this flow (Fouberg, Murphy, and de Blij 80). The United States benefits from low-wage labor on both sides of the border, in the form of cheap imports and cheap services. "Even if left conveniently unmentioned in the official policy debate," Peter Andreas contends, "illegal immigration has become an increasingly important dimension of US–Mexican interdependence" (608). In light of failures to adjust these economic push-and-pull factors of immigration, it should not be surprising that smuggling infrastructure, corruption, and environmental and human tolls rise in response.

Organ Pipe Monument is entangled in this uniquely twenty-first-century context of immigration. In the past two decades, deploying the desert against immigration ensures that migrants' bodies stay invisible and outside the economic system, while the system "accumulates" by virtue of their invisibility. Physical nature and the material bodies of migrants are the hidden costs of reconciling the dueling geopolitical need for "open" borders to benefit both the United States and Mexico economically with the need for a "closed" border in a post-9/11 national security climate. As Glenn Hurowitz observes, "Precisely because of the wall's ineffectiveness in stanching the flow of people across the border, it's the perfect solution for many members of Congress who want to show their constituents they're doing something about illegal immigration—without actually cutting off the supply of cheap labor demanded by Big Ag and the service industry." This contemporary scenario echoes Silko's depiction of the way that the materiality of vulnerable bodies supports the dominant order, which I analyze in chapter 2. Similar to how colonial-capitalism doubly exploits vulnerable groups in *Almanac,* the current system doubly extracts labor from the shadow force of undocumented immigrants; first, the facade of national security physically endangers them as they pass into the United States through the harsh desert, and secondly, their economic status once in the United States enables their further exploitation. Thus, echoing *Almanac,* Don Mitchell contends that the United States benefits from keeping this shadow labor force "invisible" in order to "extract the labor of dead bodies" ("Axiom").

The environment and immigrants are externalities of broader geopolitical imperatives. National and economic interests take precedence over environmental and humanitarian interests, producing a situation that Neil Smith calls "uneven development," in which development occurs for some at the disenfranchisement of others. Doreen Massey similarly describes the "power geometry" of globalization: "different social groups, and different individuals, are placed in very distinct ways in relation to these flows and interconnections" ("Power Geometry" 149). In the end, then, only certain people and certain territories are protected by "national security," while other groups and landscapes are made all the more *in*secure. As Sundberg concludes, "the proliferation of *insecurities* for bodies and environments resulting from the southwest border strategy entails a re-thinking of security" (2).

Reason for Hope: Activists Reframe the Debate and Influence Politics

Perhaps the best way to imagine an alternative to the dominant framing of this debate—which seeks to make the US public choose between environmental degradation and national security—is to bring other voices and perspectives to the discussion, perspectives that urge us to view the environment in alternative ways. Take, for instance, the activist Coalition to Bring Down the Wall, which sought to help shape the discussion about immigration, security, and the environment in Arizona during the time when green anti-immigrant sentiment was at its peak. The coalition is an example of environmental activism that put social justice at the center of its agenda, at the cost of support from many long-standing mainstream environmentalists who felt that "bringing down the wall"—the proposed fences, walls, and vehicle barriers along the length of the Arizona–Mexico border—was outside the purview of environmentalist concern.

The coalition united environmentalist, humanitarian, and indigenous activists in recognition that environmental and social justice concerns are structurally related. For a brief but crucial moment in 2003, the coalition successfully blocked border policies that structurally infringed on all three groups' interests. Analysis of the coalition's work highlights the mutually constitutive relationship between imagination and politics. Although the coalition was short-lived (even deliberately so, as it united for a very specific, time-sensitive political purpose), the ways in which it attempted to reframe the debate exemplify the kind of revision work that the mainstream movement will need to do to achieve its purported end of protecting the environment.

In Arizona during the early 2000s,[7] environmentalists were divided over whether immigration policy was within the purview of ecological issues, and many environmentalists were anti-immigration, drawing on a long legacy informed by fears about population growth in the United States. Mainstream environmentalists diverged from an emerging group of environmentalists, who recognized that the ecological crisis of the border was a function of colonial-capitalist relations, laws, and geopolitics. As the leading environmentalist of the coalition, Jenny Neeley, put it:

> The debate is shaped around the damage to the environment on the border. Immigrants drive cars, defecate, pollute the water, start fires, leave trash. These are definitely problems. But it's so easy to point at the immigrants as the problem. Obviously, immigration policy is at its roots. It's a very economic, a very international problem, and has to do with international economic policy; the roots are very deep and very complex. (personal interview)

Neeley reflects how the issue of "trashing" the environment divided environmentalists into two camps—those who "pointed at immigrants as the problem," and those who saw the structural, complex causes of immigration as the problem. As Neeley attests, "blame the victim" discourse was rejected because it failed to challenge dominant society's role in creating the problem for which it was blaming immigrants. Neeley's description also acknowledges the power geometry of the space of the borderland, where "international economic policy" is literally a feature of the landscape.

Not surprisingly, then, indigenous and humanitarian groups working in Tucson and in the borderland were and continue to be suspicious of environmental groups, a suspicion that exists for precisely the reasons I have been outlining in this book. Environmental groups have historically sought the support of the two other groups in efforts to save species and habitat, on the grounds of a "natural" affiliation between Native Americans and nature, for example, but rarely ever return the favor of synthesizing agendas, much less scrutinize the extent to which their agendas conflict with humanitarian and/or indigenous interests. Neeley critiques the elitism implicit in this unidirectional coalition-building among environmentalists, and why it fails.

> But there's this elitism that comes in, because, on the other hand, the environmental community is always saying "We need to outreach to the Latino community." We fail to let the Latino community bring their issues to us, to tell us what their issues are. Our idea of coalition building is a big one-way sign. We're never going to get outreach until we let them know we are about their issues. So when we're doing this outreach, we put jaguars into the conversation about humans dying, but we don't return the favor; we don't carry their water. And then we never sat down and figured out why they don't care about the environment. Hiring a Spanish-speaking environment outreach person isn't enough.

Here, Neeley articulates how environmental groups often assume that social justice works like trickle-down economics: humanitarian and indigenous groups will benefit from environmental protection since, after all, there can be no people without an environment. And, I would add, this trickle-down logic particularly undermines Native American ecological sovereignty, as their assumed status as ecological Indians makes environmental groups assume that their interests are always already in support of indigenous people. In the view of mainstream environmental groups, coalition-building has meant getting social justice groups to recognize the value of the environment, not challenging their own ideas of environmental concerns. Environmental groups therefore have rarely considered ways in which indigenous and Latino environmental concerns might be different from, or even in conflict with, mainstream concerns.

Given the tenuous historical relationship between environmental groups and groups interested in immigrant welfare or indigenous claims, it is astonishing that the coalition happened at all. It is the exception that proves the rule—that most environmentalists believe that immigration policy is not their concern. Environmentalists were divided about the environmentalist groups' participation in the coalition. In general, they would rather let Homeland Security override environmental laws in order to build walls and install ecologically destructive forms of surveillance, thereby tearing apart the border wilderness, than advocate for better immigration or drug policies, which would stem the causes of increased activity through these delicate borderland deserts. The structural relationship among immigrant welfare, issues of indigenous sovereignty along the border, and environmental destruction is not clear to them, on the whole. Neeley captures the dominant environmentalist position.

> It's hard to get the environmental community as a whole to call for immigration reform. It's very controversial to step outside of the environmental box about issues that are only seen as indirectly related to the environment. There's hesitancy to say, "We need immigration reform." They're more likely to say, "Put up more barriers." But what I spend a lot of time talking about with this group is that we can't pick just some wilderness. These walls just funnel immigrants to other environments.

Those "other environments" include the Tohono O'odham nation, as well. So, in other words, implicit in any argument to protect the borderland wildernesses is an argument to displace the ecological crisis of immigration onto the tribe and their land. Here we again see how the characteristic environmentalist position of NIMBY-ism can pit mainstream environmentalists and indigenous groups against each other.

Recognizing that the ecological problems of immigration require not defensive measures on the local and limited scale of the border, but immigration reform at a national scale, the coalition mobilized political opposition to one of the federal government's attempts to legislate the building of a wall to line three-quarters of the Arizona–Mexico border. The coalition's efforts were successful, and although the federal government continues to push, with much success, for border walls, the coalition's brief triumph created a precedent of collaboration for future campaigns. One way they did so was by framing the problem in ways that went against the dominant discourse and policy. The problems for all of these groups were the Southwest Initiative and 1990s Clinton administration policies, which the Bush and Obama administrations have maintained. Neeley reframes the debate thus: "Masses of increase in environmental degradation and deaths, racial profiling along the border, the desecration of sacred materials, impeding tribal crossing—all these are problems caused by these policies." Here, the root cause of the problem is not immigrants, but policies. Such a reframing of root causes completely shifts the narrative about environmental destruction in Arizona, challenging the status of heroes and villains in ways that have profound policy implications. The coalition rejected the dominant environmentalist and nativist immigrant-versus-nature narratives, as well as the notion that environmental and national security can be achieved only at the expense of human security and further tribal concessions. As Neeley argued, the members of the coalition "figured out quickly that we were all allies, that we are all suffering under the militarization of the border."

In addition to their general hesitation to get involved in immigration policy, mainstream environmentalists are hesitant to address their own complicity in creating the ecological crisis of the border, as Neeley observes: "We all benefit from having this shadow underclass of people, who risk their lives and pay lots of money to cross a very dangerous border to work. We need to honestly say to ourselves, 'If I don't like immigration, then I should pay more money per pound of oranges, for example, to make sure the job getting it to me is paid enough, that they have rights to unionize.'" It is not surprising that the mainstream environmental movement and public appropriation of the environmental argument against immigration insist on building more walls as the correct response; it is a lot easier to blame immigrants, ignore legal and political economic forces of immigration, and protect one's access to cheap goods and services than it is to tackle immigration reform.

Given all of these conditions, how did the coalition succeed at coming together at all? According to Neeley, it was really by luck that these otherwise disparate and often antagonistic groups got together for this end. They had previously collaborated in support of a political candidate because of his labor, environmental, and indigenous politics. When Homeland Security threatened to build a wall larger than the Berlin Wall, across three-quarters of Arizona, this prior collaboration created the conditions for collaboration around the more divisive issue of national security. Thus, the coalition was not only the exception that proved the rule that there are deep schisms between these groups, but also an example of how suspicions and divisions between interests could be overcome through awareness of shared structural disempowerment, especially on the part of the environmental groups that joined the coalition.

Conclusion

In this analysis of Organ Pipe, we can see how "nature" is deployed against immigration *rhetorically,* through the poetics of trash, and *materially,* through immigration and national security laws and policies. Meanwhile, border infrastructure damages the environment, and border policy uses the landscape as a geographical barrier, which damages the environment. Moreover, in the name of the War on Terror, the Real ID Act lifts laws that protect the environment. Coupled with the economic push-and-pull factors of immigration, these political strategies are far more damaging to the environment than the traces and trash of immigrants and smugglers, an argument that Jenny Neeley and the Coalition to Bring Down the Wall used to shift the terms of the debate.

The stories of Organ Pipe and the Coalition to Bring Down the Wall suggest that green anti-immigrant discourse has been misdirected, uninformed, and dangerous. It is misdirected because it posits immigrants as the problem while ignoring the political-economic context within which immigrants are damaging the environment, as well as the ecological impacts of increased border patrol. The alarmism is uninformed because it ignores the human history of this landscape and fails to question how the land was emptied to make it wilderness in the first place. And the alarmism is dangerous because it is readily co-opted by more extreme nationalist groups that use environmental security as a guise for more conservative politics. The case of Organ Pipe demonstrates the power of language to dictate human action and alter the natural world, both bodies and landscapes. Discourse about environmental and immigration policy can either fuel these concerns by pitting the environment against migrants, or mobilize them to unite environmental and humanitarian projects, as in the case of the coalition.

Green anti-immigrant discourse revives environmentalism's history of being dominated by elites who frame cultural contamination as an ecological issue. They thereby exonerate themselves of any racism in the name of objective science. Nature demands its others be contained. Like Frederick Jackson Turner and Theodore Roosevelt during the Progressive Era, we want nature to act as a safety valve to mitigate social forces of increased immigration and urbanization. But we also want obtrusive apparatuses of national security that threaten—even as they're called in to protect—that same wilderness. Indeed, the story of Organ Pipe extends a long history of the impossible demands on nature by the United States—to both *serve as a stage for* and *absorb the costs of* US hegemony.

The recent rhetoric surrounding immigrants in Organ Pipe revives a tradition of social exclusion in the name of nature. A well-known example of this is the Sierra Club's 1970s–'80s anti-immigration policy, which claimed that America should "bring about the stabilization of the population first of the United States and then of the world" (qtd. in Hurowitz). As Neeley observed in her environmentalist activism in Arizona, many environmentalists still hold strict anti-immigration views based on the neo-Malthusian view that the earth's "carrying capacity" can sustain only a stable human population, and that US resources should be preserved for US citizens.

Organ Pipe illustrates a nativist take on neo-Malthusianism, which frames the debate not simply as environment versus *population*, but as environment versus *immigration*. The debate crystallizes the current tension between ecology and security in this historical moment. Organ Pipe cannot be simultaneously militarized enough to deter or apprehend immigrants and smugglers (much less potential terrorists) and also "wild." Carol Ann Bassett articulates this paradox: "by increasing law enforcement in the park, there is less protection for the natural and cultural resources, which is why this national monument was created in the first place" (76). Protecting the environment and militarizing the border are fundamentally in opposition. Yet the logical response to news about the ecological impact of immigration is to demand more border security to protect nature.

Despite this dominant paradox, the Coalition to Bring Down the Wall illustrates that uniting mainstream and environmental justice concerns is possible. It will be difficult, especially because there is no one environmental model that fits all, and especially because environmentalism harbors hidden attachments to racial and colonial dominance. The identity negotiations at stake in building these coalitions and uniting agendas have as much to do with power as they have to do with protecting ecosystems, a fact that mainstream environmentalists would prefer to overlook as unrelated to the seemingly strictly empirical question of how to preserve nature.

Green alarmism about increased activity in the US–Mexico borderland is on the rise. Concerns about global climate change are only adding to this fear, as more neo-Malthusian worries about "environmental refugees" joining terrorists and economic immigrants seeking entrance into the United States take shape.[8] Fear of "invasion" is peaking, and the border landscape and migrants will continue to bear the cost of this fear. In 2007 the Senate approved a seven-hundred-mile border wall, Homeland Security invoked the Real ID Act to appropriate land from the nearby Buenos Aires Wildlife Refuge to build a fence, and Organ Pipe completed the construction of its own thirty-mile wall. Given these developments, these desert wildernesses—and the immigrants who brave them—are indeed, perhaps *more* than ever, endangered. What is at stake in this debate is the viability of environmental justice on a warming and globalizing planet, where environmental anxieties give carte blanche for the exclusion and exploitation of those deemed other.

Conclusion

Toward an Inclusive Environmentalism

I HAVE ARGUED IN THIS BOOK that the examples of the invalid, the Indian, and the immigrant are three examples of the ways in which environmentalism is complicit in maintaining social hierarchies. I have outlined some of the ways in which environmentalist discourse legitimizes and perpetuates these relations. I showed how discourses of environmentalist disgust and belief in the purity of nature reinforce distinctions between those who are ecologically correct and those who are ecologically other. Environmentalism as a social movement and as a field of study cannot continue to be successful without addressing these issues and the injustices they imply.

Gayatri Spivak's famous question "Can the subaltern speak?" captures the dilemma facing postcolonial and indigenous writers and activists. How can they articulate their own identity and political claims when the only language they wield is the language of their colonizers, and when their words and acts are so often appropriated by dominant society? To theorize an inclusive environmentalism, it is necessary to ask whether environmentalism's others can articulate—and even more importantly achieve—their own claims without "performing" or mimicking mainstream models and discourse. But ecological others are not always postcolonial subalterns. They can also be poor whites, rural people, inner-city dwellers, border crossers, climate refugees, the Chinese, American mothers (as I have argued elsewhere),[1] or any individual or group that is perceived by

179

dominant environmental thought as a threat to the environment, but whose tenuous relationship vis-à-vis nature is *blamed* for environmental crisis, even as it is more a *symptom* of broader power relations. Can their discourses be read as forms of resistance? Do the strategic advantages of performing mainstream environmentalism outweigh the problems with "using the master's tools"? In other words, can the ecological other speak?

Environmentalism's others are not silent about their exclusion; neither do they ignore environmental concerns. They negotiate their claims in ways that both challenge and reinforce, even as they tap into the power of, mainstream environmental paradigms. Environmental discourses and practices must seek more expansive ways to conceive of inclusivity, drawing on what Chela Sandoval calls "affinities," which emphasize finding common ground with others with "oppositional consciousness" and identifying along the lines of common struggles, as opposed to identity politics, which roots activism in static categories of subjectivity, such as gender, race, and class. Such traditional gender politics can make sense in some contexts, but they can be limiting in others, as *Almanac,* for example, powerfully illustrated. Thus, it is not enough to ask, as the environmental movement and ecocritics often do, "How can we make room for difference?" This approach exemplifies the tendency of pluralist and multicultural discourses to tokenize identity politics without scrutinizing the ways in which the movement fails to identify shared affinities with groups. As environmental scholars, we ignore important texts and discourses that address environmental and social justice concerns when we look only for conventional environmental themes, satirized by Sherman Alexie as "pine trees," "grizzly bears," and "rivers and streams."

Instead, a more inclusive environmentalism needs to ask, "How do othered perspectives revise mainstream environmentalism entirely and challenge assumptions of what 'environmental' means?" If identity shapes how different groups encounter and define environmental concerns, then these "may entail entirely different solutions and courses of action" from those proposed and practiced by mainstream writers and activists (Pulido, *Environmentalism* 28). There are many kinds of environmentalisms, and so new texts, genres, and voices emerge when we take seriously texts that do not center on environmental phenomena, but rather on, for example, sex tourism, food culture, genetic modification, organ theft, domestic violence, national security, and even genocide. If, like the environmentalists in Arizona who saw no relationship between immigration policy and the mandate to protect wilderness and wildlife, we fail to see the connection between these phenomena, we not only fail to "add more voices" to the movement but are actively complicit in their exclusion. An inclusive environmentalism can emerge only when it is fed by many, varying, and even competing estuaries of concern.

Competing narratives are critical because they shed light on the way that environmental discourses can be used, by environmentalists but also by others, to reinforce the status quo. In many of the narratives that I described in this book, environment rapidly becomes a form of strategic essentialism. Communities "perform" various environmental identities to align with or distance themselves from the mainstream, often in ways that reveal how mainstream discourse has been structured by US colonialism and by domestic elites. When we can see how these strategic performances expose the ways in which nature serves a political function in environmental discourse, we can understand them as forms of political resistance.

For example, just as *Almanac* provides both a critique of mainstream environmentalism and foregrounds a different set of environmental identities and concerns, it reveals problems with mainstream discourse and opens up a variety of alternative possibilities. *Almanac* articulates its own environmental ethic, which includes issues of sex, capitalism, drugs, organ trading, eugenics, and military operations. As Bridget O'Meara puts it, the novel "explores and critiques interlocking histories of oppression that inscribe the land, labor and bodies of indigenous peoples." At the same time, it "recovers and re-creates the submerged (fragmented, partial, transformed) knowledges of oppressed people, . . . affirming and strengthening vital social, ecological and spiritual relationships" (65). *Almanac* accomplishes this by insisting on an alternative to environmentalism that is rooted neither in nostalgia nor in stereotypes of the ecological indigene. It rejects purity—of land, of blood, of nature broadly conceived—as a basis for environmental and cultural preservation. It uses the master's tools—globalization, technology, literacy, military force and *environmentalism itself*—against the mainstream's master discourses and politics. In doing so, it articulates liberatory views of human relations as well as the relationship between humans and nature. Silko thus shows how nature can "come to provide a language for" as well as a "medium" to transform "the truths of bodies, selves, and landscapes" (Moore, Pandian, and Kosek 16).

Although it is crucial that we find ways to revise mainstream environmentalism, provide counternarratives of ecological identity, and attend to the social justice implications of environmental discourse, the first step is simply to acknowledge the ways that disgust activates our own environmentalism, no matter whether we are mainstream or not. We can see examples of ecological-othering occurring in popular discourse all the time, and we need to be diligent about the ways in which environmental disgust extends and masks other geopolitical, nationalist, patriarchal, colonial, capitalist, or other kinds of dominant agendas.

Take China, for example. China's environmental story is still unfolding, to be sure, but the dominant environmental view is that China is ecologically dangerous, as Solnit hinted in her article in *Orion,* to which I alluded in chapter 1. With its population size and unsustainable patterns of urban growth and consumption, the Chinese are seen as dooming the environment as they industrialize at an unprecedented and unsustainable rate. From the Three Gorges Dam to Shanghai's Baudrillardian cityscape facelift, China seems headed down the path that characterized much of the twentieth-century West, where growth for growth's sake was the driving paradigm. Yet what is missing in this narrative of China's growth is the broader global context within which it is occurring, as well as the unevenness of its development (which renders some Chinese more environmentally unethical than others, and others victims of global—not just Chinese—environmental destruction, such as e-waste recyclers), and the successful and thriving environmental movements within China, which are working hard to stem—or at least make sustainable—China's development. My point in calling "the Chinese" a potential ecological other is to highlight the complexity of China's story, in contrast to the monolithic brush with which mainstream environmentalism paints all of China un-green. The ecological-othering of China as a nation serves more to perpetuate anti-Chinese sentiment than it does to protect the environment, as protecting the environment would involve targeting much more specific (but more complex and less identifiable) sources of the problem, such as lax environmental regulations and labor laws, a point I have tried to make throughout this book.

Thus, we must be wary of the impulse to ecologically-other a community, driven as this impulse often is by other forms of nationalist, racist, gendered, sexual, religious, cultural, economic, geographical, and bodily disgust. Critical interdisciplinary scholarship on environmental security, risk theory, and disaster—emerging in a variety of fields, from postcolonial studies, epidemiology, and anthropology to political science, physical and human geography, and the health sciences—is necessary in fostering this kind of wariness of how discourses of disgust, or what Betsy Hartmann, Banu Subramaniam, and Charles Zerner call "biofears and environmental anxieties,"[2] underwrite fears of others with the authority of nature itself. As they write, "different disciplinary perspectives and theoretical insights can help illuminate how environmental and biological fears are produced and how threats to security are constructed" (2).

I have not meant to distract attention from the urgency of anthropogenic environmental crises. Critics may say that my project here undermines the environmental movement by fracturing its cause, attacking it from within, or disguising anti-environmentalism as a concern for human welfare, creating an unnecessary choice between environmental protection and social justice. On the contrary, I see the environmental work ahead as urgent, but unobtainable if it fails to account for social justice. Worse, I believe that much environmental discourse has become not environmentalism at all, but a green veneer on conservative social politics. It is this misuse of the environment—understood as both and simultaneously a discourse and an actual, material, dynamic entity—that I have taken issue with throughout the book. If we can begin to see the ways in which environmental problems are often, though not always, systemically analogous to social injustice, then we will begin to identify the ways to ameliorate both. Thus, rather than dividing the environmental movement, the

implication of this book is that to combat environmental degradation is to combat social injustice and vice versa, but only if we see
these forms of inequity in broader and more complicated economic,
historical, political-economic, and discursive contexts. We need to
take responsibility for understanding these contexts, and the ways
that environmentalist disgust reinforces rather than challenges existing power relations. What is at stake in assuming this responsibility is
the viability of environmental justice on a warming and globalizing
planet, where fear of eco-apocalypse can easily lead to discourses that
make the exclusion and exploitation of those deemed other the cost
of protecting the environment.

Notes

Introduction

1. My argument is in line with those of Charles Mills, Laura Kipnis, and others who use notions of disgust and trash to understand how dominant discourses rationalize social control based on corporeal marginality. Charles W. Mills, in "Black Trash," for instance, argues for a "shit-disturbing standpoint of black trash" (74), while Laura Kipnis, in "(Male) Desire and (Female) Disgust: Reading *Hustler,*" argues that disgust toward the female bodies in pornography reinforces elite feminist identity.

2. Environmentalist disgust toward overpopulating masses is well documented, and one need only do a cursory discourse analysis of media coverage of Occupy Wall Street to detect the anxiety about the health concerns associated with the congregating of masses of people. In this Foucauldian brave new world, "human rights" of health and safety trump the civil right to congregate, protest, and exercise free speech. As the logic goes, all those shit-producing bodies are a threat to the body politic. Similarly, thinking in terms of an ecological shitprint helps illuminate the disgust implicit in this corporeal rendering of the concept of an ecological footprint.

3. I use this term as a play on the term "politically correct," in order to point out the ways that these social categories reflect *cultural* politics, not necessarily *biological* truths, even as the full rhetorical weight of nature backs them.

4. A note on terminology: I use the term "disabled body" to refer to the associations of its social construction (maimed, lacking, dependent, physically and/or mentally "invalid" according to dominant standards of "normalcy," etc.). As I discuss in chapter 1, the category is not as stable as my use of it here might suggest, of course, and critical disability studies scholars challenge the binaries of abled/disabled, social/individual, and mental/physical that are assumed in the term. If, as I argue here, the environmental crisis is a crisis of the body, then disability is a crucial lens through which to understand the crises, or perceived crises, of both the body and nature.

5. Thanks to Rachel Ann Hanan for this insight about how our environmental values are implicit in—and indeed even constructed by—our language itself, down to the seemingly innocuous part of speech, the preposition. Such an insight suggests that language precedes, if not creates (as opposed to inhibits),

our connection to nature, an argument that is increasingly being taken seriously in the fields of ecopoetics and eco-semiotics.

6. Many theorists have thus contended that race is elided in concepts of space, such that *urban* is a metonym for *blackness*. Yet, as Linda Nash's *Inescapable Ecologies* has shown, polluted spaces are not necessarily urban, and certainly the contemporary urban dweller is more environmentalist in terms of ecological footprint than the average American rural dweller. Thus, mapping dirty spaces and dirty bodies is a much more complex undertaking than these categories allow.

7. I say "continue to be sculpted" to highlight the fact that, as I outline in this book, colonialism and capitalism were both enlivened by the sacrifice of the bodies of their others. The contemporary examples I examine herein continue a history of this phenomenon. What is new is not the use of bodies to materially support the ruling order; rather, it is the resurgence of the body in environmental discourse.

8. I use *environmentalism* and *conservation* interchangeably, although I concede that these two terms have different origins and connotations. Indeed, these two terms differ historically from the term *preservation* as well. I recognize that many historians argue that environmentalism as we know it now did not emerge until the late 1960s with the publication of Carson's *Silent Spring,* and that it could therefore be considered anachronistic to call either preservation or conservationism *environmentalism*. Given this potential historical fallacy, I want to highlight what environmental literature scholars like Mazel are trying to argue, which is that what we consider the environmental movement today had its origins much earlier than the 1960s. I am interested in the aspects of the roots of the modern environmental movement that echo both Muir *and* Roosevelt, Marsh *and* Thoreau, Carson *and* Abbey—such as the role of the pastoral and Miller's notion of nature's nation, for example.

Chapter 1

1. The distinction between valuing nature as refuge or resource occupied Progressive Era environmentalists, who were divided between conservationists (who preferred protecting nature as resource) and preservationists (who wanted to protect nature for refuge). To these groups, the projects of protecting nature as resource and as refuge were at odds, which split conservationists Pinchot and Roosevelt from preservationists such as Muir. Roderick Nash details this split in *Wilderness and the American Mind*. For my purposes here, though, both orientations toward nature amount to the same thing: nature is a safety valve for society's ills.

2. Braun offers the term "risk culture" to describe "a set of discursive operations around risk and risk taking that help constitute, and render natural, risk society's racial and class formations" (178–79). He uses the term "to call attention to the cultural and representational practices that produce risk as culturally meaningful" (178). I use the term here interchangeably with "adventure culture," although I do want to retain the connotation the term *risk* implies about the role of risk culture in a "risk society" (Beck).

3. The tension between disabled access to wilderness and the myth that wilderness should be free of mediating traces of built society is captured in an article titled "Trailblazing in a Wheelchair—an Oxymoron?" by Joe Huber. Huber asks: "Shouldn't minimum impact to the environment and safety of all those involved be balanced equally with one's right to access?" The notion of disabled people "trailblazing" in the wilderness is oxymoronic because of the implicit assumption that wilderness activities are precisely available only to those with fit, abled bodies. But even Huber fails to see the contradiction in his own language; "trailblazing" is inherently damaging to the environment in the first place. It is deemed acceptable for abled bodies only because of the myth that trailblazing is about independence and escape from technological mediation. But trailblazing with a wheelchair crosses a line because the technology involved signifies dependence. My point is that this line is arbitrary, because trailblazing—with or without a wheelchair—is unecological. The appeal of trailblazing is to fortify ableist values of independence and conquest.

4. See works by Bederman, Kosek, and Haraway for this insight.

5. For more on how spending time in wilderness became understood as a "cure" for psychological and physical maladies, see Harvey Green's chapter on "The Sanitation Movement and the Wilderness Cure" in *Fit for America.*

6. See the works by Mark Spence and Karl Jacoby for deeper historical record of this.

7. For more on Whitman's views of corporeal and national fitness, see Robert J. Scholnick, "'How Dare a Sick Man or an Obedient Man Write Poems?' Whitman and the Dis-ease of the Perfect Body." Scholnick writes, "In promoting physical health as a means of fostering national stability, control, and improvement, Whitman excluded those lacking the best blood" (249).

8. For more on Roosevelt and American empire, see Richard Slotkin, "Nostalgia and Progress: Theodore Roosevelt's Myth of the Frontier," and Amy Kaplan, "Romancing the Empire: The Embodiment of American Masculinity in the Popular Historical Novel of the 1890s." Kaplan expands on the role of what Perry Miller called America's "errand into the wilderness" in justifying expansion in "Left Alone with America: The Absence of Empire in the Study of American Culture."

9. Horsman outlines the debate between those who viewed expansion as a threat to racial purity (such as Emerson) and those who viewed it as an evolutionary imperative. Although there was no one coherent view, the debate centered on discourses of "biopower"; power residing in "species dominance" could arguably come from expansion or isolationism, depending on your view of evolution.

10. The youth were a specific target (Simon; Haraway; Selden). A popular eugenicist family film, *The Black Stork*, for example, depicted images of young boys doing physical fitness activities in natural settings. Nature was deployed as a setting for the disciplining of fit bodies, further linking ideas of what is "natural" to "nature" (Pernick, 93). Young women were also targets, but they were not framed in nature, further attesting to the link between wilderness and *masculinity* in this era. Women's professional lives could progress only to the extent that they did not compromise the national good. Women's reproductive responsibility thus

curtailed their professional options and actually reinforced their domestic duties (English). As the nation's mothers, women's bodies were enlisted as the foundation of national identity formation and the maintenance of a pure American heritage. As future patriotic mothers, young girls were encouraged to maintain physical fitness through feminine activities, such as gymnastics (Chisholm). Such activities were the feminine counterpart to outdoor adventure activities for young white boys.

11. Roosevelt's focus on the young male body as a site of national integrity was consistent with his historical moment, as Rail and Harvey argue. At this time, "sportization," as they call it, disciplined individual bodies and mobilized the population (171). Sports legitimized a "matrix of bodily surveillance technologies" (172) that helped produce the "deviant body" (173). Again, we see that the construction of the "fit" body at this moment coincided with the construction of "disability" as the deviant body.

12. "Means of subsistence" is also Marxian. Like Darwin, Marx looked to Malthus to explain the "contradictions" of capitalism. Given Malthus's theory of the tension between population growth and resource availability, capitalism would be checked by its own depletion of resources. Eco-Marxist theorist James O'Connor termed this self-defeating feature of capitalism "the second contradiction of capitalism."

13. The theory of "survival of the fittest" was advanced by Herbert Spencer, not Darwin. Unlike Darwin's theory of natural selection, the theory of the survival of the fittest inflects evolutionary progress with a moral valence and therefore justifies human interference with it. Also, to apply the rules of a species' survival to a subgroup of one species—a nation, for example—further contorts Darwin's theory. Indeed, Darwin's theories were contested and lent to as many liberatory politics as repressive ones (such as the breaking down of economic or gender-based barriers as "unnatural" blocks to evolution). Some social Darwinians rejected government interference with evolution on the grounds that interference defeated the purpose of natural selection and that the fittest would be "destined to survive." Thus, Darwin's theories were interpreted in often conflicting ways that are beyond the scope of this chapter. I restrict my discussion here to the impact of Darwin on policy and public sentiment to elucidate the relationship between nationalism, eugenics, and wilderness preservation.

14. The terms *social Darwinism, evolutionary theory, sociobiology,* and *scientific racialism* are not interchangeable and suggest varying interpretations of Darwinian theory. Sociobiologists today would not consider their theories "racist," although for more on this debate see Gould (*Ever since Darwin,* 253–59; *Mismeasure,* 326–27), Richard Lewontin's *Biology as Ideology,* and E. O. Wilson's *Sociobiology.* I use historians' preferred terms *evolutionist* and *social Darwinist* to attempt to avoid being anachronistic by projecting current debates about sociobiology onto the past.

15. The show demonstrated further simulacra in a 2007 controversy surrounding its "authenticity"; when it was revealed that the show staged many of its "wild" encounters and Grylls was often aided behind the scenes (given indoor

accommodation, assistance building rafts, for instance), the premise of the show was threatened. The Discovery Channel addressed the controversy by including a statement about these interventions at the beginning of every show.

16. Disability theorists have analyzed the way built environments create "design apartheid" that constructs disability (Gleeson; Hall and Imrie).

17. Clare's fluid sexuality and gender reassignment challenge discourses of nature beyond the ways I am examining here. Here, I focus on his explicitly environmental themes, and on how he insists on revisioning nature (the material world) to be inclusive of various kinds of body (i.e., "putting the deviant body back in nature"). But I would also argue, following the recent move in queer ecocriticism (see Mortimer-Sandilands and Erickson), that his challenge to strict gender binaries challenges dominant notions of nature as discourse (i.e., "naturalizing the deviant body"). In both these ways, then, we see not only how environments can be more inclusive but also that an inclusive corporeal ecology involves critiques of naturalizing discourses, which draw on the rhetorical power of "nature" to legitimize social control.

18. I am grateful to Elizabeth Wheeler for helping to develop this analysis of Clare, particularly Clare's attention to the healing properties of nature as a counternarrative to the wilderness plot.

Chapter 2

1. Shepard Krech's book by this name created much controversy, because of the essentializing tendency of this stereotype. For responses to his book and a review of the controversy, see *Native Americans and the Environment: Perspectives on the Ecological Indian*, edited by Michael E. Harkin and David Rich Lewis.

2. Many critics have argued that the novel is anti-gay. Silko's depiction of homosexuality in the novel is a critique of patriarchy's hostility to and disgust of all things feminine. In the Western patriarchal view that the novel rejects, feminine is messy, earthy, and impure. Alex Hunt thus nuances the novel's treatment of homosexuality: "Silko's evil characters are homosexual or asexual as a sign of their psychological sickness but also as a matter of ideological purpose. Homosexual men represent, for Silko, the ultimate denial of nature, woman, and the racial other in favor of a malign narcissism" (266). This use of homosexuality as a symbol of Western patriarchy is still troubling, but it is consistent with the connections Silko makes throughout *Almanac* between race, gender, and environmental exploitation.

3. Heteronormative "family values" rhetoric treats homosexuality as unnatural, but, as Noel Sturgeon has argued, this rhetoric could just as easily be deployed to unnaturalize heterosexuality and naturalize homosexuality. See "Penguin Family Values: The Nature of Environmental Reproductive Justice."

4. This use of blindness as a metaphor for stupidity is problematic and only reinforces my argument in chapter 1 that disability is a "narrative prosthesis" (in Mitchell and Snyder's terms) for alienation from nature. In fact, overemphasis on the visual could just as easily be the cause of insensitivity to landscape nuances,

as the insurance man's bird's-eye view of the tundra suggests. But Calabazas's point resonates regardless: a responsible land ethic requires an ability to perceive landscape nuances. Furthermore, he insists on a phenomenological interaction with the landscape that is not solely visual, but sensory, and seems to use *blindness* as a catch-all term for nonsensory knowledge broadly. Still, it remains problematic that blindness serves as a metaphor for all bodily incapacity.

5. This notion of biocultural diversity is certainly an improvement on the movement to protect biodiversity, which is often promoted at the cost of social justice and can act as a modern form of eco-imperialism. But even as biocultural diversity emphasizes the importance of preserving cultural traditions, it still upholds ecological science as the expert form of knowledge about nature, and it fails to account for how to address moments when biological and cultural "resources" are in conflict with each other.

6. As I elaborate below, the ecologist represents a distinctly mainstream form of environmentalism that Silko distinguishes from indigenous environmentalism. His specialized focus on owls is suggestive of the Western scientific habit of compartmentalizing and taxonomizing species, as opposed to an indigenous view of the interrelation of all species. This tension is an ongoing debate in the environmental movement—how to justify protecting individual species if the unit that matters is the ecosystem? How to defend ecosystems when individual species are much more effective at garnering public support?

7. This situation is not unlike the way in which pharmaceutical companies benefit twice from the spread of cancer, by producing and selling both its causes and cures.

8. Of course, there are gendered undertones to these discourses as well. Reproduction and immigration are not just racialized; they are gendered. This is especially true in the current immigration climate, as the vast majority of undocumented immigrants into the United States are women and children. Silko addresses the gendered implications of these environmental discourses of purity and pollution in the example of Serlo that I will discuss below. Women of color are ecologically other on two levels, then: they are threats to America's nature because they pollute by being nonwhite and by reproducing.

9. Serlo's disgust at women and people of color is related to his environmental sensibility in ways that are similar to how the Nazis saw genetic and environmental purity as related. Freudian historian Klaus Thewelait argues that German Nazi disgust at bodily functions, women, and racial mixing were part of the Nazi emphasis on purity of soil. Serlo shares this with Nazis, a connection Silko makes explicit: Serlo sees himself as continuing "the history of the secret agenda" that "had begun with the German Third Reich." Serlo's views about genetic purity and pollution echo what historian Robert Proctor calls "racial hygiene."

Chapter 3

1. I use the term *undocumented* instead of *illegal* to acknowledge the problem of determining "legality" when the legality of the border itself is contested.

Furthermore, calling immigrants illegal ignores how their very status as undocumented ensures their vulnerability and the state's role in keeping them that way.
Joseph Nevins explains that the term *illegal* "obfuscate[s] the role that various
agents and institutions in the US have played in encouraging and/or facilitating
unauthorized immigration" (9). Border theorists prefer *undocumented* or *unauthorized* to deemphasize the criminality of immigrants and highlight the role of
various structures in "constructing the illegal alien" (Nevins).

2. See Otto Santa Ana, *Brown Tide Rising,* for more on the pervasiveness of
these organic metaphors for Latino immigration, and Mike Davis, *City of Quartz,*
for background on "fortress" America.

3. Daylanne English remarks on the national imperative implicit in organic
metaphors: "To envision the nation as a body is to fantasize that it can and should
work as a synchronous system. . . . Even the phrase 'body politic' automatically
suggests that some body parts will be subject to Spencerian excision or excretion"
(188). English thus attests to how the very notion of the nation itself relies on
the organic metaphor of the body.

4. In this chapter, I do not provide a detailed explanation of this debate
about the environmental consciousness implied in movement versus sedentariness. Tracing this debate is a critical direction for further interdisciplinary environmental studies of globalization, transnationalism, and postcolonialism (see
Heise, *Sense of Place*). Current geographical theory and environmental history, for
example, are correcting localist environmental thought precisely because it can
be exclusionary, as I allude to in earlier chapters (see, for example, Soja; Massey;
Sassen). Border theorists also provide an important counter to the environmentalist paradigm, especially in terms of my project. If "displacement and dislocation are at the core of the invention of the Americas" (Alarcon, qtd. in Brady,
9), what kind of place-based environmental ethic is available to those who have
been displaced and dislocated? Drawing on Paul Gilroy's analysis of the diasporic
"black Atlantic," Jose David Saldivar further suggests a definition of the border
not as a static place, as many environmentalists portray it in their descriptions of
Organ Pipe, but rather as a dynamic contact zone where resistance, hybridity, and
circulation prevail. He asks a question apropos of the environmentalist investment
in purity examined above: "What changes . . . when culture is understood in
terms of material hybridity, not purity?" (19). Such a question raises the need for
a revision of the environmental narrative of the monument and wilderness spaces
in general. A full exposition of this debate is beyond the scope of this chapter,
but suffice it to say that movement is a crucial feature of environmentalism and
requires further interdisciplinary analysis.

5. I am grateful to Juanita Sundberg for this analysis of Desert Invasion's use
of the term "National."

6. These numbers have been on the increase: in 1998, 266 people died, and
that number rose to 472 in 2005 (Sundberg, 13).

7. My information about the coalition is based on field research in Arizona.
I conducted participant observation at a teach-in for the coalition in January
2006 and conducted a series of interviews between December 2005 and June

2008 with the leading environmentalist member of the coalition, Jenny Neeley, who served as the Southwest Representative of Defenders of Wildlife during this period. All quotes from Neeley herein are taken from these interviews.

8. As I argue in chapter 2, as the environment becomes a national security threat in the age of climate change, "environmental security" pundits warn of the imminent mass movement of people living in lowlands around the globe—a twenty-first-century "coming anarchy," to use Robert Kaplan's term. Not only is "nature" deployed physically and rhetorically against immigrants, as I have been describing in this chapter, it is entering national security debates through climate change discourse. This prevalent and emerging fear of environmental refugees illustrates the pertinence of the environment as a *discourse* to public policy debates. Environmental security discourse explains the rise of refugees as a result of climate change, which deflects attention from the political and economic causes of ecological marginalization, absolving these wider systems of responsibility and blame in favor of the abstract cause of climate change. These refugees' "ecological marginalization" in vulnerable environments, as Thomas Homer-Dixon terms it, exacerbates their status as national security threat and therefore as ecological others.

Conclusion

1. See Ray, "How Many Mothers Does It Take to Change All the Light Bulbs? The Myth of Green Motherhood."

2. This is the subtitle of a good example of the interdisciplinary, critical scholarship I am referring to here, a text edited by Betsy Hartmann, Banu Subramaniam, and Charles Zerner, *Making Threats: Biofears and Environmental Anxieties.*

Bibliography

Abbey, Edward. *Desert Solitaire: A Season in the Wilderness.* New York: Ballantine, 1968.

Abrams, David. *The Spell of the Sensuous: Perception and Language in a More-than-Human World.* New York: Vintage, 1996.

Adams, Paul C. "Peripatetic Imagery and Peripatetic Sense of Place." *Textures of Place: Exploring Humanist Geographies.* Ed. Paul C. Adams, Steven Hoelscher, and Karen E. Till. Minneapolis: University of Minnesota Press, 2001.

Adamson, Joni. *American Indian Literature, Environmental Justice, and Ecocriticism: The Middle Place.* Tucson: University of Arizona Press, 2001.

———. "Encounter with a Mexican Jaguar: Nature, NAFTA, Militarization, and Ranching in the U.S.–Mexico Borderlands." *Globalization on the Line: Culture, Capital, and Citizenship at U.S. Borders.* Ed. Claudia Sadowski-Smith. New York: Palgrave, 2002. 221–40.

Alaimo, Stacy. *Bodily Natures: Science, Environment, and the Material Self.* Bloomington: Indiana University Press, 2010.

Alexie, Sherman. *The Lone Ranger and Tonto Fistfight in Heaven.* New York: Atlantic Monthly Press, 1993.

Anderson, Benedict. *Imagined Communities: Reflections on the Origin and Spread of Nationalism.* London: Verso, 1983.

Andreas, Peter. "The Escalation of U.S. Immigration Control in the Post-NAFTA Era." *Political Quarterly* 113.4 (1998–99): 597–616.

Arnold, David. *The Problem of Nature: Environment, Culture, and European Expansion.* Oxford: Blackwell, 1996.

Bassett, Carol Ann. *Organ Pipe: Life on the Edge.* Tucson: University of Arizona Press, 2004.

Beck, Ulrick. *Risk Society: Towards a New Modernity.* London: Sage, 1992.

Bederman, Gail. *Manliness and Civilization: A Cultural History of Gender and Race in the US, 1880–1917.* Chicago: University of Chicago Press, 1996.

Biehl, Janet, and Peter Staudenmaier. *Ecofascism: Lessons from the German Experience.* AK Press, 1995.

Brady, Mary Pat. *Extinct Lands, Temporal Geographies: The Urgency of Space in Chicana Literature.* Durham: Duke University Press, 2002.

Braun, Bruce. *The Intemperate Rainforest: Nature, Culture, and Power on Canada's West Coast.* Minneapolis: University of Minnesota Press, 2002.

———. "'On the Raggedy Edge of Risk': Articulations of Race and Nature after Biology." *Race, Nature, and the Politics of Difference.* Ed. Donald Moore, Jake Kosek, and Anand Pandian. Durham: Duke University Press, 2003. 175–203.

Bourdieu, Pierre. *Distinction: A Social Critique of the Judgment of Taste.* Cambridge: Harvard University Press, 1987.

Brooks, David. *Bobos in Paradise: The New Upper Class and How They Got There.* New York: Touchstone, 2000.

Buell, Lawrence. *The Environmental Imagination: Thoreau, Nature Writing, and the Formation of American Culture.* Cambridge: Belknap Press of Harvard University Press, 1995.

———. *Writing for an Endangered World: Literature, Culture, and the Environment in the US and Beyond.* Cambridge: Belknap Press of Harvard University Press, 2001.

———. *The Future of Environmental Criticism: Environmental Crisis and Literary Imagination.* Oxford: Blackwell, 2005.

Cahill, Tim. "Along the Devil's Highway." *National Geographic Adventure Magazine* 8.6 (August 2006): 50–94.

Carson, Rachel. *Silent Spring.* Boston: Houghton Mifflin, 1962.

Casey, Edward. *Getting Back into Place: Toward a Renewed Understanding of the Place-World.* Bloomington: Indiana University Press, 1993.

Chase, Steve. "Changing the Nature of Environmental Studies: Teaching Environmental Justice to 'Mainstream' Students." *The Environmental Justice Reader: Politics, Poetics, Pedagogy.* Ed. Joni Adamson, Rachel Stein, and Mei Mei Evans. Tucson: University of Arizona Press, 2002. 350–67.

Chisholm, Ann. "Incarnations and Practices of Feminine Rectitude: Nineteenth-Century Gymnastics for U.S. Women." *Journal of Social History* 38:3 (Spring 2005): 737-63.

Churchill, Ward, and Winona LaDuke. "Native North America: The Political Economy of Radioactive Colonialism." *The State of Native America: Genocide, Colonization, and Resistance.* Ed. M. Annette Jaimes. Boston: South End Press, 1992. 241–66.

Clare, Eli. *Exile and Pride: Disability, Queerness, and Liberation.* Cambridge: South End Press, 1999.

Coates, Bill. "Tide of Humanity Tramples on Organ Pipe Cactus National Monument." *Arizona Capitol Times* (October 13, 2006): Accessed on highbeam .com, January 2008.

Coates, Peter. *American Perspectives of Immigrant and Invasive Species: Strangers on the Land.* Berkeley: University of California Press, 2006.

Comer, Krista. *Landscapes of the New West: Gender and Geography In Contemporary Women's Writing.* Chapel Hill: University of North Carolina Press, 1999.

Cosgrove, Denis. "Habitable Earth: Wilderness, Empire, and Race in America." *Wild Ideas.* Ed. David Rothenberg. Minneapolis: University of Minnesota Press, 1995. 27–41.

Cresswell, Tim. *Place: A Short Introduction.* Malden: Blackwell, 2004.

Cronon, William. *Nature's Metropolis: Chicago and the Great West.* New York: W. W. Norton, 1991.

———. "The Trouble with Wilderness." *Uncommon Ground: Rethinking the Human Place in Nature.* Ed. William Cronon. New York: W. W. Norton, 1996. 69–90.

Dare, Martha. "Biological Toxins Found at Arizona's Southern Border." *Sierra Times* (May 19, 2003). November 2005 <sierratimes.com>.

Darwin, Charles. *On the Origin of Species.* Ed. Gillian Beer. Oxford: Oxford University Press, 1996.

Davis, Diana K. *Resurrecting the Granary of Rome: Environmental History and French Colonial Expansion in North Africa.* Athens: Ohio University Press, 2007.

Davis, Mike. *City of Quartz: Excavating the Future in Los Angeles.* New York: Vintage, 1992.

Deleuze, Gilles, and Felix Guattari. *A Thousand Plateaus: Capitalism and Schizophrenia.* Trans. Brian Massumi. Minneapolis: University of Minnesota Press, 1987.

Desert Invasion. November 2005 <www.Desertinvasion.org>.

Di Chiro, Giovanna. "Beyond Ecoliberal 'Common Futures': Environmental Justice, Toxic Touring, and a Transcommunal Politics of Place." *Race, Nature, and the Politics of Difference.* Ed. Donald Moore, Jake Kosek, and Anand Pandian. Durham: Duke University Press, 2003. 204–32.

Dixon, Melvin. *Ride out the Wilderness: Geography and Identity in Afro-American Literature.* Chicago: University of Illinois Press, 1987.

Dorn, Michael. "Beyond Nomadism: The Travel Narratives of a Cripple." *Places through the Body.* Ed. Heidi Nast and Steve Pile. New York: Routledge, 1998. 136–52.

Dougherty, John. "One Nation, under Fire." *High Country News* (February 19, 2007): 8–13.

Douglas, Mary. *Purity and Danger: An Analysis of the Concept of Pollution and Taboo.* 1966. New York: Routledge, 2002.

———. *Risk and Culture: An Essay on the Selection of Technical and Environmental Dangers.* Berkeley: University of California Press, 1982.

English, Daylanne. *Unnatural Selections: Eugenics in American Modernism and the Harlem Renaissance.* Chapel Hill: University of North Carolina Press, 2004.

Evans, Mei Mei. "'Nature' and Environmental Justice." *The Environmental Justice Reader: Politics, Poetics, and Pedagogy.* Ed. Joni Adamson, Mei Mei Evans, and Rachel Stein. Tucson: University of Arizona Press, 2002. 181–93.

Figueroa, Robert M. "Other Faces: Latinos and Environmental Justice." *Faces of Environmental Racism: Confronting Issues of Global Justice.* Ed. Laura Westra. Lanham: Rowman and Littlefield, 2001. 167–86.

Food, Inc. Dir. Robert Kenner. Perf. Eric Schlosser, Michael Pollan. Magnolia Pictures, 2008, 2009.

Fouberg, Erin H., Alexander B. Murphy, and H. J. de Blij. *Human Geography: People, Place, and Culture.* 10th ed. Hoboken: John Wiley and Sons, 2012.

Foucault, Michel. *History of Sexuality.* New York: Pantheon, 1978.

Freund, Peter. "Bodies, Disability, and Spaces: The Social Model and Disabling Spatial Organisations." *Disability and Society* 16, no. 5 (2001). 689–706.

Garland-Thomson, Rosemarie. *Extraordinary Bodies: Figuring Physical Disability in American Culture and Literature.* New York: Columbia University Press, 1997.

———. "The Politics of Staring: Visual Rhetorics of Disability in Popular Photography." *Disability Studies: Enabling the Humanities.* Ed. Sharon L. Snyder, Brenda Jo Brueggemann, and Rosemarie Garland-Thomson. New York: Modern Languages Association, 2002. 56–75.

Germic, Stephen. *American Green: Class, Crisis, and the Deployment of Nature in Central Park, Yosemite, and Yellowstone.* Lanham: Lexington Books, 2001.

Gibson, Barbara E. "Disability, Connectivity, and Transgressing the Autonomous Body." *Journal of Medical Humanities* 27.3 (Fall 2006): 187–196.

Giddens, Anthony. *The Consequences of Modernity.* Cambridge: Polity Press, 1990.

Gleeson, Brendan. *Geographies of Disability.* New York: Routledge, 1999.

Gould, Stephen Jay. *Ever since Darwin.* New York: W. W. Norton, 1977.

———. *The Mismeasure of Man.* New York: W. W. Norton, 1981.

Green, Harvey. *Fit for America: Health, Fitness, Sport, and American Society.* New York: Pantheon, 1986.

Grove, Richard. *Green Imperialism: Colonial Expansion, Tropical Island Edens, and the Origins of Environmentalism, 1600–1860.* Cambridge: Cambridge University Press, 1996.

Grylls, Bear. *Bear Grylls Born Survivor: Survival Techniques from the Most Dangerous Places on Earth.* N.p.: Channel 4 Books, 2007.

Guha, Ramachandra, and Juan Martinez-Alier. *Varieties of Environmentalism: Essays North and South.* London: Earthscan, 1997.

Hall, Peter, and Robert Imrie. "Architectural Practices and Disabling Design in the Built Environment." *Environment and Planning B: Planning and Design* 26.3 (1999): 409–25.

Haraway, Donna. "A Manifesto for Cyborgs: Science, Technology, and Socialist Feminism in the 1980s." *Australian Feminist Review* 2.4 (1987): 1–42.

———. *Primate Visions: Gender, Race, and Nature in the World of Modern Science.* New York: Routledge, 1989.

Harkin, Michael E., and David Rich Lewis. *Native Americans and the Environment: Perspectives on the Ecological Indian.* Lincoln: University of Nebraska Press, 2007.

Hartmann, Betsy, Banu Subramaniam, and Charles Zerner. *Making Threats: Biofears and Environmental Anxieties.* Oxford: Rowman and Littlefield, 2005.

Harvey, David. *The Condition of Postmodernity: An Enquiry into the Origins of Cultural Change.* Oxford: Wiley-Blackwell, 1992.

———. *Justice, Nature and the Geography of Difference.* Cambridge: Blackwell, 1996.

Heise, Ursula K. "Ecocriticism and the Transnational Turn in American Studies." *American Literary History* (2008): 1–24.

———. *Sense of Place and Sense of Planet: The Environmental Imagination of the Global.* New York: Oxford University Press, 2008.

Hepworth, James R. *Stealing Glances: Three Interviews with Wallace Stegner.* Albuquerque: University of New Mexico Press, 1998.

Higham, John. *Strangers in the Land: Patterns of American Nativism, 1860–1925.* New Brunswick: Rutgers University Press, 2002.

Himot, Kate. "America's Ten Most Endangered National Parks." *National Parks* 78.2 (2004): 32–33.

Hobsbawm, Eric. *Nations and Nationalisms since 1780: Programme, Myth, Reality.* Cambridge: Cambridge University Press, 1992.

Homer-Dixon, Thomas. "Environmental Scarcities and Violent Conflict: Evidence from Cases." *International Security* 19.1 (2004): 5–40.

Horsman, Reginald. *Race and Manifest Destiny: The Origins of American Racial Anglo-Saxonism.* Cambridge: Harvard University Press, 1981.

Hsu, Hsuan, and Martha Lincoln. "Biopower, *Bodies . . . The Exhibition,* and the Spectacle of Public Health." *Discourse* 29:1 (Fall 2007): 15–34.

Huber, Joe. "Trailblazing in a Wheelchair—an Oxymoron?" *Palaestra* (28 July 2005): 52.

Huhndorf, Shari. *Going Native: Indians in the American Cultural Imagination.* Ithaca: Cornell University Press, 2001.

Hunt, Alexander. "Narrating American Space: Literary Cartography and the American Southwest." Diss. University of Oregon, 2001.

———. "The Radical Geography of Silko's *Almanac of the Dead.*" *Western American Literature* 39.3 (Fall 2004): 256–78.

Hurowitz, Glenn. "Prairie Chicken: Why Environmental Groups Have Been Slow to Fight the Border Wall." *Grist.* (October 16, 2007). October 2007 <www .grist.org>.

Imrie, Robert, and Peter Hall, eds. *Inclusive Design: Designing and Developing Accessible Environments.* New York: Spon Press, 2001.

Jackson, Jean. "Culture, Genuine and Spurious: The Politics of Indianness in the Vaupés, Colombia." *American Ethnologist* 22.1: 3–27.

Jacoby, Karl. *Crimes against Nature: Squatters, Poachers, Thieves, and the Hidden History of American Conservation.* Berkeley: University of California Press, 2001.

Jamie Oliver's Food Revolution. ABC. 21 March 2010–24 June 2011.

Kang, Ja-mo. "An Ecological Reading of Leslie Marmon Silko's *Almanac of the Dead.*" *English Language and Literature* 49.4 (2003): 731–54.

Kaplan, Amy. "'Left Alone with America': The Absence of Empire in the Study of American Culture." *Cultures of United States Imperialism.* Ed. Amy Kaplan and Donald E. Pease. Durham: Duke University Press, 1993. 3–21.

———. "Romancing the Empire: The Embodiment of American Masculinity in the Popular Historical Novel of the 1890s." *American Literary History* 2:4 (1990). 659–90.

Kaplan, Caren. *Questions of Travel: Postmodern Discourses of Displacement.* Durham: Duke University Press, 1996.

Kaplan, Robert. "The Coming Anarchy." *Atlantic* (February 1994). 44–76.

Karalus, Dan. "Between Nature and Nation: Organ Pipe Cactus National Monument and Its Borders." Unpublished paper. Provided by author, 2009.

Kevles, Daniel. *In the Name of Eugenics: Genetics and the Uses of Human Heredity.* New York: Knopf, 1985.

Kingsolver, Barbara. *Animal, Vegetable, Miracle: A Year of Food Life.* HarperCollins: New York, 2007.

Kipnis, Laura. "(Male) Desire and (Female) Disgust: Reading *Hustler.*" *Cultural Studies.* Ed. Lawrence Grossberg, Cary Nelson, and Paula A. Treichler. London: Routledge, 1992. 373–91.

Kloor, Keith. "Sonoran Storm." *Audubon* 106.3 (July–August 2004): 11–12.

Kollin, Susan. *Nature's State: Imagining Alaska as the Last Frontier.* Chapel Hill: University of North Carolina Press, 2007.

Kosek, Jake. "Purity and Pollution: Racial Degradation and Environmental Anxieties." *Liberation Ecologies: Environment, Development, Social Movements.* Ed. Michael Peet and Richard Watts. New York: Routledge, 2004. 115–52.

Krakauer, Jon. *Into Thin Air.* New York: Anchor, 1997.

Krech, Shepard, III. *The Ecological Indian: History and Myth.* New York: W. W. Norton, 2000.

Kuletz, Valerie. *The Tainted Desert: Environmental Ruin in the American West.* New York: Routledge, 1998.

LaDuke, Winona. *All Our Relations: Native Struggles for Land and Life.* Cambridge: South End Press, 1999.

Lappé, Frances Moore. *Diet for a Small Planet.* New York: Random House, 1971.

Lewkowicz, Bonnie. "Accessible Outdoors: Opening the Door to Nature for People with Disabilities." *Bay Nature Magazine* (October–December 2006): 21–34.

Lewontin, Richard. *Biology as Ideology: The Doctrine of DNA.* New York: Harper, 1993.

Li, Tania Murray. "Articulating Indigenous Identity in Indonesia: Resource Politics and the Tribal Slot." *Comparative Studies in Society and History* 42.1 (January 2000): 149–79.

Limerick, Patricia Nelson. *Legacy of Conquest: The Unbroken Past of the American West.* New York: Norton, 1988.

Lohmann, Larry. "Green Orientalism." *Ecologist* 23:6 (December 1993): 202–4.

Lowenthal, Abraham F. Personal interview. 23 December 2005.

Lowenthal, David. *George Perkins Marsh, Prophet of Conservation.* Seattle: University of Washington Press, 2000.

Luke, Timothy. *Ecocritique: Contesting the Politics of Nature, Economy, and Culture.* Minneapolis: University of Minnesota Press, 1997.

Ma Agustín, Laura. "Still Challenging 'Place': Sex, Money, and Agency in Women's Migrations." *Women and the Politics of Place.* Ed. Wendy Harcourt and Arturo Escobar. Bloomfield: Kumarian Press, 2005.

MacCannell, Dean. *The Tourist: A New Theory of the Leisure Class.* Rev. ed. New York: Schocken, 1989.

Macnaghten, Phil, and John Urry. "Bodies of Nature: Introduction." *Body and Society.* Vol. 6. Ed. Phil Macnaghten and John Urry. London: Sage, 2000. 1–11.

Mairs, Nancy. *Waist-High in the World: A Life among the Nondisabled.* Boston: Beacon, 1996.

Malthus, Thomas. *An Essay on the Principle of Population.* Oxford World's Classics reprint: xxix Chronology. 1798.

Man vs. Wild. Discovery Channel. 2006–.

Marx, Leo. *The Machine in the Garden: Technology and the Pastoral Ideal in America.* New York: Oxford University Press, 1964.

Massey, Doreen. *For Space.* Thousand Oaks: Sage, 2005.

———. "A Global Sense of Place." *Space, Place, and Gender.* Minneapolis: University of Minnesota Press, 1994.

———. "Power Geometry and a Progressive Sense of Place." *Mapping the Futures: Local Cultures, Global Change.* Ed. Jon Bird et al. London: Routledge, 1993. 60–70.

Mayer, Sylvia. *Restoring the Connection to the Natural World: Essays on the African American Environmental Imagination.* Munster: LIT Verlag, 2003.

Mazel, David. "American Literary Environmentalism as Domestic Orientalism." *The Ecocriticism Reader: Landmarks in Literary Ecology.* Ed. Cheryll Glotfelty and Harold Fromm. Athens: University of Georgia Press, 1996. 137–48.

McAvoy, Leo. "Outdoors for Everyone: Opportunities That Include People with Disabilities." *Parks and Recreation* (2001): 24–36.

Merchant, Carolyn. *The Death of Nature: Women, Ecology, and the Scientific Revolution.* New York: HarperOne, 1990.

———. "Reinventing Eden: Western Culture as Recovery Narrative." *Uncommon Ground: Rethinking the Human Place in Nature.* Ed. William Cronon. New York: W. W. Norton, 1995. 132–70.

Miller, Perry. *Nature's Nation.* Cambridge: Belknap Press of Harvard University Press, 1967.

Mills, Charles W. "Black Trash." *Faces of Environmental Racism: Confronting Issues of Global Justice.* 2nd ed. Ed. Laura Westra and Bill E. Lawson. Lanham: Rowman & Littlefield, 2001. 73–90.

Mitchell, David, and Sharon L. Snyder. *The Body and Physical Difference: Discourses of Disability.* Ann Arbor: University of Michigan Press, 1997.

Mitchell, Don. *The Lie of the Land: Migrant Workers and the California Landscape.* Minneapolis: University of Minnesota Press, 1996.

———. "A New Axiom for Reading Immigrant Landscapes." Conference paper, Association of American Geographers Annual Conference. San Francisco. 2007.

Momaday, N. Scott. *The Way to Rainy Mountain.* Albuquerque: University of New Mexico Press, 1976.

Moore, Donald, Anand Pandian, and Jake Kosek. "Introduction: The Cultural Politics of Race and Nature: Terrains of Power and Practice." *Race, Nature, and the Politics of Difference*. Ed. Donald Moore, Anand Pandian, and Jake Kosek. Durham: Duke University Press, 2003. 1–70.

Morrison, Toni. *Playing in the Dark: Whiteness and the Literary Imagination*. Cambridge: Harvard University Press, 1992.

Mortimer-Sandilands, Catriona, and Bruce Erickson, eds. *Queer Ecologies: Sex, Nature, Politics, Desire*. Bloomington: Indiana University Press, 2010.

Morton, Timothy. *Ecology without Nature: Rethinking Environmental Aesthetics*. Cambridge: Harvard University Press, 2007.

Nabhan, Gary Paul. "Destruction of an Ancient Indigenous Cultural Landscape: An Epitaph from Organ Pipe Cactus National Monument." *Ecological Restoration* 21.4 (2003): 290–95.

———. "Land of Contradictions." *Audubon* (March–April 1999): 84–89.

Nagel, Carlos. *Special Report No. 8: Report on Treatises, Agreements, and Accords Affecting Natural Resource Management at Organ Pipe Cactus National Monument*. Tucson: Cooperative National Park Resources Studies Unit, University of Arizona, 1988.

Nash, Linda. *Inescapable Ecologies: A History of Environment, Disease, and Knowledge*. Berkeley: University of California Press, 2006.

Nash, Roderick. *Wilderness and the American Mind*. 1967. New Haven: Yale University Press, 2002.

Nast, Heidi, and Steve Pile. *Places through the Body*. London: Routledge, 1998.

"National Park 'Endangered' by Migrants." *Hispanic* 17.3 (March 2004): 14.

Neeley, Jenny. Personal interviews, December 2005, January 2007, June 2007.

Nettleford, Peter A., and Elaine Stratford. "The Production of Climbing Landscapes-as-Texts." *Australian Geographical Studies* 37.2 (1999): 130–41.

Neumann, Roderick. *Imposing Wilderness: Struggles over Livelihood and Nature Preservation in Africa*. Berkeley: University of California Press, 1993.

Nevins, Joseph. *Operation Gatekeeper: The Rise of the "Illegal Alien" and the Making of the U.S.–Mexico Boundary*. New York: Routledge, 2002.

Nussbaum, Martha. *Frontiers of Justice: Disability, Nationality, and Species Membership*. Cambridge: Belknap Press of Harvard University Press, 2006.

O'Meara, Bridget. "The Ecological Politics of Leslie Silko's *Almanac of the Dead*." *Wicazo SA Review* 15.2 (Fall 2000): 63–73.

Ortiz, Simon. *from Sand Creek*. Tucson: University of Arizona Press, 2000.

———. *Woven Stone*. Tucson: University of Arizona Press, 1992.

Peña, Devon. "Tierra y vida: Chicano Environmental Justice Struggles in the Southwest." *The Quest for Environmental Justice: Human Rights and the Politics of Pollution*. Ed. Robert Bullard. San Francisco: Sierra Club Books, 2005. 188–208.

Pernick, Martin S. "Eugenics and Public Health in American History." *American Journal of Public Health* 87.11 (1997): 1767–772.

Pollan, Michael. *The Omnivore's Dilemma: A Natural History of Four Meals*. New York: Penguin, 2006.

Proctor, Robert. *Racial Hygiene: Medicine under the Nazis*. Cambridge: Harvard University Press, 1988.

Pulido, Laura. "Ecological Legitimacy and Cultural Essentialism: Hispano Grazing in the Southwest." *Capitalism, Nature, Socialism* 7.4 (December 1996): 37–58.

———. *Environmentalism and Economic Justice: Two Chicano Struggles in the Southwest.* Tucson: University of Arizona Press, 1998.

———. "Race, Immigration, and the Border." *Antipode* 36.1 (2004): 154–57.

———. "Rethinking Environmental Racism: White Privilege and Urban Development in Southern California." *Annals of the Association of American Geographers* 90.1 (2000): 12–40.

Pyle, Robert Michael. "The Extinction of Experience." *City Wilds: Essays and Stories about Urban Nature.* Ed. Terrell Dixon. Athens: University of Georgia Press, 2002. 257–67.

Rabinow, Paul. *The Foucault Reader.* New York: Pantheon, 1984.

Rail, Genevieve, and Jean Harvey. "Body at Work: Michel Foucault and the Sociology of Sport." *Sociology of Sport Journal* 12 (1995): 164–79.

Ramos, Alcida. "Pulp Fictions of Indigenism." *Race, Nature, and the Politics of Difference.* Ed. Donald Moore, Jake Kosek, and Anand Pandian. Durham: Duke University Press, 2003. 356–79.

Ray, Sarah Jaquette. "How Many Mothers Does It Take to Change All the Light Bulbs? The Myth of Green Motherhood." *Journal of the Motherhood Initiative for Research and Community Involvement* 2:1 (Spring/Summer 2011): 81–101.

Razack, Sherene. "When Place Becomes Race." *Race and Racialization: Essential Readings.* Ed. Tania Das Gupta. Ontario: Canadian Scholars' Press, 2007. 74–82.

Reed, T. V. "Toward an Environmental Justice Ecocriticism." *The Environmental Justice Reader: Politics, Poetics, and Pedagogy.* Ed. Joni Adamson, Mei Mei Evans, and Rachel Stein. Tucson: University of Arizona Press, 2002. 145–62.

Rich, Adrienne. *Of Woman Born: Motherhood as Experience and Institution.* New York: W. W. Norton, 1976.

Rome, Adam. "Political Hermaphrodites: Gender and Environmental Reform in Progressive America." *Environmental History* 11.3 (July 2006): 440–63.

Rosaldo, Renato. *Culture and Truth: The Remaking of Social Analysis.* New York: Beacon, 1993.

Rose, Gillian. *Feminism and Geography: The Limits of Geographical Knowledge.* Minneapolis: University of Minnesota Press, 2003.

———. "Looking at Landscape: The Uneasy Pleasures of Power." *Space, Gender, Knowledge: Feminist Readings.* Ed. Linda McDowell and Joanne Sharp. London: Arnold, 1997. 193–200.

Rosen, Elizabeth. "Somalis Don't Climb Mountains: The Commercialization of Mount Everest." *Journal of Popular Culture* 40.1 (2007): 147–68.

Said, Edward. *Culture and Imperialism.* New York: Knopf, 1993.

———. *Orientalism.* New York: Pantheon, 1978.

Saldivar, Jose David. *Border Matters: Remapping American Cultural Studies.* Berkeley: University of California Press, 1997.

Sandoval, Chela. *Methodology of the Oppressed.* Minneapolis: University of Minnesota Press, 2000.

Santa Ana, Otto. *Brown Tide Rising: Metaphors of Latinos in Contemporary American Public Discourse.* Austin: University of Texas Press, 2002.

Sassen, Saskia. "Women's Burden: Counter-Geographies of Globalization and the Feminization of Survival." *Nordic Journal of International Law* 71 (2002): 503–25.

Scholnick, Robert J. "'How Dare a Sick Man or an Obedient Man Write Poems?' Whitman and the Dis-ease of the Perfect Body." *Disability Studies: Enabling the Humanities.* Ed. Sharon L. Snyder, Brenda Jo Brueggemann, and Rosemarie Garland-Thomson. New York: MLA, 2002. 248–59.

Scott, James C. *Seeing like a State: How Certain Schemes to Improve the Human Condition Have Failed.* New Haven: Yale University Press, 1999.

Seager, Joni. *Earth Follies: Coming to Feminist Terms with the Global Environmental Crisis.* New York: Routledge, 1993.

Segee, Brian P., and Jenny L. Neeley. *On the Line: The Impacts of Immigration Policy on Wildlife and Habitat in the Arizona Borderlands.* Washington, DC: Defenders of Wildlife, 2006.

Selden, Steven. "Eugenics and the Social Construction of Merit, Race, and Disability." *Journal of Curriculum Studies* 32.2 (2000): 235–52.

Sewall, Laura. *Sight and Sensibility: The Eco-Psychology of Perception.* New York: JP Tarcher/Putnam, 1999.

"Shifting to the East: U.S. Fights to Close Gaps from Otay to Jacumba." *San Diego Union Tribune* 26 May 1996.

Shildrick, Margrit, and Janet Price. "Breaking the Boundaries of the Broken Body." *Body and Society* 2:4 (1996): 93–113.

Silko, Leslie Marmon. *Almanac of the Dead.* New York: Penguin, 1992.

———. *Yellow Woman and a Beauty of the Spirit: Essays on Native American Life Today.* New York: Simon and Schuster, 1996.

Simon, Bryant. "'New Men in Body and Soul': The Civilian Conservation Corps and the Transformation of Male Bodies and the Body Politic." *Seeing Nature through Gender.* Ed. Virginia Scharff. Lawrence: University of Kansas Press, 2003. 80–102.

Slicer, Deborah. "Toward an Ecofeminist Standpoint Theory: Bodies as Grounds." In *Ecofeminist Literary Criticism: Theory, Interpretation, Pedagogy.* Ed. Greta Gaard and Patrick Murphy. Champaign: University of Illinois Press, 1998. 49–73.

Slotkin, Richard. "Nostalgia and Progress: Theodore Roosevelt's Myth of the Frontier." *American Quarterly* 33.5 (1981): 608–37.

Slovic, Scott. "Editor's Note." *ISLE: Interdisciplinary Studies in Literature and Environment* 14.1 (Winter 2007): v–vii.

Smith, Neil. *Uneven Development: Nature, Capital, and the Production of Space.* New York: Blackwell, 1990.

Soja, Edward. *Postmodern Geographies: The Reassertion of Space in Critical Social Theory.* London: Verso, 1989.

Solnit, Rebecca. "Looking away from Beauty: What Remains Hidden behind the Nationalism of the Olympic Games." *Orion* (July/August 2008): 16–17.

Spence, Mark. *Dispossessing the Wilderness: Indian Removal and the Making of the National Parks.* New York: Oxford University Press, 1999.

Spivak, Gayatri. "Can the Subaltern Speak?" *Marxism and the Interpretation of Culture.* Eds. Cary Nelson and Lawrence Grossberg. Urbana: University of Illinois Press, 1988. 271–316.

Spurr, David. *The Rhetoric of Empire: Colonial Discourse in Journalism, Travel Writing, and Imperial Administration.* Durham: Duke University Press, 1993.

Stallybrass, Peter, and Allon White. *The Politics and Poetics of Transgression.* Ithaca: Cornell University Press, 1986.

Stanescu, Vasile. "'Green' Eggs and Ham? The Myth of Sustainable Meat and the Danger of the Local." *Journal of Critical Animal Studies* 7.3 (2009): 18–55.

Stegner, Wallace. *Angle of Repose.* New York: Penguin, 1992.

Stein, Rachel. *Shifting the Ground: American Women Writers' Revisions of Nature, Gender, and Race.* Charlottesville: University of Virginia Press, 1997.

Steingraber, Sandra. *Living Downstream: A Scientist's Personal Investigation of Cancer and the Environment.* New York: Vintage, 1997.

Stevens, Sharon. *A Place for Dialogue: Language, Land Use, and Politics in Southern Arizona.* Iowa City: University of Iowa Press, 2007.

"Stompin' on the Saguaro." *Environment* 44.9 (2002): 7–8.

Sturgeon, Noel. "Penguin Family Values: The Nature of Environmental Reproductive Justice." *Queer Ecologies: Sex, Nature, Politics, Desire.* Ed. Catriona Mortimer-Sandilands and Bruce Erickson. Bloomington: Indiana University Press, 2010. 102–33.

Sundberg, Juanita. "Feminist Geo/Political Ecology and the Politics of Security." (2006). Manuscript provided by author.

Sundberg, Juanita, and Bonnie Kaserman. "Cactus Carvings and Desert Defecations: Embodying Representations of Border Crossings in Protected Areas of the U.S.–Mexico Border." *Environment and Planning D: Society and Space* 25.4 (2007): 727–44.

Sutter, Paul. "Terra Incognita: The Neglected History of Interwar Environmental Thought and Politics." *Reviews in American History* 29 (2001): 289–98.

Sze, Julie. "Boundaries and Border Wars: DES, Technology, and Environmental Justice." *American Quarterly* 58:3 (September 2006): 791–814.

Taylor, Peter, Saul Halfon, and Paul Edwards, eds. *Changing Life: Genomes, Ecologies, Bodies, Commodities.* Minneapolis: University of Minnesota Press, 1997.

Thacker, Andrew. *Moving through Modernity: Space and Geography in Modernism.* Manchester: Manchester University Press, 2003.

Thewelait, Klaus. *Male Fantasies: Women, Floods, Bodies, History.* Minneapolis: University of Minnesota Press, 1987.

Thoreau, Henry David. "Walking." *Wild Apples and Other Natural History Essays.* Ed. William Rossi. Athens: University of Georgia Press, 2002. 59–92.

Thornton, Thomas F. *Being and Place among the Tlingit.* Seattle: University of Washington Press, 2007.

Tillett, Rebecca. "Reality Consumed by Realty: The Ecological Costs of 'Development' in Leslie Marmon Silko's *Almanac of the Dead*." *European Journal of American Culture* 24.2 (2005): 153–69.

Touching the Void. Dir. Kevin Macdonald. Perf. Simon Yates, Joe Simpson, and Brendan Mackey. IFC Films, 2003.

Tremain, Shelley, ed. *Foucault and the Government of Disability*. Ann Arbor: University of Michigan Press, 2005.

Tuan, Yi-Fu. *Landscapes of Fear*. New York: Pantheon, 1979.

———. *Space and Place: The Perspectives of Experience*. Minneapolis: University of Minnesota Press, 1977.

Unger, Nancy C. "Women, Sexuality, and Environmental Justice in American History." *New Perspectives on Environmental Justice: Gender, Sexuality, and Activism*. Ed. Rachel Stein. New Brunswick: Rutgers University Press, 2004. 45–62.

Villa, Raul Homero. *Barrio Logos: Space and Place in Urban Chicano Literature and Culture*. Austin: University of Texas Press, 2000.

Wald, Priscilla. *Contagious: Cultures, Carriers, and the Outbreak Narrative*. Durham: Duke University Press, 2008.

Watson, Julie. "Unruly Trample National Parks." *Associated Press* (12 July 2002).

Weir, Daniel, and Irisita Azary. "Quitovac Oasis: A Sense of Home Place and the Development of Water Resources." *Professional Geographer* 53.1 (2001): 45–55.

Wendell, Susan. *The Rejected Body: Feminist Philosophical Reflections on Disability*. New York: Routledge, 1996.

Wheeler, Elizabeth. "Don't Climb Every Mountain." Unpublished paper. Provided by the author.

White, Richard. *The Organic Machine*. New York: Hill and Wang, 1995.

Williams, Raymond. *The Country and the City*. New York: Oxford University Press, 1973.

Williams, Trevor, and Peter Donnelly. "Subcultural Production, Reproduction, and Transformation in Climbing." *International Review of the Sociology of Sport* 20.1 (1985): 3–15.

Wilson, E. O. *Sociobiology: The New Synthesis*. Cambridge: Belknap Press of Harvard University Press, 2000.

Worster, Donald. *The Wealth of Nature: Environmental History and the Ecological Imagination*. Oxford: Oxford University Press, 1993.

Ybarra, Priscilla Solis. *Walden Pond in Aztlan? A Literary History of Chicana/o Environmental Writing*. Rice University, 2006.

Zehle, Soenke. "Notes on Cross-Border Environmental Justice Education." *The Environmental Justice Reader: Politics, Poetics, and Pedagogy*. Ed. Joni Adamson, Mei Mei Evans, and Rachel Stein. Tucson: University of Arizona Press, 2002. 331–49.

Index

About the Author

SARAH JAQUETTE RAY is Assistant Professor of English and Coordinator of the Geography and Environmental Studies Program at the University of Alaska Southeast in Juneau, where she teaches literature and environment, geography, and writing. Ray received a doctoral degree in Environmental Sciences, Studies, and Policy from the University of Oregon, a master's in American Studies from the University of Texas at Austin, and a bachelor's in Religious Studies and Women's Studies from Swarthmore College. Recent publications include "How Many Mothers Does It Take to Change All the Light Bulbs? The Myth of Green Motherhood," in the *Journal of the Motherhood Initiative for Research and Community Involvement;* "Risking Bodies in the Wild: The 'Corporeal Unconscious' of American Adventure Culture," in the *Journal for Sport and Social Issues;* and "Endangering the Desert: Immigration, the Environment, and Security in the Arizona–Mexico Borderland," in *ISLE: Interdisciplinary Studies of Literature and Environment.*

Ray's research interests are environmental justice, ecofeminism, disability theory, environmental security, environmental refugeeism, critical human geography, political ecology, and the cultural politics of "sense of place." Ray is particularly interested in the ways in which discourses of nature and the environment are deployed for the purposes of social control but also for political empowerment by marginalized groups. This research interest has taken new shape during her time in southeast Alaska, where racial, gender, class, and political conflicts are often negotiated through narratives of nature.